KU-189-302

WE ARE NATURE

TV presenter, instructor and bestselling author Ray Mears has become recognised throughout the world as an authority on the subject of bushcraft and survival. TV series including *Ray Mears' Bushcraft, Ray Mears' World of Survival, Extreme Survival* and *Ray Mears Goes Walkabout* have made him a household name over the past two decades, but he has spent his life learning these skills, and founded Woodlore, The School of Wilderness Bushcraft, over thirty-five years ago. He was awarded the RGS Ness Award in 2003 and the Mungo Park Medal in 2009. This is his fourteenth book.

WE ARE NATURE

How to Reconnect
with the Wild

RAY MEARS

EBURY
PRESS

Ebury Press, an imprint of Ebury Publishing
20 Vauxhall Bridge Road
London SW1V 2SA

Ebury Press is part of the Penguin Random House group of companies
whose addresses can be found at global.penguinrandomhouse.com

Penguin
Random House
UK

Copyright © Ray Mears 2021

All photos © Ray Mears, except: photos 4, 5, 6 and 8 in section one
© Jonathan Buckley; photo 11 in section one © Martin Hayward Smith;
and photos 6 and 10 in section two © Phil Coles

Illustrations by David Wardle

Ray Mears has asserted his right to be identified as the author of this Work
in accordance with the Copyright, Designs and Patents Act 1988

First published by Ebury Press in 2021

www.penguin.co.uk

A CIP catalogue record for this book is available from the British Library

ISBN 9781529107982

Printed and bound in Great Britain by Clays Ltd, Elcograf S.p.A.
The authorised representative in the EEA is Penguin Random House Ireland,
Morrison Chambers, 32 Nassau Street, Dublin D02 YH68.

MIX
Paper from
responsible sources
FSC
www.fsc.org   FSC® C018179

Penguin Random House is committed to a sustainable future
for our business, our readers and our planet. This book is
made from Forest Stewardship Council® certified paper.

For Ruth

Thank you for your unwavering love and support.

Darling, you are the most incredible force of nature,

but not even you can call YOO HOO! to sleeping lions.

Contents

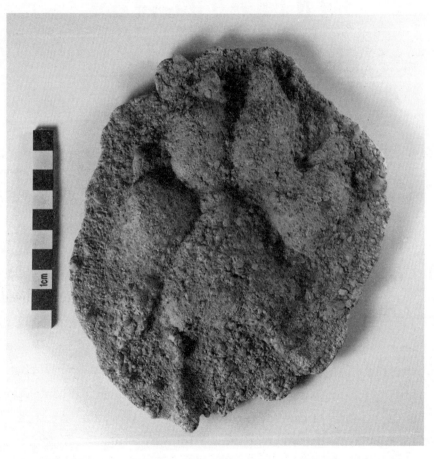

Footprint of an alpha-male grey wolf, cast in dental stone on
1 May 2009 in the Sawtooth Mountains, Idaho, three days
before their controversial delisting as an endangered species.

INTRODUCTION
The Wolf

The old Lakota was wise. He knew that man's heart, away from nature, becomes hard; he knew that lack of respect for growing, living things soon led to lack of respect for humans too.

Chief Luther Standing Bear, *Land of the Spotted Eagle*

Like many travellers, I have over the years amassed an eclectic collection of mementos, reminders of people, places and experiences lived. There is for example a representation of a honey ant, hand moulded in spinifex resin by an elderly Pitjantjatjara Aboriginal woman. We had travelled in the desert together collecting honey ants and witchetty grubs. Her dreaming was honey ant, so she had a special connection with and duty of care for honey ants. In an extraordinary gesture of friendship, she had etched her true Aboriginal name into the figurine with a hot wire. When she gave it to me, she pressed it deeply into my hand. It was a gift to remind me always of her and the journey we had made together. Not surprisingly, I have never forgotten.

There are many other items, such as a *pierre noire*, the fabled African black stone, a traditional treatment for venomous snakebites, or shoes woven from lime bark by a Belarusian man. Each item has a story; each item stirs an emotion. But of all these personal

1

treasures, my favourite is a plaster cast of a grey-wolf footprint. I made it while tracking wolves in the Sawtooth Mountains for an ITV documentary. Humble as it is, that plaster cast and its story is the inspiration for this book.

Canis lupus, the grey wolf, is an adaptable creature able to live in a wide variety of habitats, from the barren arctic tundra, through the great boreal forest, the diminishing broadleaved woodlands and prairie grasslands to the forbidding desert. The wolf once ranged across most of the North American continent. While the species has always persisted in Canada, within the United States the grey wolf was effectively eradicated from the country by the westward expansion of the population during the nineteenth century and the years which followed. 'Manifest Destiny' for the fledgling America nation spelled 'Merciless Doom' for the American grey wolf.

Today, though, through the reintroduction efforts of conservationists, grey wolves have established populations in northern Wisconsin, northern Michigan, northern Minnesota, western Montana, the Yellowstone area of Wyoming, Idaho, Washington State and Alaska. And in southwest New Mexico and eastern Arizona, a Mexican subspecies of the grey wolf was reintroduced to protected parkland. Successful reintroductions, however, as I would find out, are not always welcomed.

My wolf track is from the Sawtooth Mountains of central Idaho. In 1995, fifteen grey wolves were released, followed the next year by another twenty. While no one knew at the time whether or not the reintroduction would prove successful, the painstaking work of the biologists paid off. When I cast my track in 2009, the population stood at more than 800 wolves. In fact, so well had the population recovered that in just a few days the wolf was to lose its protected status in Idaho and licensed wolf hunting would be permitted.

It was an interesting time to be in Idaho. Tensions were high: on one side stood the federally backed conservationists; on the other a powerful local lobby of hunters and ranchers who were complaining that the wolves threatened their livelihoods and way of life. Both sides had valid arguments, which they expounded with heartfelt passion, while in between, as is so often the case, the wolves stood in the dock, under sentence of death, oblivious to the human debate, simply living according to their nature. Here was an experiment at the frontier of rewilding, teetering on a knife edge.

What I found most alarming, though, was the widespread, profound hatred towards the wolf which I encountered – a hatred fuelled and fanned by the malicious lies and anti-wolf propaganda touted by extremists, heating emotions to boiling point, while making no sensible contribution to the debate. So frenzied was the atmosphere that there was a belief that wolves were everywhere and that the community was under siege. It was a bizarre and ridiculous situation.

From a filming perspective, even with the assistance of top local wolf biologists and two of the most experienced American wildlife cinematographers, finding wolves to film proved to be incredibly difficult. A long time had to be spent glassing the terrain in the hope of spotting wolves or, more likely, the ravens that so often follow a pack. Even when we found wolves, they had the edge in the steep mountainous terrain, easily loping up slopes in minutes that would take us as many hours to climb. When I eventually did rest the lens of my scope on a wolf pack, contrary to the propaganda, they were hunting voles not elk.

I was driving one morning when the vaguest movement caught my eye from across a damp meadow. I pulled into a large layby and set up my spotting scope on my tripod. There in the distance were four wolves hunting voles. It was a bad time for the voles: spring meltwaters had evicted many of their number from the security of their burrows, and the wolves were happily cleaning up on the abundance. Off to one side, a large female was sat very forlornly licking a clearly painfully injured foot. Even from my far vantage point, the blood of the wound could be seen. In the background, a large male was more difficult to keep track of.

I estimate that I had been watching the wolves for no more than two minutes when a white station wagon pulled into the layby and parked beside me. Given that the parking area could easily have accommodated two articulated lorries, I realised that my activity was the cause of interest, which was confirmed when a woman stepped out of the driver's door, leaving it open. She was wearing glasses and walked over to me while peering in the direction my scope was pointing. 'Are those wolves?' she asked. When I confirmed her suspicion, she let fly her total venom at such terrible animals. I listened patiently to her rant. She was obviously aware that I was with the film crew – word spreads like wildfire in small mountain communities. When she had finished, I asked her if she would like a better look and showed her how to focus and adjust the scope.

To my surprise, she accepted the invitation and started to watch the wolves. Then a strange thing happened – her tone softened. I explained that they were hunting for voles, and from her descriptions of the way they pounced, it was clear that she enjoyed watching them. I then pointed out the injured wolf, and there was a volte-face in her attitude. All of a sudden, while not defending the depredations of the wolf on cattle, she showed much greater tolerance. We talked for a while, and I explained a little about the true biology of the wolf. It transpired that she had not personally lost livestock to wolves but had heard that some other ranchers had. As she left, she confided in me that she didn't really mind the wolves, but her husband wanted them dead. Clearly that was the party line she felt obliged to support.

The next morning, the cameras were due to film aerial views from a helicopter and then general views of the Sawtooth Range. For me, it meant a rare quiet morning. Packing some forensic dental plaster and my brew kit into my daypack, I returned to that layby and hiked out into the mountains in search of tracks to cast. It was a cold, damp day, and the terrain was beautiful, with the dusky green sage brush having mostly emerged from under a thawing mantle of snow. I walked for some five miles trying to avoid breaking the ice that was glazing the large puddles so as to remain silent and improve my chance of seeing some wolves. A wolf's sense of hearing is estimated to be sixteen times more sensitive than ours.

I remember that walk well. I had packed my trusty, old and well-worn-in hiking boots for the trip only to discover that by the end of this day's walking the midsole had completely disintegrated. Five miles in, I found day-old tracks of a lone wolf following the trail I was on, which followed the contour at the base of a slope. The wolf had been walking on coarse sand on the right-hand side of the track in the opposite direction to me. Walking to the side of the track in this way had put the wolf tight up against the slope, keeping it well out of sight of any prey higher up the hill.

Unfortunately, the melting snow meant that the sand had the consistency of wet porridge, so none of the tracks retained sufficient detail for casting. I followed the trail regardless, relishing the opportunity to learn more about how a wolf moves in such a landscape. A mile further on, still following the base of the hill, the trail and the wolf tracks turned right towards a new valley.

Here I found what I was looking for – a series of well-defined imprints. Taking clear, icy meltwater from a small stream, I mixed the plaster and filled the tracks I had selected. The instructions promised that the plaster would be set in fifteen minutes. From experience, I knew this was a gross underestimation and that having used very cold water it would take even longer. I estimated at least ninety minutes, probably two hours. I decided to wait.

On the opposite side of the track was a slight rise covered in sage brush. I walked up this rise for fifty metres and sat down. Given the frantic pace at which we had been working, I decided a short nap would be wise. I put on my Buffalo mountain jacket for its warmth and windproof quality and lay down. Submerged in the fragrant sage brush and breathing the cleanest mountain air, I soon drifted off to sleep.

I am not certain how long I had dozed for when my subconscious alarm roused me. Lying down in the sage brush, I was hidden, so I used the opportunity to allow my eyes to adjust to the bright light. Then I sat up very slowly and carefully and peered across the tops of the sage brush. There, not thirty metres from me was a wolf, stood stock still staring at the puddles of slowly hardening plaster. It was huge, and I realised that it was the alpha male of the pack, the same male which had proved elusive the day before. Unaware of my presence, he was motionless, staring with wary curiosity at those strange blobs of plaster.

Moments such as this are wonderful and oh so rare. Luckily for me, the wind was not blowing from behind me. Had it been, I would never even have known the wolf was around. Raising my binocular very slowly, not just to avoid a betraying movement but also to reduce the possibility of stray noises and even scent, I could see the wolf more clearly, and from the way that the wind was moving his fur I was able to discern that the breeze was passing diagonally between us from his left to my right.

After watching for what seemed like an age, I smiled to attract his attention – it worked. The tiny movement caught his eye, and the wolf looked straight at me. Wolves have the most purposeful gaze of any creature that I have tracked; they seem to look through you with an X-ray intensity. I quite expected him to show a sign of fright, surprise or even irritable disdain, all reactions I have witnessed when surprising other predators. But not this wolf. His eyes met mine with profound confidence. I swear that had I been carrying a rifle, he would have dared me to shoot. He clearly recognised what I was. We stared at each other for a minute, maybe two, before I spoke to him, and then he calmly and effortlessly sprung around to his right and departed. What a privilege, a moment never to be forgotten. After a few minutes, I examined his footprints. They matched precisely those that I was casting.

Three days after I cast that track, wolves in Idaho lost their endangered-species status and tags were issued to hunters. That first year the state issued 26,428 tags to fulfil a strict cull quota of 220 wolves. Overall, at the end of the 2009 wolf-hunting season, 135 wolves had been culled, proving that despite the high skill level of the local hunters, the wolves were a more challenging prey than anticipated. Sadly, I learned that my wolf was one of those culled. Since then, the pattern has continued – the wolf population has continued to increase, and they are now being found in an ever-widening range of locations. Naturally, conflicts with ranchers have also increased, although not as dramatically as forecast. Unfortunately, in a few cases, individual ranchers have suffered devastating losses that are no longer compensated, as the ranchers now have the right to protect their stock against wolf predation. As always, conservation comes at a financial price that somehow has to be met. Most hearteningly, though, some of the heat from the extremists has been cooled as people have adjusted to the wolves return.

Rewilding works largely on restoring ecosystems with the minimum of interference by humans. Wolves, though, pose a challenge for rewilding, as they are both an apex predator and a keystone species. While they can pose a threat to human livestock and domestic animals, they can equally have a profoundly beneficial impact on whole ecosystems. More importantly, removing them can cause an ecosystem to collapse.

Studies from places such as Yellowstone have shown that reintroducing wolves has had some dramatic impacts, most notably keeping the resident elk (*Cervus canadensis*) population on the move, which reduces localised overgrazing pressure, allowing trees to re-establish themselves. This in turn increases woodland, providing more habitat for birds and other wildlife. Increased woodland also slows the runoff of water, reducing soil erosion and establishing improved freshwater and riverine habitats. These impacts have been widely hailed as vindication for the concept of rewilding, but it is worth noting that this effect has not proved to be as widespread in Yellowstone as was originally expected. Nature once again demonstrating her mysterious complexity.

In truth, the wolf reintroduction is still a work in progress, with many lessons yet to be learned. It will take much longer until we fully understand the role of the wolf in the larger ecosystem. One thing, though, that the majority of biologists agree about is that it would have been far better to have protected the wolf, rather than having to reintroduce the species after an absence of many decades. As we face up to the reality of global warming and the consequences of our impact on our natural environment, we need to work much harder at restoring ecosystems not just in prescribed wilderness areas and national parks but everywhere, even within our cities.

Making that documentary back in 2009, I had one other great privilege. I had the opportunity to work with members of the Native American Nez Perce nation, who had been the sponsors for the wolf reintroduction back in the 1990s. They were fascinating. When I interviewed them, they told me that as a people they had lived alongside wolves for thousands of years, and that throughout this time they had made their living as hunter-gatherers in direct competition with the wolf for food, but that they had never hated it. Far from it. For them, the wolf was known as a creature that cared for its young, that worked in a society just like people, and above all was a master hunter to be revered and emulated. Competition from the wolf made them stronger; indeed, they wished to be more like the wolf. Helping to reintroduce the species was to welcome back a brother and to restore spiritual balance to the land, land which they hold to be sacred.

What was apparent in talking with the Nez Perce was that their attitude to the wolf was based upon a keen observation and understanding of wolf biology. It made me think back to that lady I had shared my spotting scope with. Perhaps the secret to a more spiritual involvement with nature lies in a closer observation of wildlife and the understanding that results.

In my life, I have had the opportunity to work with and learn from tribal peoples worldwide. I have travelled widely in some of our most remote and pristine wildernesses. I find myself being constantly asked if I am frightened by the creatures or hostile dangers of the wild – I am not. To me, it seems the strangest question. I wonder, have we become so removed from nature that we now fear our original home? I do not travel in wild places to challenge myself or to conquer nature. I travel there to better understand nature, to gain physical and spiritual enrichment. I have taken the time to learn about and understand what I may encounter, a process which has taught me to respect and not fear the challenges of the wild.

Being in wild places where there are potentially dangerous predators heightens the senses wonderfully, with a rewarding sense of being alive, a feeling that is otherwise totally dulled by the security of safety-obsessed urbanity. As human society grasps the consequences of centuries of environmental abuse and we begin to work to rewild our damaged ecosystems, I am interested in the damage that those centuries have wrought on humanity itself. If we are to adapt to restored environments, we surely need to rewild ourselves too. Along the way, we will perhaps learn to know ourselves better and to come closer in understanding to the other creatures that we share our lifetimes with. With that wolf in mind, with whom I shared but a few minutes of my existence, this is my humble contribution to this vital cause.

The caribou feeds the wolf,
but it is the wolf who keeps the caribou strong.

Inuit proverb

SMELL

Smell is a potent wizard that transports you across thousands of miles and all the years you have lived.

Helen Keller, *The World I Live In*

Just two days ago, I was asked what subject I find the most rewarding to teach. Having assumed that it would be fire lighting or the identification of wild foods, my inquisitor was astonished when I answered that I take the greatest reward from teaching the uses of our senses. I felt it was necessary to elaborate, explaining that this subject, more than any other, underpins every other aspect of bushcraft, connects each branch of the study, can find daily application wherever we are and has beyond all else the most profound capacity to improve the quality of our experience of life. I have received many letters from former students supporting my assertion, some detailing how it has beneficially changed their lives. As we start out together on a journey in search of a stronger connection with nature, nothing can be of greater fundamental importance.

Our journey has already begun. In fact, it started on the day that we were born, even before we opened our eyes. When we drew our first sweet breath of life-giving air into our tiny pristine lungs, we unwittingly embarked on a sensory exploration of the world, employing our oldest and most enigmatic sensibility, our ability to detect chemicals by their smell.

Our sense of smell is mysterious. Only in recent years have researchers had the tools to better investigate its unique sensory relationship with our brain. Quite unlike any other sense, our ability to detect and interpret odours is instinctive and intuitive, a response that triggers emotions and memories. In a world that is overloaded by precisely resolved audio and visual stimuli, our sense of smell seems vague, difficult to quantify, resistant to the scrutiny of science. But as we shall discover, it is an incredibly powerful, sophisticated genetic legacy that nature has endowed us with, to a degree above our other senses, for not only is it one of our first stimuli in life, it is also the one sense that does not fade or diminish when we pass middle age. Throughout our lives, our sense of smell will refresh itself every four to eight weeks.

The nebulous nature of our sense of smell has frustrated empirical scientists and philosophers through the ages. In *Treatise on the Sensations*, published in 1754, Étienne Bonnot de Condillac summed up an attitude to our sense of smell which persists to this very day: 'Of all the senses it is the one which appears to contribute least to the cognitions of the human mind.' But it is its very obscurity to conscious investigation that I believe reveals our sense of smell's importance.

Scents float through the air carried on vacillating currents. The strength of the odour can vary in intensity and significance. Despite this, we can establish both the direction from which the odour originates as well as gauging the distance of the odour source. One year I was searching for a bushman village that had moved in the intervening two years since my last visit. I was told that it was close to the carcass of a rogue elephant that had recently been culled by the authorities. With only a rough description of the location of the carcass, I and a colleague drove north through the flat landscape of comiphora bushes, in which for many miles, in all directions, visibility is reduced to fifty metres. Having once before had to locate an elephant carcass like this, I planned on using my sense of smell. Crossing a shallow depression that during the rainy season fills and becomes a life-bringing water pan for the local wildlife, we could find no indication of either people or elephant, nor were there vultures circling to indicate its location.

Then, as we were scanning the skies, the faintest hint of decay reached our nostrils. A scent not dissimilar to a beef stock cube, slightly sweet and meaty, it was also lightly tinged with the corruption of death. But it was faint. It seemed to be coming from our right towards the north-northeast. Turning the vehicle in that direction, we drove a track that approximated the direction of the odour. After half a mile, we stopped and sniffed the air again. The smell was slightly stronger and now hinted at a more northeasterly direction. At the first opportunity, we turned on a more eastward-leading track.

Another mile and we stopped. There was no scent on the air. Establishing the wind direction from the colder, more evaporative side of my licked finger, we discovered that it was still coming from the northeast. We had probably overshot the scent trail.

Turning and driving back, we stopped every two hundred metres to sniff the air. Eventually, after about four such halts, we caught a whiff of the scent from our right. It felt as though we were on the eastern edge of the scent trail. This was ideal, as it is easier to estimate the trail direction on its edge, where there is strong scent contrast for comparison.

We turned north towards the scent at the first opportunity. We realised we were closing in on the source from the increasing intensity of the smell, and then suddenly it was gone. We had driven out of the far western side of the scent plume. There was no passable track to drive up towards the scent, so we looked for opportunities to circle right. What was interesting was that we both agreed on the estimate of the distance to the source. Continuing in this way, taking suitable turnings afforded by the bush, occasionally squeezing the 4x4 through the deadly barbed thorns and avoiding becoming stuck in patches of soft sand, I estimated that we had overshot the source and were circling around it.

Through the undergrowth I could see a distinct mass, like a large termite mound but without a spire. A little further and there was a foot trail which showed a lot of recent barefoot traffic. Investigating the trail on foot, it led directly towards the mound, and now the scent became overpowering.

We had found the elephant carcass. It was surrounded by the ashes of small campfires and flattened piles of leaves. The local San people had made fires to cook meat whilst they'd butchered the carcass. The leaves were to provide a sand-free surface on which to collect and pack the meat. Little was left. Using the foot trail to provide a bearing, we headed in that direction until we located our friends and their little grass huts. It was a wonderful exercise to track a scent like a bloodhound. I have long remembered it and wondered at the capacity for olfactory awareness that our distant ancestors might once have demonstrated.

What we know of our sense of smell is still very basic. We understand the mechanisms by which we detect scents but very little about the way our brains process these signals. When we breathe in through our nose, we draw air into our nasal cavity. Every breath is laden with tiny scent molecules called ligands. Inside the nasal cavity, the air circulates, passing over the sticky tissue of the olfactory mucosa, which lines the roof of the nasal cavity. In the process, ligands adhere to this mucus and diffuse within it. Here they are received by millions of tiny cilia, the multibranched ends of our olfactory receptor neurons. The axons of these neurons pass through perforations in the cribriform plate of our skull's ethmoid bone, which separates the nasal cavity from the brain cavity. Inside the cranial cavity, they connect to our brains via our olfactory bulbs. We have two olfactory bulbs, which are located centrally, beneath the front portion of the brain. Here, signals from the olfactory receptor neurons synapse, or connect, with mitral cells within spherical structures known as glomeruli and the process of smell interpretation begins.

A complex miracle of biology, our olfactory bulbs are the primary reception centre for smell stimuli. In ways still under investigation, they seem to function somewhat like a radio tuner, able to filter out background odours and discriminate between them. They can adjust the sensitivity and volume of odour detection and allow other areas of the brain to selectively tune in to specific odours of interest, even, as we have seen, establishing the direction and distance of an odour source. They can also respond very swiftly to changing environmental circumstances.

Signals leaving the olfactory bulbs pass into the hippocampus, amygdala and orbitofrontal cortex, regions of the brain that are responsible for memories, emotions and decision-making. Precisely how these regions of the brain process olfactory signals remains somewhat elusive, but through these organs we can learn odours and store memories of smells we consider important by association with their pleasantness, unpleasantness, reward or threat. These associations are often strongly linked to emotional life events, so much so that an odour can trigger the recall of a vivid memory of that event as well as the emotional response felt at the time.

My own strongest experience of this kind was smelling diesel fuel at a filling station for the first time after surviving a helicopter crash.

The scent instantly triggered a strong physiological response. For a moment, I lost track of where I was, powerfully charged emotions transporting me back to that experience, its place, its time, complete with the sound of the crash and the feeling of the environmental atmosphere at the crash site, even generating a rush of adrenalin.

Fortunately, since then my brain has had time to process the experience and refile it in a more historic region of my memory, and I have never since experienced this response. Now when I detect the scent of diesel, I have a choice over whether to recall that memory or not. But why is there such a powerful link between scent and emotion? There are perhaps many reasons which yet elude us, but such responses certainly have survival value.

By connecting odours to our emotions, nature has not only provided us with an excellent means of remembering and cataloguing scents and their meanings, it has also provided us with an incredible early warning system. Emotional responses occur quickly. Scent warnings are plugged directly into these rapid responses and as such are capable of initiating action without the need for cognitive processing. In a crisis, this can eliminate a step in the decision-making process, enabling us to respond almost instantaneously to a life threat detected by its associated odour. It may well be that when we describe a physical response to a situation as having been instinctive, it was driven by an olfactory warning.

Our sense of smell is extraordinary. It can pick out significant odours from within a complex melange of scents. The range of smells which we can detect is unimaginably vast, hence there are far too many to be individually named. In some ways, our sense of smell is a hidden superpower. When I am walking in wild country, particularly where I might encounter dangerous animals, I think of my olfactory sense as a valuable scouting capability, constantly alert to dangers that are obscure or hidden from my other senses. Scent alerts are frequently very subtle and may pass totally unheeded by those who choose to disregard them or do not value their olfactory capacity. I have learned through experience to trust this sense and to allow it to feed into my overall sensory assessment of my environment. With practice, I have learned to recognise the feeling that I am smelling something of interest. At these moments, I allow the olfactory report to raise the alertness of my other senses, whilst I interrogate my sense of smell more carefully.

I clearly remember the first time that I made this work. I was walking in old hornbeam coppice when I felt that I was close to something. I stopped and raised my sensory alertness and sniffed the air. Instantly, I caught the faintest odour. My feeling was that it was a deer scent, although I could not say with certainty that I was correct. Working on my feeling, assuming that it was deer, I rationalised that if I could smell it, then it must be very close. I scrutinised every possible hiding place with my eyes and the aid of my binocular. Nothing. Nor was there any sign of droppings. I sniffed the air again and established what direction the scent was coming from. Silently I walked towards the source, being extremely careful not to break any twigs under foot. It was a still, late-summer day – the scent trail I was following could hardly be moving as I stalked it.

In this way, I followed the scent for 200 metres through the woods, at which point the odour was clearly much stronger. I was now certain that it was a deer scent. Then, led totally by my nose, my eyes recognised the outline of a fallow buck sitting in the shadows at the base of a bushy field maple, just ten metres in front of me. He was totally motionless and very well hidden, his pelage blending perfectly with the ground, enhanced further by the disruptive dappling of shadows and sunlight.

Even though I am used to spotting deer, I do not think I would ever have seen him, unless he had moved in some way, without following his scent. It was a revelatory moment. Since that now long-distant day, I have concentrated harder on using my sense of smell. I now regularly detect deer by their scent before I can see or hear them.

That it is possible to use our sense of smell in such a proactive way seems contrary to accepted wisdom. Whenever we discuss our ability to detect odours, we inevitably make comparisons to other animals, such as bears and bloodhounds for whom smell is the dominant sense, but we make no comparison to those animals for which it is not. Consequently, we create the impression that our sense of smell is in some way substandard.

Nothing could be further from the truth. We have a balance of sensory abilities that provide us with an astonishing capacity to detect nuanced changes in our environment. Our sense of smell is an intrinsic part of that ability, as testified to by the way our olfactory centre connects with our brain. It is not that we cannot smell things, more the case that we do not choose to use our sense of smell. Modern research by Matthias Laska from Linköping University has established that we hold our own in comparison to other animals. His 2017 paper *Human and Animal Olfactory Capabilities Compared* concludes that

> qualitative comparisons of olfactory capabilities suggest that human subjects have at least the basic ability of using their sense of smell in all behavioural contexts in which animals are known to use their noses. This includes gathering of information about the chemical environment, food selection, spatial orientation, social communication, reproduction, as well as learning and memory.

Taken together, these findings suggest that the human sense of smell is not generally inferior compared to that of animals and much better than traditionally thought.

When I first started researching our sense of smell nearly forty years ago, it was estimated that humans could differentiate between 10,000 different odours. While this sounded impressive, it never seemed enough to explain the delicacy of our sense of smell, certainly not that demonstrated by wine tasters. Today, research has updated the estimate to a whopping 1 trillion odours – 1,000,000,000,000. Little wonder that we do not have words to describe all these smells.

It is also astonishing how low our threshold for detecting an odour can be. It has been discovered that some people are able to smell trichloroanisole, the chemical that is responsible for the odour of a corked bottle of wine, at concentrations of parts per trillion. Maybe a love of good wine is the perfect motivation for human olfactory excellence.

While some odours are easily detected and recognisable, such as the smell of smoke, blood or putrefaction, others are more subtle, such as the approach of rainfall in the desert. This is a scent that desert nomads recognise at unbelievable distances, but which novices only detect when the rain is almost upon them or becomes visible in the sky. I was once advised by a desert Bedouin that we should 'hurry before the water floods the wadi'. The wadi was yet a day's drive ahead across the desert. Puzzled, I asked him why he thought the wadi would flood. Without translating the question, my young Bedouin interpreter smiled, and, pointing to the distant, very flat horizon, explained, 'He smells the rain in the mountains.' Nothing more needed to be said, and, yes, he was right.

Such odour sensitivity reveals how good the human sense of smell is and that we become especially alert to those odours that have special significance to us. But unless tainted by contaminants, water is considered odourless, so what do we smell when we smell rain? It is the interaction of the precipitation and its attendant humidity meeting the parched desert ground that produces the distinctive scent of rain. This moisture liberates a range of fragrant chemicals called petrichor, which become aerosol when rain splashes from the ground surface. The petrichor odour is a cocktail of fragrances, some produced by volatile plant oils, with the most prominent being geosmin, which results from actinobacteria that break down organic matter.

This rain odour can also be smelled when rain falls on a concrete conurbation after a period of hot, dry weather, although it is less pleasant than the desert version, in which the fragrant aromas from volatile, ultraviolet protective plant oils sweeten the edge of the more sweaty-sock or old-laundry-basket-like actinobacteria scent. But even though rainfall can be smelled, I have never yet travelled with a desert nomad capable of locating ground water by its scent or, for that matter, by divination.

That the full capability of our sense of smell reveals itself in life-threatening circumstances, such as the arid desert, reinforces my belief in its survival value. It also becomes apparent under stressful circumstances, when our other senses are in some way reduced. There are many references of heightened olfactory awareness from warfare in thick forest or rainforests, where dense vegetation reduces visibility and increases the potential for an enemy to lay an ambush from concealment.

During the tropical conflicts in Vietnam, Borneo and the Malay Peninsula, and in other theatres of the Second World War, soldiers were taught to avoid the use of scented items such as boot polish, soap and toothpaste to avoid their inapposite odours betraying their presence to their foes. This was particularly the case during the Mau Mau emergency of the early 1950s during which the elusive Mau Mau freedom fighters living close to the ground developed a legendary ability to detect their enemies by scent:

> *In the Mt Kenya forests a surrenderee guiding a patrol detected*
> *the presence of another patrol three hours after it had passed and*
> *ten yards from the track it had used. Their presence was given*
> *away solely by the powerful smell left by their clothes brushing*
> *the bushes on either side of the track.*
>
> Notes on Forest Lore, Operations and Training

Our sense of smell, then, is an important defence mechanism, forewarning us of a multitude of dangers, such as, for example, a gas leak. However, there are some dangers which cannot be smelled, such as carbon monoxide, which is invisible, odourless and toxic. It is vitally important to deploy electronic carbon monoxide alarms where such a threat is known to exist.

As a field naturalist, my sense of smell is very important to me. I love to explore the countryside with my nose sniffing wild mint, marjoram and wild garlic leaves. It adds a whole new dimension to the experience of nature. One of the greatest scent delights of all occurs at night during the English summer: honeysuckle perfuming the forest, compelling moths to unwittingly assist in its pollination. But it is in support of one of my greatest passions, the study of fungi, that I find the greatest use of my olfactory sense.

Fungi are fascinating in every respect but without access to a microscope many have such subtle differences that they can be difficult to distinguish between. Here scent is one of the tools in the mycologist's arsenal, for it is often possible to differentiate between two similar species by their scent. Some of the fungal odours are fascinating. For example, consider the following fungal pairings easily mistaken by sight:

The panther cap (*Amanita pantherina*) smells of cut potato
while
The blusher (*Amanita rubescens*) smells indistinct

The fools webcap (*Cortinarius orellanus*) when cut smells faintly of radish
while
The chanterelle (*Cantherellus cibarius*) smells lightly of apricot

The ivory funnel (*Clitocybe dealbata*) smells delicately sweet
while
The miller (*Clitopilus prunulus*) smells strongly of flour

In fact, there are some wonderful odours in the fungal flora: coconut, aniseed, curry, radish, gunpowder and so on. But there is a problem – scent is a very personal, subjective sense. While one person might describe a fungal scent as being like old motor oil, another person sniffing the same fungus might perceive it in a totally different way. This can also be influenced by our genetics, for people from differing races and genetic strains can have widely differing olfactory perception. It may even be that one person simply cannot smell an odour that is overpowering to another. When learning to recognise fungi, it is essential to tune into one's own sense of smell and to calibrate it to that recorded in the field guides; for this, there is no substitute to accompanying an expert in the field when clear identification of a species can be taught and its scent learned.

It may, however, be encouraging to learn that professional tasters and perfumers who rely on their sense of smell in their work are not born with their olfactory sensitivity. It is something they develop with long training, a considerable part of which is learning the language and classification methodology employed in their industry.

Doctors also employ their sense of smell. A friend who is a consultant plastic surgeon once explained that he is able to differentiate between infections by their odours. But even this is a basic level of skill compared to that of Joy Milne, a retired nurse from Perth, who astonished the world with her ability to recognise sufferers with Parkinson's disease by the disease tainting their body odour. Clearly the boundaries of human olfactory capability are still being defined.

The great thing about our sense of smell is that the more we exercise it, the better it becomes. In 2019, Johannes Frasnelli's team at Université du Québec à Trois-Rivières, found that after just six weeks of olfactory training there is a measurable thickening of the brain's cortex. His team had previously discovered that people with a thicker cortex had better olfactory perception.

Considering the poor regard in which we generally hold our sense of smell, we manage to surround ourselves with an astonishing diversity of overpoweringly pungent fragrances. This is not a new phenomenon. We have been anointing ourselves with bouquets, balms, fragrant oils and distillations for thousands of years. The oldest known perfume maker, and therefore chemist, was Tapputi-Belatekallim, described in a Cuneiform tablet dated to 1200BCE, from Babylonian Mesopotamia. She is described using water and other solvents to distil fragrances from flowers, oils, calamus, myrrh and cyperus. Perhaps Tapputi knew as well as modern chemists that beyond reason and logic, humans desire an agreeable scent for our foods, our living spaces and for our bodies.

Modern fragrances are chemical cocktails cunningly designed to win our attention and ultimately to encourage us to part impulsively with our hard-earned wages. Perfumeries are keenly aware of this and actively encourage their consumers to associate fragrance offerings with a desired lifestyle. A fragrance alone cannot achieve this, so they marry their scent to branding and compelling imagery designed to conjure a visual association which stimulates an emotional response, deploying advertisements which are provocatively suggestive of cherished, perhaps secretly indulgent, desires – the more luxuriant the association, the higher the price of the perfume. It is a winning combination that perhaps reveals we are not masters of our sense of smell but its servants. Today, the global worth of the fragrance industry is said to be in the region of $50 billion, which is not to be sniffed at!

Although it is not always in the forefront of our minds, our sense of smell is constantly functioning. If we wish to develop it, we must practise using it, most particularly in the field of activity we most intend to deploy it. But all olfactory practice will be beneficial, particularly when assessing scents against others. Learning to describe smells assists us in building a framework in our minds for scent investigation. Above all we, need to give ourselves time to notice odours and to learn to recognise them, paying special attention to scents at those times when their source is apparent. If we wish to sniff an odour more efficiently, we can direct our nostrils towards it and take several short sniffs to draw in the ligands we are searching for. Sometimes closing our eyes can also assist in an odour assessment.

Consider scent for what it is: a whole separate dimension to the world, one which most of us walk through without even noticing. It has been my experience that actively practising using our sense of smell can also switch on our other senses, increasing our overall alertness and perception.

As in so many cases, it is when we are stripped of a sense that we discover its true value. Being unable to detect odours is a condition called anosmia; it can be a temporary or permanent condition that results from injury, illness or genetic difference. Without the ability to detect the odours of smoke or putrefaction, anosmia can lead to higher incidences of burn injuries and food poisoning. Particularly for those who develop anosmia later in life, the loss of the sense of smell is often associated with depression. Much of the joy of life is related to scent, particularly the flavour of our food. As we shall discover, our sense of smell is also closely linked to our enjoyment of flavours.

TASTE

Watch a French housewife as she makes her way slowly
along the loaded stalls ... searching for the peak of ripeness
and flavour ... What you are seeing is a true artist at work.

Keith Floyd

By comparison to the esoteric complexity of our sense of smell, our sense of taste appears positively bland, mundane and mechanical. Yet taste is vitally important for our health and wellbeing and is complex in its own unique way.

While eating is essential for life, it is not without risk. The first important role our sense of taste fulfils is as the gatekeeper to our mouths, protecting us from consuming poisons or otherwise harmful substances. It also enables us to identify food stuffs that offer the most nutrients and calories vital for production of life's energy. I would also argue that before the advent of modern chemical analysis, our sense of taste in conjunction with our sense of smell was our principal means of recognising medicinal compounds found in plants and the primary way in which we determined edible from poisonous foodstuffs, particularly plants.

But more than just protecting us, our sense of taste also greatly enriches our lives, for we all must eat. We each have an inbuilt curiosity about new flavours and cuisines. Talking food is one of the few truly cross-cultural experiences of life, and one which transports us back to the earliest days of cooking when we first shared meat grilled on the latest technological discovery, fire.

One of the best meals I have eaten was in the company of an artisanal cheesemaker in the French Alps. We had just walked her goat herd up to an ungrazed mountain pasture. The air was crisp and thin, the sun warming and the pasture verdant, the lush grass barely finding space to grow between the abundance of edible herbs. We spent a few minutes picking lady's mantle, salad burnet and other edible leaves, then spread a small red checked cloth under the shade of a tree. I sliced an artisanal baguette with an Opinel No08 pocketknife. It so perfectly matches the bread that I have often wondered which came first, the loaf or the knife? As I did so, my host produced a jar of dandelion jam and a paper package of soft white goat's cheese from her knapsack.

I learned from the expert cheesemaker that in the mountains the local cheesemakers consider this to be the best goat's cheese. It is delicate, creamy, barely solid, with a delightful flavour a far cry from the hard cheese we find on the refrigerated shelves of supermarkets. Historically, this cheese was too fragile to be transported out of the mountains by pack animals and consequently was only tasted by mountain folk, or those prepared to hike in. It was a simple poetic repast, enjoyed in the very meadow that had been converted into the cheese. Interestingly, eating that cheese, as fresh as it can ever be eaten, I could pick out the flavours of the pasture. It was a sensory epiphany – for the first time in my life, I truly understood the meaning of the French word *terroir*: the concept that the flavour of locally produced food can embody the environment of the region, the uniqueness of the growth habitat and the quality of the production method.

I also realised in those few mouthfuls that the term has been misappropriated by large-scale commercial producers. Like a three-star Michelin dish, every molecule of flavour in that humble meal spoke of the meticulous attention paid to the ingredients, from the grass in the meadow to the loving care afforded the goats, the cheese-maker bringing everything together with the dedicated virtuosity of a conductor leading a great orchestra. The whole process was avowed without compromise to provide quality of flavour rather than quantity of production.

All of our senses are meant to function in concert with their partner senses, but perhaps none more so than our sense of taste, which depends also on our sense of smell and our trigeminal nerves' ability to detect texture, temperature and pain. When we eat, the aromas from our food are also able to reach the olfactory mucosa in our nasal cavity via our nasopharynx opening at the back of our mouth. These scents in combination with our taste detection are critical to our perception and appreciation of flavour. We see this when a diner breathes in deeply to imbibe a plate of fine food's aromas before taking a bite. In the process, she explores a kaleidoscope of odours that will increase her salivation, raising and improving the sensory alertness of her taste buds in anticipation of the mouthwatering flavours flooding the brain. It is a joyous engagement with a process that perhaps evolved primarily as a defence mechanism. Long before restaurants, this olfactory contribution to our sense of taste enabled us to detect the volatile odours of food that was putrefying, tainted by harmful bacteria or which carried other volatile scents warning of danger. Given the sensitivity and swift response of our olfactory sense, we can think of it as an early warning system, alerting our taste senses to pay greater attention.

When I started to explore the use of our senses for fieldcraft, the doctrine being espoused was that different parts of our tongue were responsible for detecting different taste modalities: the tip of the tongue for sweet, the sides for salt and sour, and the back of the tongue for bitter. Despite the widespread acceptance of this theory, it never seemed to be clearly demonstrable when tested. Now research has disproven the concept.

Today, taste receptors have been found for five tastes: bitter, sour, salt, sweet and umami (savouriness). And research continues to attempt to identify whether we might also have other taste senses, but more of that later.

The human tongue is covered with papillae, the little bumps that we can see covering our tongues. There are four different forms of papillae. Filiform papillae are the most common and create the white surface of our tongue. These do not contain taste buds but are responsible for grip, cleansing the mouth, and aiding chewing and speech. The other three types of papillae each contain taste buds. Fungiform papillae are red and, as their name suggests, mushroom-shaped and found across the front two thirds of the tongue. Foliate papillae are mostly found towards the rear sides of the tongue and are crease-like folds in the tongue's surface, while circumvallate papillae, of which we have only ten to fourteen, are ring-shaped depressions located at the rear of the tongue.

On average, a taste bud survives for just ten days, and we each have between 2,000 to 8,000. After the age of fifty, just as some might argue we are becoming most appreciative of the finer tastes in life, there is a reduction in the number of taste buds. Nature is a cruel mistress.

Each taste bud has a pore that opens out to the surface of the tongue. This allows taste molecules and ions to enter. Regardless of its location on the tongue, each taste bud contains the taste chemoreceptors necessary to identify any of the five tastes, which means that we can detect any taste on any part of the tongue. Each chemoreceptor reports individually to its specific part of the brain's taste-perception centre, the gustatory cortex. Every sweet receptor reports to a sweet nexus. Every bitter receptor reports to a bitter nexus, and so forth.

Bitter

Although it is not strictly accurate to suggest there is a hierarchy to our taste capabilities, I cannot help thinking that our ability to detect bitter compounds is our most important. It has even been suggested that our bitter response may be a reflex. Strongly bitter substances can trigger a gag reflex, our body effectively and forcefully rejecting them. Infants are particularly sensitive to bitterness, suggesting that this sensory ability is inherited not learned. There is good reason for this: many poisons that can harm or kill us are bitter in taste, particularly plant toxins such as:

~ Cyanide, found in many plants such as cherry and
   apple seeds
~ Ricin, found in castor bean
~ Saponin, found widely in plants such as soapwort,
   horse chestnut and many legumes
~ Progoitrin, commonly found in plants in the cabbage
   family

While infants universally reject bitter tastes, adults can learn to tolerate some bitter compounds such as coffee, chocolate and beer, each containing psychoactive substances such as caffeine and alcohol. Perhaps this is because of the increased sense of inhibition and wellbeing that result, or perhaps they have other hidden medicinal benefits yet to be identified. Even so, the bitterness in coffee and chocolate is routinely mellowed by the addition of milk products and sugar.

It fascinates me that our hunter-gatherer ancestors ate a much wider range of plants species than we do today. The majority of the wild greens they relied upon are far more bitter than we are willing to tolerate today. In my lifetime, even the tomatoes most popular in supermarkets have gravitated to sweeter varieties. Were our ancestors less sensitive to bitterness, or were they able to interpret its value differently than we do today? Certainly, by eating a wide diversity of wild greens, they accessed a nutritional treasure trove that makes our modern vegetable offerings appear nutritionally lacking.

While our sensitivity to bitterness can detect many chemical poisons, there are some which can bypass this defence mechanism. If we consider the aptly named death-cap fungus (*Amanita phalloides*), we encounter a wild mushroom that victims have described as being delicious to eat but which contains particularly toxic substances. Death-cap poisoning is particularly fascinating. After dining on this delicious fungus, victims do not experience any signs of poisoning for between six to twenty-four hours. For this reason, the symptoms – abdominal cramps, vomiting and diarrhoea that causes severe dehydration – are not always associated with the fungus meal. Aggressive hydration to counteract the dehydration and maintain healthy kidney function is essential first aid. By the time victims of death-cap poisoning are diagnosed, the toxins have often passed beyond the reach of usual liver-poisoning protocols. Only a small quantity – one quarter to half a cap of death cap – can prove fatal.

The fungus contains amatoxins that are absorbed by the liver and the kidneys. In the liver, the amatoxins inhibit cell regeneration and cause cell necrosis. The amatoxins are then ejected into bile, which becomes concentrated in the gall bladder. After eating a meal, the gall bladder releases bile into the gut along with the amatoxins. At the end of the small intestine, the bile is reabsorbed into the liver along with the amatoxins and so the vicious cycle of poisoning repeats itself, each cycle resulting in ever greater liver-cell necrosis. In the kidneys, assuming they are healthy, amatoxins are separated from the blood and sent to the bladder from where, if there is hydration to permit it, they can be voided by urination. Until the kidneys have removed all the amatoxins, the liver will continue to be damaged. As already stated, the kidneys must be kept well hydrated to function normally. Failure to maintain adequate hydration will lead to the amatoxins damaging kidney cells as well. If the kidneys fail, death usually follows shortly behind.

Treatment for death-cap poisoning is incredibly complicated. While several medicines, including one derived from milk thistle (*Silybum marianum*), seem to have shown promise, there is, as yet, no specific antidote. This should be a reminder of how we need all our senses for life. The death cap is an easy fungus to learn to recognise by sight and thereby to avoid.

Sour

Our ability to detect sour flavours enables us to identify and gauge bacterial decay, ripeness and fermentation processes. In this way, it also acts as a protection, warning us of potentially harmful bacteria in rotting meat and vegetables, which produce characteristically sour compounds. But our response to sourness is nowhere near as strong as our bitter response. This reflects our need to be able to determine ripeness in fruits by tasting.

Our sense of taste coupled with our sight, smell and touch provide a sophisticated means of evaluating the ripeness of wild fruits, differentiating between unripe, ripe and overripe. So precise is this evaluation that foragers can monitor the fruit on wild bushes and accurately predict the perfect moment to return to harvest it, even allowing for some tart fruits to decay slightly, a process which renders them more palatable. Experimenting with the decay of wild fruits in this way led our ancestors to the discovery of the fermentation process, managing beneficial sour decomposition processes to make bread and brew alcohol.

Salt

Our ability to sense saltiness is a fascinating aspect of our taste that remains puzzling to scientific investigation, despite humans having had a long relationship with the substance. Until the advent of refrigeration, the use of salt was one of our most important means to preserve foods. Today, salt is used by societies worldwide to enhance the flavours of food.

Salt, however, has its own tastes. Indeed, chefs utilise different salts for their specific flavours: sea salt rich in minerals such as magnesium and chloride provides a taste reminiscent of the ocean; Himalayan pink salt gives a mild pleasant taste; and delicately flavoured fleur de del, the most expensive salt of all, a fine crusting hand-gathered from the surface of salt marshes but only when the weather allows, is used only for finishing fine dishes of fish, eggs, meat, chocolate, caramel or the very freshest of salads. Salt enhances our foods by reducing bitterness and enhancing sweetness and umami. These effects cause us to crave salt, perhaps even becoming addicted to its flavour. We need salt for our wellbeing, but too much is unhealthy for us, causing raised blood pressure, which can exacerbate other health conditions.

Umami

The most recently accepted taste modality, umami is related to savouriness, specifically to the glutamate molecule. The ability to detect this flavour enables us to identify protein-rich foods and is closely linked to meat eating. But in addition to meat and poultry, umami is also found in fish, eggs and dairy, seaweed, dried tomatoes, garlic, onion, carrots, celery, potatoes, sweet potatoes, corn, soybeans, soya sauce, ginger, and broccoli, to mention just a few. Surely umami represents the joy of cooking. Just writing this list has set my mouth watering, and will send me in search of a cooking pot and a flame to cook over. Perhaps it was this taste that inspired our ancestors to master the making of fire.

Sweet

For much of the human population, calories are easily available in the form of high-energy starchy foods, sugary drinks and sweets. But for the remaining indigenous communities living a traditional life, the story is quite different. One of the constants of day-to-day living in hunter-gatherer communities is the search for sugar. This is not an easy food to obtain. Berries are mostly seasonal and for nomadic people can be difficult to store.

Around the world, many people have instead looked to insects that store sugar to provide life's sweetness. In their search for sugar, indigenous communities demonstrate an incredible taste-driven determination and an astonishing knowledge of natural history. I have watched in Indonesia as a man reached into a bee's nest for honey, with only a blindfold and a black bin liner over his arm for protection. I can still see his pained grimace. I have helped rainforest Indians in the head waters of the Orinoco River scoop the sweetest lemony honey from a tree felled to collect it, shared wild honey with the Bayaka people in the Central African Republic and delighted at the flavour of Australian trigona-bee honey with Aboriginal honey gatherers, who call it 'sugar bag'.

There are some places on our planet that are extraordinarily beautiful – the central Australian desert is one such example. Standing there in 1998 on the paprika-coloured earth, I watched with fascination as my Aboriginal guide, the one who had given me the honey ant made from resin, carefully scanned the ground. An old lady with white hair poking from under a woolly hat, she was clad, as Aboriginal ladies usually are, in a brightly coloured floral dress. In her leathery hands, she carried a metal digging stick five feet long that she referred to as a crowbar, and in her other hand a small short-handled shovel. Behind her, a young woman was following with a wooden *coolamon* under her arm. A *coolamon* is a tray made from wood used for digging, for transporting foods, as a mixing bowl and even as a cradle.

The old woman was watching carefully. 'There's one, see.' She pointed to a scurrying insect with the tip of the crowbar, one ant amongst many. Now she followed it, a tiny, fast-moving ant with a lightly banded abdomen. Tracking an ant is difficult, especially when you have never tried before. Several times I lost sight of the scurrying creature but could pick it up again by reference to where the old woman was looking. She of course never lost sight of it. And then she did. She shook her head and laughed, then resumed her search, quickly finding another ant.

This we followed until it vanished into a tiny hole in the sand. Carefully, she scraped the light scattering of dead leaves from around the hole to expose it and then, seating herself to one side, she began to dig with the tiny shovel. She was carefully following the hole down into the ground. I could not believe what I was watching. The skill level required to carry out that simple task was astounding. As she followed the tiny opening just four millimetres in diameter downwards into the ground, using the shovel and crowbar, she excavated a hole, a metre in diameter, in which she could sit. As she dug deeper, she started to sink from sight into the earth.

Eventually, five feet deep, with only the top of her woolly hat, incongruous in the scorching desert heat, showing above ground, she laid the shovel to one side and continued to dig very carefully into the dark-orange soil with her hands. Gently, the sand fell away from the face of her excavation to reveal a horizontal chamber, a hand-span wide and four centimetres tall, extending into the earth. Hanging from the roof of the chamber were rows of what resembled golden marbles. These were ants, each with a distended abdomen filled to bursting with a golden liquid, the plates of the abdomen stretched taught, creating black bands on the surface – honey ants, a legendary Aboriginal delicacy. With great finesse, she picked these ants from the roof of the chamber and passed them up to her young assistant to place in the *coolamon*.

But as she passed each one up it didn't go into the *coolamon*; instead, the young girl grasped the ant by its head and sucked out the sweet amber nectar from the abdomen, grinning with great pleasure. As fast as the old lady was harvesting them, the young woman was eating them. It was funny and a reminder of just how desirable sweet treats are in such a landscape. I am happy to report that I was also able to enjoy the delicious sweet taste of the honey-ant nectar.

At the end of our foraging session, we walked back to our Landcruiser to drive back to the community. The old lady was happy that I had assisted her in the digging, but mostly that I was genuinely interested to learn the process. Like many communities, hers had seen too many youths, seduced by the distractions of the modern technological world, failing to complete their schooling in traditional knowledge. I pondered the human desire for sugar and its ability to motivate the discovery of such a subterranean desert secret.

But Australia is not alone in providing surprising examples of ways in which people find sugar. In Tanzania, around Lake Eyasi, there are vast forests of baobab trees (*Adansonia digitata*). An incredibly beautiful landscape, particularly when the baobab are in flower, it is also one that has been greatly diminished in neighbouring regions, with trees felled by land-hungry farmers wielding chainsaws. Here in these forests live one of the last hunter-gatherer communities of Africa, the Hadza. They have an ancient association with this landscape, replete with incredible forest lore acquired over millennia. Walking with Hadza hunters is always fascinating, their knowledge of the flora and fauna extensive, their interaction with nature direct and immediate.

Sitting under the shade of a bush late one morning, their bows all carefully hung in the branches, for it is taboo to place a bow on the ground, we were interrupted by the persistent chattering of a light-brown thrush-sized bird. To my ears, it reminded me a little of a great-spotted woodpecker's chick-chick sound but was delivered with an insistence and urgency even a chiff chaff would be envious of. This bird was a greater honeyguide, which has the most appropriate scientific name of any creature I know: *Indicator indicator.*

One of the men answered the bird's call with a whistle, and we were up on our feet and following it. Chattering and flitting from tree to tree, it gradually led us to a baobab, where one of the men spotted honeybees entering and leaving from a crevice in the crotch of one of the upper branches. While one man made a fire with his hand drill, the other men cut green branches and saplings with their axes. The saplings were cut into pegs forty centimetres long, pointed at one end and roughly chamfered at the other. These pegs were then placed onto the fire to harden.

While this was happening, several large bundles of green branches were tied together with bark, and long strips of bark were tied together to make a cord. With the pegs deemed sufficiently hardened, one man began to hammer them into the soft, almost spongy, bark of the baobab with the back of his axe. Each peg acted as a foot support, forming a ladder to the bees' nest twenty feet above us.

Once within arm reach of the nest, which was now emanating a deep menacing hum of irritation, the man hooked his axe over his shoulder and used the cord to pull up one of the bundles that the others had ignited in the fire. This bundle was used to smoke the bees' nest, subduing them to allow the man to steal their honey. It would take four such bundles to subdue the bees. With his axe, the honey gatherer now chopped into the tree and pulled out large sheets of wax comb heavy with honey and threw them down.

As soon as they landed, the men below feasted on the sweet honey. Once again, tough luck for the man being stung up in the tree. Realising that he was missing out, he started to eat the honey as he pulled it out of the nest. This raised complaints from his colleagues below, whose faces were already covered in the sticky sugar. One man complained that he no longer had teeth and could not bite into the waxy comb well enough to take his portion.

However, on this occasion no one went without. There was plenty of honey for all and enough to carry back to the village. Some wax comb was left for the honeyguide to feast upon, which was the bird's reward. Collecting honey in this way is incredibly dangerous in such remote circumstances. Should a man fall and break his leg, the consequences are likely to prove fatal.

The cooperative relationship with the greater honeyguide is one of the most fascinating in the natural world, both in terms of the two-way communication between people and the free-living bird and the resulting increased success in obtaining food for both humans and the honeyguide. Having seen the whole process, I started to notice pegs in virtually every baobab tree in the forest and scars where pegs had formerly been hammered, testimony to the continuation of this ancient relationship, and, once again, all driven by our insatiable desire for the taste of sweetness.

Unfortunately, our desire for sugar can also be dangerous, particularly for indigenous communities. Sugar and fat are generally difficult to obtain in nature, which results in a strong desire for both amongst the world's indigenous communities. In a traditional lifestyle, this desire has beneficial survival value. However, a modern diet can be disastrous for hunter-gatherers. As they fall victim to the easy availability of sugar, fat and processed foods of low nutritional value, the result is an increase in diabetes, high cholesterol, heart disease, other associated health conditions and premature death. It also causes a loss of mobility and morale, which can lead to an unwillingness to continue with the hard labour of traditional life and a consequential loss of culture, hastened further by the premature mortality.

One of the saddest ironies is that we do not always recognise that sugar is an ingredient in modern food. Our tongues can be fooled by other flavour components, and we are unable to determine the concentration of sugar present. In one Canadian first-nation reservation shop I visited, a display at the checkout counter indicated graphically how much sugar was contained in the canned goods by placing a clear bag alongside each, with the sugar content represented by sugar cubes.

• • •

Bitter, sour, salt, umami, sweet: these are the predominant five tastes, but how do we explain other taste phenomenon, such as our ability to taste fatty foods, spicy foods, cool foods or astringent, drying substances? Umami was not officially recognised as a human taste modality until receptors cells for it were identified, and researchers continue to explore our sense of taste. Do we have receptors for pinguis, the taste of fat? It is highly likely that we do. Fat is a high-energy food resource, one that we have a craving for. Discovery of such a capacity might help to shed light on human obesity.

Our ability to taste spicy-hot foods and menthol-cool foods is attributed to what is described as a common chemical sense. It does not have a more succinct name yet. It is believed that this sense protected us from plants that concentrate spicy compounds to deter insects and other predators. If you have ever chewed a small part of a water-pepper leaf (*Polygonum hydropiper*), you will have quickly identified its burning, spicy defence. But none of our main five taste modalities can adequately account for our ability to taste this.

Both our sense of taste and sense of smell can vary widely between individuals due to genetic differences. This can result in some people being unable to detect some tastes such as umami. These genetic differences may shed light on our complex relationships with foods, our preferences, our dislikes and our cravings, some of which can result in overindulgence. As time goes on, I eagerly await researchers unravelling the remaining mysteries of taste and our wonderful evolutionary gift that equips us so well to explore our world through this sense. Until then, I shall enjoy the scent of umami-rich foods simmering in a cooking pan, anticipate the different food sensations of the changing seasons, and enjoy discussing cuisine with my friends and family certain in the knowledge that I am exercising one of our oldest inherited faculties for survival.

TOUCH

See how she leans her cheek upon her hand.
O that I were a glove upon that hand,
That I might touch that cheek!

William Shakespeare,
Romeo and Juliet, Act II, Scene II

Fungi fascinate me – they are mysterious, unpredictable and beguiling, and searching for them is like treasure hunting. Perhaps deep down I sense our connection with them, for humans are more closely related to fungi than to plants. Certainly, pursuing fungi is like no other form of nature study that I have ever encountered.

With experience, field mycologists sense the presence of fungi before they see them: perhaps they can smell them; perhaps they are just more alert to the enigmatic set of environmental conditions that trigger mycelium to bear fruit and produce mushrooms. Whatever it is, fungi demand total dedication before even the most rudimentary progress can be made in their identification. While serving out their apprenticeship in fungus recognition, every field mycologist has been inexorably drawn into the dappled shade of old-growth forests, where the fungi reward only the highest level of attention.

Although olfactory alertness is a must for mushroom hunters, our sense of taste can also play an important role in fungus identification. But I fear that a novice attempting to identify fungi with their mobile phone, rather than a tutor, might come to grief attempting to taste one of the more deadly species that we know are best left alone. This is where our sense of touch as an important way to assess fungi comes in.

When I arrived at the gates of the Jodrell Laboratory of the Royal Botanic Gardens Kew to begin my exploration of the world of fungi in the early 1980s, I did so, like most before me, having already become familiar with the shapes and forms of birds, trees and plants. Arrogantly, I felt well equipped for my new interest – how foolish the notion. Never before or since has a field of natural science been so engulfing, a sink or swim experience. Floundering in the tide of information imparted by my tutor, the incredible Dr Derek Reid, I swam for my life, determined to stay afloat. Eventually, I realised that the only way to progress was to go with the flow and give myself up totally to the study, allowing myself to be absorbed into the fascinating world of mycelium. With each fungus I encountered, I would sit beside it and respectfully ask it, 'Tell me about yourself?' One by one, the fungi revealed their secrets, and it became the journey of a lifetime.

One particular fungus taught me an important lesson about our senses. It was a glorious autumn afternoon, and although the leaves were still on the trees, they were now displaying the stunning yellows, reds and browns that define the season. There before me, having emerged from a pillow-like mound of hard ground with a covering of short moss, I found a small boletus mushroom. Boletes are stemmed fungi that in place of the bladelike gills found in field mushrooms are equipped with a spongey layer of tubes for their spore dispersal. A good many of the most popular edible fungi are boletes, so as a novice mushroom hunter with a special interest in the edible and useful varieties I was immediately fully alert. 'Who are you?' I asked. Pulling my field guide out, I laid it on the ground beside the fungus and knelt to take a closer look at this new friend. The cap of the mushroom was a dark umber colour, slightly lighter towards the cap margin. I always revel in finding fungi in pristine condition before slugs munch their way into the caps, and this fungus was perfect, standing proud with its soft, velvety cap. I reached out to stroke it only to discover that to my touch the cap felt waxy. I thought I was hallucinating. I touched it again, and once more it was waxy, even though it was perfectly velvety to look at. I laughed – what an amazing trick. But why? Such are the mysteries of the mushroom world. It was a true revelation. That little bolete taught me that fungi, like a stage magician, can deceive our eyes. Ever since, I have always paid the closest attention to details, never making a snap identification after a cursory glance.

But how are we able to identify the touch of something that feels waxy? That cap was cool and smooth but not without texture; it had the faintest irregular ripples. That we can detect these details instantly with a fingertip reveals something of our somatosensory system, our incredible sense of touch.

Touch is the sense we take the most for granted, but without it life borders on the impossible. It is our sense of touch that enables us to understand our body position, to stand upright, to direct the move-ment of our limbs, to detect injury, illness, heat and cold, or to detect whether something is sharp, blunt, wet, slippery or dry. In conjunc-tion with our curiosity and our memory, we can recognise a wide range of substances and objects by their touch alone, and we can use our sense of touch to help us carry out the finest of motor tasks. In an emergency, it is our sense of touch that quietly, invisibly supports us, enabling us to tie knots in darkness, to pick our way across a rubble field, or to maintain our balance on a plank bridging a chasm as we try to reach a casualty trapped by an earthquake. Then by touch alone we can feel for a life pulse, and while waiting for assistance we can gently hold their hand, reassuringly conveying the warmth of human kindness, care, hope and love.

Our somatosensory system is a marvel of nature that functions through a network of neural receptors that are found all over our bodies in our skin, but also internally in muscles, joints, epithelial tissues, bones and the cardiovascular system. Broadly speaking, we have nerve receptors sensitive to five specific stimuli: mechanoreceptors for pressure and touch; thermoreceptors for temperature changes; nociceptors that detect harmful stimulus from mechanical injury and thermal damage that result in discomfort and pain; chemoreceptors that react to harmful chemicals; and proprioceptors that enable us to judge the position and movement of our body. While we describe this as our sense of touch, it is a multisensory system through which we can also feel subtle changes in atmospheric conditions, detect internal injury and much more, so much so that it seems poorly served by the specifically narrow word 'touch'. Perhaps 'contact sense' or 'sensatory sense' would better describe such a broad capability. However we choose to define it, this system constantly feeds information gathered by these receptors to the brain, which in turn works miracles with the harvest, interpreting, cataloguing and inferring from the data, enabling us to build a picture of the environment outside of our skin as well as within it.

When we disassemble our sensory capabilities, it is easy to become fixated on the mechanism of the sense and to forget its larger influence. That is certainly the case for our sense of touch. It is now well accepted that touch plays a vital role in an infant's healthy development. Loving touch is the soil in which the seeds of human emotion and physical wellbeing are nurtured. Research has shown that denied such care, children may exhibit emotional harm and in extremis can experience a higher incidence of long-term physical health problems throughout their lives.

Touch is also a method of communication that can cross cultural and linguistic divides. I have had many experiences which lead me to believe that touch can also allow cross-species communication. While I generally avoid handling wildlife – on the basis that if I was in the animal's place, I would not want to be picked up by a giant – there are inevitably circumstances when it is necessary. For example, my dog Jag once led me to a bird in my garden, a hawfinch (*Coccothraustes coccothraustes*) that had clearly injured a wing. Having fetched a suitable old shoe box as temporary ambulance, I lifted it very carefully, always talking to it but mostly trying to convey a sense of kindness, aid and safety through my touch. I was, I admit, wary of being pinched by the bird's powerful bill that is strong enough to crush a cherry stone but resolved to accept the risk as the bird was in need of help. Despite its fear, the hawfinch responded, and whilst remaining wary I felt it relax to my grasp, allowing me to assist it, a miraculous act of trust in contradiction of every survival instinct a totally wild creature normally lives by.

When a representative from the local wildlife hospital arrived, they did so with a very different attitude, dismissively telling me that it was unlikely to be a hawfinch and more likely a greenfinch (*Chloris chloris*). On lifting the lid from the box, the man ate humble pie: 'Oh, it is a hawfinch.' Resisting the urge to say I told you so, I watched with fascination as the professional, perhaps intimidated by the bill, rather roughly grasped the bird and demonstrated beautifully, with words I shall not repeat, that the hawfinch can indeed bite with the strength of a pair of pliers. I am glad to say that the wildlife hospital redeemed themselves, nursing the bird back to full health, and it was successfully released back into the wild a few weeks later.

The very next year, I watched with fascination as a Scottish bird ringer examined barn-owl chicks (*Tyto alba*), something I have witnessed on many occasions. Bird ringers have a wonderful caring touch with the birds they record, but this ringer stood out. He had the most extraordinary gift – his gentle touch was miraculous, the chicks responding as calmly as though he was their grandfather. He was a real bird whisperer. If we are sensitive, our sense of touch can in this way convey our innermost thoughts and intentions.

While we are equipped with many different types of somatosensory receptors to detect a wide variety of different stimuli, the most directly relevant to our fieldcraft are the tactile receptors that are found in our skin, our largest sense organ. The most numerous of these are our free nerve endings, found just below the skin surface in the mid layers of the epidermis, the outermost layer of skin. These are receptive to gentle touch, temperature, pressure, stretching and pain. They have large diameter nerve fibres encased in a substance called myelin, which facilitate good neural conduction and consequently fast communication with the brain. For example, if you touch a metal surface, it immediately feels cold as we sense the conductivity of the material as a cooling sensation.

As a tropical species by origin, we are well equipped in a biological sense to cope with warm temperatures, able to lose heat to our environment by radiation and the evaporation of sweat. By contrast, we are poorly equipped to cope with cold temperatures and can only survive in cold environments by using our intellect to provide ourselves with shelter, specialised clothing and fire. This vulnerability to cold is reflected in our ability to sense changes in temperature. We have two specialised thermoreceptors: warmth receptors, which register increases in temperature, and cold receptors, which register decreases in temperature. We have more cold receptors than warmth receptors, and our cold receptors report to the brain ten times faster than our warmth receptors.

The deepest layer of the epidermis is the *stratum basale*, which attaches the epidermis to the dermis and generates new epidermal cells. In this layer, we have Merkel discs. These cells are specialised tactile mechanoreceptors, providing sensitivity to fine touch. Responsive to vibrations from ten to fifteen hertz, they detect over a small field and are closely grouped, which enables us to discriminate between fine details, particularly shapes and edges, as well as locating a stimulus; for example, detecting when and where a mosquito lands on our face. Merkel disc receptors are particularly densely clustered in the fingertips and lips. In the spring, you might like to explore this sensitivity by exploring the fine hairs on the edge of a beech leaf. While easy to see, they are so soft that it is difficult to detect these hairs by the touch of a fingertip, but easy using our lips. Like our free nerve endings, they also communicate quickly with the brain.

Just below Merkel discs we find Meissner's corpuscles distributed in the *stratum papillare*, the very uppermost region of the dermis. These mechanoreceptors, sensitive to vibrations of fifty hertz, also contribute to our sense of fine touch. While Merkel discs adapt slowly to stimuli, Meissner's adapt swiftly. This means that when we put on a glove, we immediately we feel its presence with both of these mechanoreceptors, but we quickly lose the report of glove wearing from the Meissner's corpuscles while the Merkel discs continue to register the stimulus. Meissner's corpuscles are mostly located in hairless regions of our skin, particularly on our fingertips and eyelids.

Deeper in the dermis are Ruffini endings, which detect stretching of the skin, deformation within joints and warmth. Accounting for 20 per cent of the receptors in a human hand, they are also important to our proprioception, enabling us to detect slippage and thereby to finely adjust our finger position. Due to their deep location in our skin, they are slow to detect heat and provide the lasting sense of pain after a burn is sustained.

Even deeper in the skin are Pacinian, corpuscles located in the skin's hypodermis, its lowermost layer, as well as within joints, the vascular tissue surrounding bones, the pancreas and other organs. These receptors detect pressure responding to deep touch and vibrations with a frequency between 200 to 300 hertz. They allow our hands to detect fine textures.

Hair follicles are also enveloped in several specialised touch receptors and can enable us to detect a variety of stimulus from the very lightest touch to constant pressure, such as that experienced when wearing a hat.

I have only mentioned the most understood or common touch receptors, and some are yet only poorly understood. Our sense of touch is extremely complex, and our brain has the capacity to garner and interpret a plethora of stimuli from a multitude of different touch-sense receptors for the protection of our body from environmental threats such as stings, sharp items, environmental changes and internal disease. But we can also reach out in curiosity and touch things to improve our sensory understanding of them. As children, we do this naturally. As we mature, we become more reticent to engage in a tactile exploration of our surroundings. But if we can learn anything of our sensory capability, it is that all our senses are interlinked and that stimulating one heightens the alertness of the others. I make a point of engaging with the natural world in a tactile sense. It can be especially useful in the identification of plants. For example, felt textures, such as the ribbing on the stem of a hard rush (*Juncus inflexus*) or the sandpaper-like surface of elm leaves (*Ulmus spp.*) to say nothing of the mysterious waxy sensation of the boletus cap that fooled my eyes.

I have found that using my sense of touch helps me enormously when tracking: feeling the ground for a textural comparison of tracks with the surrounding surface, determining if dew has been dislodged from grass, or feeling for residual warmth where an animal has slept or to estimate the age of an abandoned campfire. In poor light, when it becomes more difficult to visually determine depth in a track, I explore track impressions with my fingertips to better evaluate the depression.

Like all of our senses, our sense of touch can be improved with practice, as is so aptly demonstrated by concert violinists who combine their sense of hearing with a highly developed tactile sensitivity to and connection with their instrument to produce music imbued with emotion and passion. This ability to align our tactile awareness to that of an instrument, connecting with an inanimate object as an as an extension of ourselves through our sense of touch, is one of the most fascinating attributes of this sense. In effect, it allows us to plug ourselves into the tool, sensing responses far beyond the instrumentation, whether it be a racing car, an off-road 4x4, a bicycle, a fighter plane or a simple surgeon's scalpel. With much practice, and a mind willingly receptive to the tactile feedback, we can master the tool by becoming one with it.

So how might this assist us in our pursuit of nature? Firstly, using our sense of touch more fully can provide a richer experience of life. Reaching out and feeling the surface tension of a pool of water, or exploring the texture of barks, mosses, lichens and plants, is to investigate the familiar in an unfamiliar way, rewarding us with the revelation of a hidden dimension. Comparing the textures of leaves – contrasting, for example, the downy plush of a fleabane leaf with the leatheriness of a pussy-willow leaf, or the springy stiffness of a pine needle with the tissue-like softness of a newly unfurled lime leaf – not only assists us in identifying these plants, it also stimulates and enlivens our tactile sense and thereby all our senses, heightening our connection with the natural world. When we are walking quietly in search of wildlife and we need to tread lightly, feeling the ground with our feet enables us to maintain our balance and to keep our eyes up and scanning the landscape.

To improve our tactile sensitivity, there are many small exercises we can perform. Have a friend hand you an unknown object in darkness or when wearing a blindfold. Explore the object by touch and afterwards make a sketch of what you discovered. With practice, you will begin to identify tiny details that your eyes might ignore. When camping, do not reach for your torch but locate and operate your equipment by touch. Practise tying knots, writing notes and even making fire in total darkness. Who knows, one day these abilities might be important to your physical wellbeing?

Practise moving quietly, feeling the ground, particularly by walking at night when deprived of the sense of vision. Start by wearing thin-soled shoes and progress to your hiking boots. Begin in safe, open ground, without dangers such as rocks, ditches, water features or other obvious hazards, and progress to moving through woodland. Go slowly, feeling your way and allowing your hair to warn of branches and other obstructions in the darkness and learning to relate your body position to your somatosensory map of your surroundings. This is a real challenge but one that greatly improves our ability to move quietly at any time. In the darkness of a moonless night, try to identify the trees and shrubs around you, feeling for their leaves, noticing the nature of the spring in the branches, feeling for the now familiar texture of the bark.

Never hesitate to combine your senses. In midsummer, challenge yourself to locate a honeysuckle purely by its scent and walk to it in darkness, silently, following the smell, finding your way by touch, then reward yourself by sucking the sweet nectar from the flower once you have found and identified it. These are simple little exercises that most people would never bother with but which will greatly enhance your overall sensory alertness and receptiveness, and your confidence to be out in darkness.

Touch – we take it so much for granted, but it is vital for our lives and has the potential to bring so much reward to the very experience of living.

THE DOMINANT SENSES
– HEARING AND SIGHT

A terrifying sight confronted me. Luckily, through sitting in the darkness of the hole for so long, my eyes had grown accustomed to the gloom, so that I could see, only a few feet away, and lying broadside on, the enormous form of a tiger …

Kenneth Anderson, 'The Bellundur Ogre'
in *Tales from The Indian Jungle*

That our senses of touch, taste and smell are essential for our normal health and wellbeing should now be apparent, and I hope it is also obvious that most of us can make far better use of these faculties to amplify our experience of nature. But as we shall discover later, making full use of our sensory modalities is more than just an enhancement to our enjoyment of life; it can also be essential to its preservation, maintaining our safety outdoors.

That we do not generally make full use of these reflects on how wedded we are to our most dominant senses of hearing and sight. But even with these preferred senses, there is room for improvement. Living in a high-fidelity, stereoscopic world, we are bombarded daily by highly defined audio and visual input. Although invisible to us, the air is crowded with radio waves delivering constant stimuli for our insatiable auditory and optic nerves. In the frenzied commercial competition for our attention, our suitors make it easy for us, appealing to us with catchy jingles and bright-neon sale signs in well-illuminated supermarket aisles. Through our mobile phones, social-media companies make their fortunes by holding our attention, luring us with colourful graphics and reward schemes, perniciously using our own data against us to exploit our interests, habits, psychological biases and natural human desire to be liked. Not only do these insidious algorithms rob us of precious hours from our lifetimes, they also are altering human values. Couple these processes with the search for a mate, and it is easy to understand how our youth are becoming addicted to social media, obsessed with presenting themselves camera ready and wearing make-up that suits transmission through the tiny lenses of the mediocre cameras built into mobile phones but which in reality does nothing to improve on nature's touch.

As new generations stare into their phones, developing repetitive strain injury to their thumbs, stooped necks and the now clinically recognised 'social-media addiction', I cannot help wondering if humanity has not enslaved itself to this technology. What started out as exciting entrepreneurism by inspirational young computer experts has turned into a nightmare that is eroding the very fabric of human society; one day history may judge this malaise as having been started by child entrepreneurs who were savvy in new technology but lacking in the maturity and life experience necessary to exercise wise restraint and sensible safeguards.

Unsurprisingly, social media has been linked to increased anxiety, psychological fragility, self-harm and increased suicide rates amongst the under thirties. What is even more saddening is that this technology is seducing us away from using the full range of our senses of hearing and sight. As we have already discovered, if we do not use our senses, we lose them. Using our senses dynamically to explore the natural landscape around us is exciting and spiritually rewarding, enlivening in a way that a device powered by a silicon chip never can be. Believe it or not, there truly is a hidden world out there waiting to be discovered; all we have to do is to listen and open our eyes.

Although it is of course possible to explore our auditory and our visual senses individually, when we employ them in the wild, we do so in a totally integrated, mutually supportive way, steering them by very similar psychological processes. For that reason, we will explore them together. Moreover, I hope to encourage you to always employ them simultaneously, for that is how nature intended us to use them.

When we are outdoors, our senses of hearing and sight work in perfect synchrony to detect, locate and identify surrounding wildlife. To make the most of both, we must practise using them and construct a sensory archive of sounds and sights for comparison. As we shall explore later, a great deal of our sensory interpretation must be achieved in our subconscious mind. For that reason, the data we need must be stored in our cerebellum, where it can be instantly accessed and cross-referenced with the input from our other senses. To use both our hearing and our sight well, we must understand their function and train in their use as well as actively demanding that our brains pay full attention.

Hearing

In the animal world, there are some extraordinary listeners. Dolphins, for example, can detect sound frequencies as high as 150,000 hertz, while bats who navigate and locate their prey by echolocation of high-pitched sounds detect frequencies up to 100,000 hertz. At the opposite end of auditory reception, elephants rumble messages over long distance using low-frequency sounds below twenty hertz.

While this is impressive, human hearing is not to be ignored. Our hearing is very good, and we are theoretically capable of detecting sounds in an impressive frequency range of twelve to 28,000 hertz, although mostly less than this depending on our age, health and whether we have taken good care of our hearing. Our auditory range is strongest between 2,000 and 5,000 hertz. For comparison, the average frequency range for a dog's hearing is sixty-four to 44,000 hertz, which means we can hear some lower-frequency sounds than dogs, but they outstrip us with their ability to hear high-frequency sounds. Thus, at home a dog will easily hear the movement of a distant gate latch that is totally undetectable to us, but when walking in the countryside our dog might not hear a nearby low-frequency animal disturbance that to us seems obvious.

Our hearing enables us to explore the surrounding landscape, sometimes to astonishing distances. Subconsciously, we are aware that high-frequency sounds dissipate over distance faster than low-frequency sounds, and consequently we generally perceive low-frequency sounds as being of a more distant origin than high-frequency ones. However, we are sometimes mistaken in such assumptions, reflecting the difficulty we have in accurately determining the distance of a sound source. Our best means of judging distance is to record the bearing of a sound and then take a second bearing by relocating ourselves. By triangulation, the intersection of these two bearings will indicate both the direction and distance to the sound source. On wilderness expeditions, every member of a party is trained to respond to an emergency-whistle signal by immediately pointing in the direction of the sound. Bearings can then be recorded and the signaller's location determined.

If we know their meaning, sounds alone can be definitive proof of an animal's presence. Just three years ago, I heard the call of a Tengmalm's owl (*Aegolius funereus*) in woodland near to my home. Normally a resident of the boreal forest, from which it receives its alternative name, the boreal owl, it is bird I am well familiar with but which was far outside of its usual range. Although I heard it on many occasions, it was eighteen months until my wife eventually managed to spot it, seeing it before me.

Beyond recognising the distinctive calls of wildlife, we can also determine some animals from the sounds they make while moving about; for example, the distinctive disturbance made by blackbirds foraging in forest leaf litter, a sound that is uncannily like human footfall, or badgers munching bluebell bulbs, which sounds like a human eating a pickled onion.

Within our auditory frequency range, our hearing is incredibly sensitive. The delicate mechanisms of our ear are extremely responsive to sound stimuli. It has been discovered that when we hear the faintest sounds, the human eardrum vibrates less than the diameter of a single molecule. No wonder that our hearing is easily damaged by exposure to loud sharp sounds – if you value your hearing, take care of it. We are also able to determine the direction of sounds with great precision. Research has demonstrated that we can differentiate between sounds separated by only three degrees. It is these last three auditory virtues that define the importance of our sense of hearing: we can hear the faintest sounds, determine their direction of origin and can learn to understand their meaning.

In the wild, these qualities have value without measure. Combined with our intellect, they enable us to find our way, listening for natural features beyond our sight that might guide us, such as waterfalls or the sound of human activity. They enable us to detect a call or sound signal for help and to accurately determine the direction in which to search. But most of all they enable us to identify animals hidden from sight by the densest vegetation or under the cover of total darkness, such as the sawing call of a leopard.

Working in television, I am particularly conscious of sound. We have a saying, 'you only notice poor sound'. Apart from errant wind currents playing across the radio mic, the greatest auditory hindrances are sounds such as overhead aircraft, refrigerator condensers, chainsaws and outboard motors. When we are talking, our brains filter out these irritating background noises so that we can concentrate on our conversations. But a microphone is unable to filter such sounds out, resulting in interminable delays while film crews wait for the interference to stop.

This ability to hear selectively has probably saved many marriages but must be managed with care in the wild. We even actively block out distracting noises; for example, commuters on trains wear headphones connected to tablets and other electronic devices to access more pleasing auditory stimuli. But in the wild, we must turn up the background sound and allow our mind to explore it. With practice, we can use our mental sound filter to allow us to selectively interrogate the noises around us. To do this requires that we be still and thereby perfectly silent. It can help at first to close our eyes and to clear the pressure in our eustachian tubes by moving our jaw, leaving our mouth slightly open. Now we can reach out with our sense of hearing to receive sounds from the different quarters around us, one by one, penetrating our immediate surroundings and reaching to mid distance and out to the distant horizon. Try for yourself, then compare what you have heard to what you can see. You may be surprised to discover it is possible to hear sounds emanating from far-distant activity. With practice, this will become second nature and will not require you to close your eyes.

Many significant sounds in nature are subtle and pass unnoticed. From late July to the middle of August, a classic sound of this sort can be heard if you listen carefully: the mating call issued by a roe doe to attract a roebuck. While to untutored human ears it is inaudible amongst the multitude of other natural sounds, to a roebuck this delicate squeak is an irresistible lure. Once you have learned to recognise it, you will notice it more easily. Just as top musicians develop an incredible ear for music through practice, we too need to practise using our hearing, tuning it to the symphony of nature's melodies. In many cases, it will be our hearing that first alerts us to the presence of an animal and directs our eyes to search in the right direction for a revealing sign of movement.

Twenty something years ago, I was leading a guided walk in a beautiful nature reserve in Essex. When we stopped for lunch, one of the participants came over to talk to me. He was wonderfully keen on wildlife and seeing more of it, and he had been reading a range of books on the subject – some good, some perhaps a little flowery in their teaching. He asked me about our sense of sight, and just as I was about to provide an answer to his question he suddenly and awkwardly froze and stared over my shoulder, like a pointing gun dog on a scent, indicating something behind me. His dramatic behaviour was for effect. He was trying to live up to an idea he had read in one of the more esoteric books. After a long moment, during which I patiently observed his bizarre and some might say rather rude behaviour, he announced with great drama, 'A robin!'

Without turning to look, I said to him, 'Yes, it has been there for some time. It keeps turning its head on its side and staring up at the sky. If you look carefully, you will see a kestrel.' He scanned the sky and at first saw nothing. I looked up, and very high above the distinctive silhouette of a kestrel's pointy wings and straight tail could be seen.

As if to provide confirmation in case of any doubt, it momentarily came to a hover before gliding away on patrol. Tired of the charade, I packed to move on. The man sat on his haunches, giving me a weird look – perhaps he thought I was something of a mystic.

At the end of the walk, the man approached me and politely asked the right question: 'How did you know about the kestrel? Did you hear it?'

'No,' I answered. 'The robin was telling me it was there. When a robin spots a kestrel, it often peers intently at the sky and gives that high-pitched whistle of alarm that it was making.' I then explained that awareness of nature is allowing all your senses to work simultaneously, and that when watching wildlife it is vital to listen with our eyes and to watch with our ears. In this way, we can visualise actions from their sounds and know what a distant event sounds like from what we are observing. This enables us to remain aware of what is going on around us without necessarily having to always confirm sounds by sight and vice versa. He walked away deep in thought. I was simply glad that the robin hadn't let me down.

That the soaring kestrel was little more than a speck in the sky, but the robin could see it with its tiny eye is an obvious indication that something is different about avian eyesight compared to our own. But as we shall discover, our own eyesight is also pretty amazing.

Sight

Some people insist that it is foolishness of the greatest order to venture into wilderness alone. They clearly never have. Travelling alone in wilderness is one of the most life-affirming things you can experience.

I have spent all of my adulthood exploring our beautiful planet's wildest regions. In these places, I have come to know myself, and I have discovered hope that in nature's astonishing power of regeneration she will be able to overcome humankind's folly. But most importantly of all, I have learned that we are never alone. Without the disturbance of another human, creatures of the wild come closer and introduce themselves. Of all these wild companions, it is the ever-watchful eagle that is most fascinating to me.

It was whilst paddling alone on a remote lake in Northern Ontario that I first realised this. I was nearing the end of my ten-day excursion, and the moment was approaching to make for the trailhead rendez-vous with my outfitter in three days' time. Deciding that time was now too short to explore the northeast arm of the lake ahead of me, I reached out widely from the right gunwale of the canoe, and with a powerful drawing stroke that defined this moment in my journey, I spun the bow towards the next portage trail that lay three hours south-east of me. As I turned, two bald eagles (*Haliaeetus leucocephalus*) passing overhead came into my view. I paused and called up to the first and nearest bird. It was surprised and lost its composed rhythm of flight. Regaining composure, it circled around me, looking down and calling back. I smiled. In a way that is difficult to explain, we had an under-standing. I had no doubt that those same birds had been watching me for days – they had been my neighbours. They were a particularly welcome sight that reminded me of the value of wilderness areas. The bald eagle was declared a provincially endangered species in Ontario in 1973. Since then, their numbers have been growing. Here in this quiet backwater, I felt that I had entered their world.

Two days before, from their lofty perches, they had watched my canoe buck on the waves as I'd battled my way into the lake against strong winds that were a gift from a hurricane passing up the eastern seaboard.

They had seen me stretch my tarp and kindle my fire on the small island in the western arm of the lake, and they were the same eagles that had feasted on the trimmings of the pike I'd caught for my dinner.

All was mysteriously calm now. The night before, the temperature had dropped, raising a thick dawn mist over the lake. There was a change in the air, and the forest seemed quieter than before the storm. I noticed subtle changes: true bulrush (*Scirpus lacustris*) wilting and a beautiful scarlet red maple (*Acer rubrum*) leaf held proud on the mirror-like meniscus of the lake's dark water indicated that summer was officially over. In a few weeks, this lake would be frozen, the forest blanketed in snow. Someone once said to me at the end of an arduous trip, 'I am glad to be leaving, but I am sad to be leaving.' That sentiment really struck a chord.

Eagles to me symbolise wilderness. There are few animals that I envy, but when it comes to their ability to soar over the land, surveying it with their superlative vision, I am awed. Eagles are believed to be able to spot a rabbit at two miles, and their visual acuity is often cited as being 20/4 compared to our 20/20 vision. This means that what we can see at four metres, an eagle can see at twenty metres. The secret to their vision is the design of their eye. Eagles have a greater density of cone cells concentrated in their fovea, the small central part of the retina responsible for vision of the sharpest acuity. The fovea is also pit shaped, which is believed to provide something equivalent to tele-photo vision. And they have better colour vision to us, seeing colours more vividly, differentiating between a greater range of colour shades and being able to see ultraviolet. This equips them superbly to locate their prey from altitude, differentiating between the mute colours of a rabbit from the surrounding moorland, – they may even be able to see the urine of their prey. Their field of view is 340 degrees – nearly all-around vision.

Other animals also have some visual advantages. If you catch a cat in the beam of a torchlight, their eyes shine brightly. The same is true of many of other animals, but not humans. This eyeshine is the result of a tissue called the *tapetum lucidum*, which reflects light back through the eye, a simple explanation of its function being that it provides the eye a second opportunity to receive the light photons. A cat's *tapetum lucidum* reflects 130 times more light than us, giving them far superior night vision. However, even with this advantage, even a cat cannot see in total darkness, such as experienced in a cave.

Despite this, human eyesight should not be underestimated. Although we do not have a *tapetum lucidum*, we do have some night vision, and we have an impressive field of view. Horses have a 350-degree field of view, like many other prey species, while predators such as dogs and cats have 150-degree fields of view. Our field of view extends to 210 degrees horizontally and 150 degrees vertically, providing a clue to our evolutionary past, in which we were both predatory and vulnerable to predation. Where we excel is in the extent of our binocular vision, which extends to 120 degrees, providing excellent perception of depth compared to a dog's 85 degrees. While not matching an eagle, our visual acuity is also excellent: 20/20 on average and 20/10 at best, compared to 20/50 in dogs and 20/100 in cats, which indicates that what a cat can see at twenty metres, we can see at 100. We also see in full colour, whereas many mammals see in a limited colour range; cats and dogs, for example, see in a way similar to humans who are red-green colour blind, red appearing dark and green a light monotone hue. They are, however, very sensitive to yellow and blue, good colour choices to avoid when dressing for concealment.

The human eye functions like a camera. We have a lens that focuses light rays onto the retina, our light sensor. The brightness of light reaching the retina is controlled by the iris, which determines the size of the pupil, a hole in the eye that allows the light through. In bright light, our pupils contract; in low light, they dilate. Stress can also change our pupil size: adrenalin causes our pupils to dilate, improving our poor-light vision and helping us to cope with threat conditions.

Just as in a camera, the image received by the retina is inverted, our brains correcting the orientation later. The retina of our eye comprises two types of photoreceptors: rods and cones. In the human eye, there are 120 million or more rod cells, but only six to seven million cone cells. Our rod cells are concentrated towards the outer edge of our retina, while the cone cells are clustered in the macula, the 5.5-millimetre diameter region of our retina that is effectively the centre of our visual field, with the highest density at the fovea centralis, which is 0.3 millimetres in diameter.

Cone cells require bright light and connect individually to their interneurons. These cells provide the highest acuity in our vision as well as our colour perception. We have three types of cone cell: L-cones that are sensitive to long-wavelength light (564 to 580 nanometres); M-cones that are sensitive to medium-wavelength light (534 to 545 nanometres); and S-cones that are sensitive to short-wavelength light (420 to 440 nanometres).

Colour blindness results from genetic differences in these cells, falling into three basic types: blindness to red-green colours, blindness to blue-yellow colours and total colour blindness. Being colour blind can interfere with the reading of the subtle colour hues in nature, such as those encountered when identifying fungi, but should not be considered a hindrance to the enjoyment of nature; in fact, I have many times worked with excellent trackers who are colour blind but whose ability to read fine colour changes in ground spoor is exceptional.

Our rod photoreceptor cells, meanwhile, are highly sensitive to light. Able to detect single photons, they connect in groups of fifteen to thirty to a connecting neuron called an interneuron. It is believed that this amplifies their signal to the brain but results in reduced visual acuity.

In daylight, we only perceive full colour and fine detail in the central region of our visual field, with less-defined vision and reduced colour perception from the outer region. Our brain then takes the relatively small amount of detailed colour imagery it is presented with and uses it combined with the less-colourful, less-defined peripheral imagery to decipher the image by comparison to memories stored throughout life. If we see a Y-shaped image on a page, for example, we can interpret it as a three-dimensional representation of a corner, which can in turn be perceived either protruding from the page or depressed within it. Most people see it as a projecting corner, perhaps recalling an early memory that a corner is hard and sharp, discovered when exploring on all fours as an infant. What is important to understand here is that our memory plays a critical role in the interpretation of the visual signals we receive from our photoreceptors. If we wish to become good at spotting things, we need to have built up a substantial store of imagery for comparison.

Travelling with hunter-gatherers in a foreign land, this is immediately obvious, for even the best-trained observers are outmatched by the ability of the locals to spot things of value. For this reason, when we have an opportunity to study an animal, we must drink in the details, scanning its shape, colours and textures carefully: what is the angle of the neck and head? The shape and movement of the tail and ears? What colour are the legs? Are their scent glands visible? And so forth. If using a field glass or scope, study these details carefully and repeatedly. In this way, we begin to prepare ourselves to spot wildlife through a tiny gap in vegetation, to identify wildlife at great distance, or when only briefly glimpsed.

I am often faced with the task of spotting rare wildlife that I have never seen before. To do so, I study multiple field guides and sketch the animal. Drawing skill is not important; it is the process of identifying the diagnostic features and how they may be apparent that is the point. By this procedure, we can provide our brain the advantage of a template to fit actual sightings within. Just this morning, there was a story in the news that a shadow of a big cat had been spotted on CCTV in a seaside town. At one glance, it was clearly not a cat but a dog, most likely a greyhound, so defined was its outline. Making reliable sightings of wildlife requires attention to details and an understanding of the diagnostic features.

At night, however, our cones are far less effective, and we rely almost entirely upon the rod cells of our peripheral vision. Looking directly at an object, placing it in our central vision as we would in daylight, does not work, as this region of our vision is devoid of rod cells and effectively night blind. If instead we look off slightly to one side, we place the object in the more rod-endowed region of the retina. Denied detail and colour, our night vision depends on interpretation of what we might consider fuzzy images. The more memories for comparison the better, the more we are used to searching for things visually the better, but most importantly the more time we have spent outdoors observing at night the better. This night-time observation develops more than just our ability to interpret peripheral imagery in poor light; it also greatly improves our visual perception in daylight.

We can gain an idea of the differences between our rod and cone vision by a couple of simple exercises. If we look into a circle, formed by stretching our arms out straight in front of us with our palms forward and the tips of our thumbs and index fingers touching, we can see the full-colour detail of our central vision. Without moving our eyes and focusing on an object seen through the circle formed by our hands, we can gain an impression of the surrounding peripheral vision and its limitations. Now if we stretch out one arm, making a fist and staring at the back of it, we obstruct our central vision and can only explore the world with our peripheral vision. This provides an insight into how our vision functions in low light.

It would appear that our peripheral vision is sorely lacking compared to our focused vision; however, it has one more trick up its sleeve. Although rod cells react more slowly to light stimulation than cone cells, our peripheral vision is excellent at detecting movement. Perhaps this is a result of the rod cells signalling in arrays, rather than individually like cone cells. If you are walking with a friend in the countryside and they spot something and say, 'Look over there, a deer!' but despite looking in the right direction you do not see the animal until it is fleeing, the reason is that you are searching with the narrow field of your focused vision. Unless you look at it directly, your focus is too narrow. Eventually, the movement of the fleeing animal is detected by your peripheral vision. Rather than searching for the animal with your focused vision, it is better to simply turn to face the general direction and allow your peripheral vision to lead the visual search. Its superior motion detection will quickly pick up any movement and you can then focus your central vision upon it. You may also discover that you detect several animals while your friend's focused vision is myopically fixated on only one.

Hopefully, you are ahead of me now. We detect a sound with our hearing, turn towards it using our peripheral vision and when motion is detected focus on it, identify it and observe it. Better still if you thought about using your sense of smell before your sense of hearing.

It is also possible to use our peripheral vision whilst also simultaneously using our focused vision, and to use our hearing while we are using our eyes. But to do this we must train. Judo players routinely demonstrate this sort of situational awareness during the free practise they call *randori*, when many players are competing within the confines of the *tatami* practice area. To avoid dangerous collisions while at the same time focusing on defeating their opponent, they must maintain overall situational awareness, listening for and peripherally noticing the presence and movement of other players in close proximity.

Outdoors, we need to do the same thing, only on a far grander scale, alert to movement from our toes to the distant horizon. To train ourselves, we can start by separating the processes of peripheral and focused viewing. To do this, scan the landscape with your peripheral vision. First, look forwards and without moving your eyes focus your attention to reach for the far edges of your field of vision, receptive to movements, shapes and colours that stand out. Then deliberately explore each with your full-resolution central vision. If you keep practising, you will notice that your peripheral vision is passive, responding to stimuli, whereas your focused vision is active and searching. Every time you go out, spend a few minutes doing this exercise. We are training the mind to recognise the potential of our peripheral vision and to value its contribution. At first, this will seem awkward, and you might find yourself doing a pretty good imitation of a zombie. However, as you detect more, your brain will warm to the process, it will become more natural and you will be able to utilise both styles of vision simultaneously without contrivance or effort.

How to Indicate an Observation

When outdoors, it is commonly the case that people struggle to successfully indicate a visual sighting to a colleague. Here the best way is to follow a set protocol and train in its use. It is well worth the effort. Should you see something rare, you can quickly, accurately and easily direct other eyes onto the subject.

Assuming you see the head of a leopard in the far distance, whilst maintaining your watch on the subject your description to other onlookers might go like this:

Watcher: 'TO THE RIGHT ... LONE BLACK TREE ON SKYLINE.'

Onlooker: 'SEEN.'

Watcher: 'BASE OF TREE ... EIGHT O'CLOCK ... LARGE BLACK BOULDER.'

Onlooker: 'SEEN.'

Watcher: 'THREE O'CLOCK ... STATIONARY YELLOW CIRCLE ... LEOPARD'S HEAD.'

Onlooker: 'SEEN.'

This is usually followed by, 'Amazing! Good spot!'

The principle is simple: find an obvious feature that everyone can easily recognise as a visual reference and use it to direct others by a clock-face method to the subject. In this case, the clock face is first centred on the base of the tree and then onto the large black boulder from which the leopard becomes visible. As the onlooker finds each object, they acknowledge with 'seen', triggering the next reference, while all the time using both focused vision and peripheral vision to detect movement. The secret is to choose the most obvious reference markers, to keep the steps to as few as possible and to not be too descriptive of the finer details. Distances are difficult to estimate, so try to avoid them and, only if absolutely necessary, use terms such as 'far distance', 'middle distance' and 'close to'.

Night

The darkness of night has a profound effect on our primary senses, most notably our sight because of our cone cells struggling to function. But if we instead rely on our rod cells and our peripheral vision, we can see better than many people think is possible. At night-time, the signals from our sense of hearing are also raised in importance. When watching a television in an unlighted room, you may have noticed that the volume seems to increase after the sun has set. The sound, though, has not altered; it is our brains turning up the volume in our minds.

To assist our hearing in darkness, we can stop frequently and listen while motionless. The quieter we move, the less we betray our presence, but also the less noise we make that may obscure significant sounds around us. Quiet clothing such as wool and fleece are good for their silence. Interestingly, when we are moving as quietly as possible, we might think that our clothing is very noisy, when actually the sounds being generated cannot be detected beyond two metres.

After nightfall, our sense of smell also registers more clearly, particularly if we have been developing it. Two nights ago, I went for a night walk, choosing not to use a torch so that could I rely on my senses to find my way around, a typical training hike. In woodland, it is usually possible to locate the course of a path by looking up to where the lighter sky shows through the associated gap in the forest canopy. Crossing open ground is much easier, but as I approached a corner of a field where there is a gate, I could see nothing due to the deep shadows from the surrounding woodland. Sixty metres from the gate, I detected a very strong scent of cattle. I was able to determine that it was coming directly from the corner I was approaching. As I moved closer, I eventually heard the tell-tale sound of an animal urinating. With no moonlight to aid me, the shadow was impenetrable to my vision, and I decided it was time to check with a torch. Switching my head torch to its lowest setting, and holding it so that only a tiny beam of light penetrated the darkness, I played it on the corner to find a group of bullocks crowded together by the gate, a perfect demonstration of integrating the sense of smell to augment the dominant senses.

Night vision

For our eyes to function at all in darkness, they need to adapt to the dark, a process which takes thirty to forty minutes. During this time, our rod cells generate rhodopsin, also known as visual purple, a protein pigment that is responsible for our monochromatic night vision. While it takes time to generate, rhodopsin is destroyed in seconds by exposure to bright light. For this reason, it is wise to guard our dark-adapted night vision by using red-coloured light sources or white light on very low settings if our torch facilitates this. If unavoidably encountering someone else with a bright light or oncoming vehicle headlights when on foot, we should close our dominant eyes to preserve some night vision. Dazzled by a light, we see the purple colour in our vision.

Our visual acuity is greatly reduced at night by the available moonlight – what we normally would see at 200 hundred metres under a full moon may only be perceived in darkness at twenty, while on a very dark night it can be considerably less. However, the more we use our senses at night, the better we cope with darkness. Many times, while travelling in remote regions of the world where there is no electricity supply, I have been astounded by the excellent night vision of the local people, some even riding bicycles in what I would otherwise have considered total darkness.

One of the key problems at night is that it becomes especially difficult to see into shadows, as they are darker than the surrounding area but also because the overall contrast in our vision prevents it – my inability to see the cattle in the field was a good example of this. One way to overcome this is to cup our hands as if mimicking a binocular and to look through the tubes our hands create. In this way, we narrow our field of view, localising the contrast and allowing us to better see into shadows. This is also one of the reasons that a binocular functions so well in darkness.

OPTICAL TOOLS

The Loupe or Hand Magnifying Lens

A magnifying lens is the first optical tool any naturalist should equip themself with. While any handheld magnifier is better than none, the large magnifying glass employed by Sherlock Holmes can be rather cumbersome and is easily damaged during rigorous field use. For this reason, most naturalists carry a small folding field loupe. These can be found in differing magnifications and lens diameters, some with multiple lenses, some with inbuilt illumination.

My preference is for a folding loupe of metal construction, with a 10x magnification and a diameter of twenty-one millimetres, with inbuilt LED illumination. The latter greatly aids vision when used in poor light or the shadows of a forest. While the very best illuminated loupes, such as the Lichen candelaris, are expensive and mostly used by professional or serious amateur bryologists, perfectly adequate illuminated loupes can be purchased today at very reasonable prices (less than £50) and will almost certainly be your most cost-effective optical tool. Choose only those loupes that are achromatic. These are normally made from the combination of three lenses, known as triplets. Beware lenses that proclaim that they are triplets when in fact they are not. It is also a good idea to purchase a protective case for the storage of your lens between trips or, failing this, to use a small water-tight box with a silica-gel sachet inside. In the field, though, most naturalists carry their loupe on a neck lanyard.

Field loupes have a very close focal length. To use one, having opened the loupe, hold the shell casing between your thumb and the inside of your curled index finger. Then support your thumb knuckle against your cheek, below your eye socket. The lens needs to be held so that your eye looks centrally through the lens. When this is achieved, you should not notice any visual disturbance from the lens; if it is slightly misaligned, the image will appear distorted. This is a principle that will apply to all the optics we shall employ. Anything you wish to examine is now brought up to the loupe with your free hand until it is in sharp focus. I support my object-holding hand against my lens holding hand for stability. As you will discover, it is important to ensure that the object that you are studying is well illuminated. With such close focus, you will need to adjust your body position so that it does not fall into the shadow cast by your head, hence the great advantage of a loupe with built in illumination.

If you cannot bring the object to the lens, 'Mohammed must go to the mountain', and you may have to kneel to make your observation. However, you can be content that you are well on your way to the seemingly bizarre, eccentric behaviour common amongst naturalists. What casual observers cannot discern, though, when they see you crawling around watching a beetle through your tiny lens are the myriad natural wonders you are exploring. Apart from merely deciphering features that can be diagnostic for the identifying of species, once we start to magnify the minutiae of nature around us, we embark on a bewildering journey into an otherwise hidden world, discovering wonderous details that mostly pass totally unnoticed, such as the intricate fusilli-shaped anthers of the common centaury (*Centaurium erythraea*) flower.

Like leaving the normal world on a voyage of discovery, exploring the natural world through a magnifying lens is a mind-expanding experience. But beware – you may soon want to delve deeper and find yourself browsing catalogues for field microscopes.

The Binocular or Field Glass

The binocular is the single most important item of equipment we can carry to improve our power of vision, transforming our experience, understanding and interpretation of nature, so much so that it should be always within arm's reach when we are out.

The history of the binocular

Two years ago, when guiding a safari in Namibia, I led my party up onto a high *kopje* at the beginning of an evening's tracking to scan the landscape for wildlife with our binoculars, a process called 'glassing'. From this vantage point, a few giraffes (*Giraffa camelopardalis*) and blue wildebeest (*Connochaetes taurinus*) could be seen with the naked eye, but through my binocular the whole ecosystem opened up, beautifully illuminated in the golden light of the late afternoon. Now, in the near distance, I watched a rush of banded mongooses (*Mungos mungo*) dashing from a termite mound towards some dead logs, while in the mid distance the pastel pelage of impalas (*Aepyceros melampus*) grazing on the edge of clearings seemed almost translucent, and the dark forms of baboons (*Simia hamadryas*) could be seen patrolling boldly through the scrub. In the far distance, there were more giraffes, with elephants and rhinos discreetly camouflaged despite their size.

I have always enjoyed observing from high ground, and I relished this opportunity to glass the veld. With the binocular mounted on a tripod, I could clearly see many miles of the landscape, my view only obscured by the vegetation as gradually the increasing distance diminished the advantageous angle provided by my elevation on the *kopje*. Scanning a dark *kopje* more than five kilometres away, I noticed a tiny movement. Centralising my field of vision on the site of the disturbance, I settled in to watch. Just to the left and below the crest of the dark volcanic boulders was a light-golden circle that seemed out of keeping with the surroundings but was indistinct in the shimmer of the intervening heat haze. After a few moments, it ducked out of sight and emerged again slightly to the right. I realised at once from the size, colour and way it moved that it was the head of a leopard, spotted and observed from what would have otherwise seemed an impossibly long distance.

I was pleased, for we would now head out in search of the tracks of that particular leopard and discover whether it was a male or female, reading the story of its life imprinted on the ground. But I was equally amazed at how well my relatively small 8x32 field glass had performed. It is experiences such as this that build faith and confidence in one's tools. Twelve months later, I would use that same binocular in the same way to observe one of the most elusive animals on the planet.

As we drove the dusty trails towards the leopard *kopje*, I thought about the miracle of glass. I felt a tangible connection to the people of the ancient Levant, who around 3,500BCE first experimented in making glass; if only they could see what their discovery is now capable of. It took 5,000 years until what started out as ornamental beads would be turned into lenses. When lens makers in the Netherlands first worked out how to make a telescope at the beginning of the seventeenth century, they unwittingly transformed human understanding of our place in the universe.

The first written description of a telescope is a letter dated 25 September 1608, recommending the patent application of spectacle maker Hans Lipperhay, 'who claims to have a certain device by means of which all things at a very great distance can be seen as if they were nearby, by looking through glasses which he claims to be a new invention'. Although his patent application would fail, as it was felt that the design was already in general usage and therefore lacked novelty, Lipperhay would be commissioned by the States General of the Netherlands to make a binocular version of his telescope. On 2 October 1608, he was requested to ascertain 'whether he could improve it so that one could look through it with both eyes'. On 15 December 1608, the first record of a binocular entered written history: '[I] have seen the instrument for seeing far with two eyes, invented by the spectacle-maker Lipperhay, and found the same to be good'. Perhaps it was an unknown practically minded civil servant who first saw the potential and suggested mounting two telescopes parallel to each other; whoever it was, they were a genius. However, having a good idea and bringing it to fruition are two different processes. Although both the telescope and binocular began to be developed at roughly the same time, manufacturing a binocular would prove to be a far greater engineering challenge than simply making a telescope.

Once Lipperhay's invention became public knowledge, it attracted the attention of scientists and astronomers worldwide. On the 26 July 1609, an English scientist by the name of Thomas Harriot used a Dutch telescope to draw the first map of the moon, four months ahead of Galileo, the father of modern science, who would improve on the 3x magnification of the Dutch telescopes, producing his own with a magnification of 30x and using it to make his famous depictions of the moon, to describe the rings of Saturn and to conduct other important astronomical observations. Today, telescopes and binoculars made to this simple design are referred to as Galilean.

In 1617, Johannes Kepler offered a new design. He lengthened the telescope, improving the magnification and broadening its field of view, but his design inverted the image seen through the ocular lens at the eyepiece. In 1635, Christopher Scheiner added a lens to the eyepiece to erect the image (set it the right way up), and ten years later Anton Maria Schyrle de Rheita employed a three-lens eyepiece that would become known as the Schyrle Erecting System, producing a practical telescope with an erect image, good field of view and magnification.

Gradually, by small improvements, the optics of telescopes were improving, but the greatest advances would not occur until the middle years of the eighteenth century when brass could be accurately fashioned into robust tubing and Chester Moore Hall recognised that different glass types could have different refractive indices. He used this discovery to combine two lenses of different glass types, enabling red and blue light to focus at the same point, producing the first achromatic telescope, thus reducing colour aberrations and improving resolution. This work was further refined by John Dollond, who brought telescopes to the mass market, his name becoming synonymous with the telescope.

Binocular design

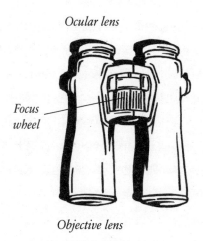

Ocular lens

Focus wheel

Objective lens

Binocular design is based upon either simple Galilean telescopes or the more complex but potentially more useful Keplerian telescopes. For both, the difficulty of finding an effective way to mount the telescopes with precise parallel alignment while enabling simultaneous focus and adjustment of the distance between the telescopes – the inter-pupillary distance that accommodates the varying facial dimensions of different users – was, to say the least, problematic.

While the better field of view and higher magnification of Keplerian binoculars were attractive, their length was challenging, being both cumbersome and magnifying any defects in alignment. Unsurprisingly, the best progress was initially made with the Galilean approach. Miniature telescopes called spyglasses were mounted in pairs to produce the first opera glasses, a use to which their low magnification was well suited. Considerable advances were subsequently made in the production of opera glasses, such as adjustable bridge mounts that allowed for inter-pupillary adjustment and central focusing wheels, both features common in binoculars today. The compact size and shape of opera glasses would also inspire the design of field glasses.

The earliest practical military field glasses were of Galilean design, and they would remain in wide use into the First World War. The engineering breakthrough that would advance the Keplerian model in binocular design was the invention of a prism mechanism to erect the image at the eyepiece, patented in 1854 by its inventor, the Italian optician Ignazio Porro. Using a prism to replace the bulky lenses necessary to erect the image at the eyepiece, he was able to shorten the binocular. His concept was developed further still, enabling the folding of light within the binocular to the point where the length of the binocular was reduced until it was shorter than the focal length of the binocular.

The first prism binocular that we can describe as modern was produced in 1894. Once light and strong aluminium tubing became available, it was swiftly adopted by binocular manufacturers as a marriage made in heaven, while following on from the Porro prism, newer prism designs, such as the Abbe-Köenig and the Schmidt-Pechan roof prisms, mastered the folding of light rays, revolutionising binocular design and resulting in the wonderful optics available to us today.

Galilean binoculars that generally have low magnification, a narrow field of view and a large exit pupil are still manufactured for opera glasses, children's binoculars and spectacle-mounted jeweller's or surgeon's loupes, for which purpose their designs are particularly well suited. But the majority of contemporary binoculars are of the more versatile Keplerian model, with good fields of view and higher magnifying power. With the advantage of recent advances in lens coatings, computer-aided design and high-quality glass, the designers of top-quality modern binoculars work at the theoretical frontier of optical design. When you purchase a top-quality binocular, you access the very highest quality materials and design.

Purchasing a binocular

When selecting a binocular for field use, we currently have two basic styles to choose from: those with a Porro prism design, which are the classic-shaped binocular with widely separated objective (front) lenses, or those with roof prisms, which allow for a slimmer design. While most modern binoculars incorporate a roof prism, top-quality Porro prism designs are still available and are often less expensive than their roof-prism counterparts. Theoretically, the wider separation of the objective lenses of Porro prism binoculars provides better perception of distance; however, in practice any advantage is unnoticeable.

If you are new to binoculars, I would advise you to avoid the gizmos and gimmicks. A binocular or field glass will have a rough life; it therefore needs to be strong and resilient, as well as optically superb. A good quality, straightforward binocular is ideal. Zoom binoculars that offer a variety of differing magnifications, even amongst the top brands, are an optical compromise and unnecessarily complicated, as are image-stabilised binoculars. What we shall be needing is a tough binocular, light and compact enough that it will always be with us but not so compact that it cannot gather enough light for use at dusk or even at night. Equally, it should not be so large that it is tiresome to carry or so awkward that it reduces our willingness to move lithely through the landscape. Inevitably, in pursuit of the perfect field binocular, we will have to make some compromises based upon well-informed choices. In my professional life, I have had the opportunity to use many of the world's best binoculars and to compare them with an astonishing range of other brands, some remarkably good, some I doubt even Galileo would have thought worthy.

When we first consider purchasing a binocular, the price tags can seem breathtakingly high; however, generally speaking, with binoculars, and certainly with the top brands Swarovski, Zeiss and Leica, you very much get what you pay for. A well-made binocular has expensive coatings and the best glass to provide the clearest view. They are engineered to the highest standards from the finest materials, are expertly assembled and should, if well cared for, last a lifetime, even becoming a family heirloom. That having been said, there are also many midrange brands, such as Opticron, Nikon, Steiner and others, that also provide high-quality optics at very reasonable prices, while in the wake of technological advances it has become common for the top manufacturers to reduce the price of their former top-line range once it is superseded by a new design; this in particular can provide an affordable way into binocular use.

Are the top brands really so good? Yes, they are. While the days of the best binoculars being crystal clear while the cheaper alternatives were like peering through fog have gone, the top brands still have the optical edge, advantaged by their years of dedication and research. They also stake their reputations on the quality of their products. Modern optics are simply superb. That binocular manufacturers can truly find room for improvements is both astonishing and testimony to their ongoing dedication to support our desire to see more. However, I caution you to beware the binocular that is dressed up to resemble the top brands but is only a cheap imitation. The best way to choose is to stick with well-established brands made in Austria, Germany, the UK or Japan. To gain an impression of what the best quality is like, look at a Swarovski NL Pure 8x42, arguably the very best binocular available at the time I write these words.

Binoculars are made to support a wide range of observational needs, from watching birds to sport, sailing, hunting and general travel. This has resulted in a wide range of binocular shapes and types. We need a binocular suited to birdwatching or hunting. The basic parameters are that it should be strong and not cumbersome, it should be equipped with a central focusing wheel so that we can easily maintain focus on a subject moving towards or away from us, it should function well in low light, and it should ideally be sealed against the elements, the best models being nitrogen filled to prevent internal fogging by condensation.

Beyond the brand, which is usually determined by our budget, we must choose by the magnification and the size of the objective lens. Binoculars are defined by these features, so you will see them labelled 12x50, 10x50, 8x56, 8x42, 7x50, 10x25, 8x25, and so on. In each case, the first number defines the magnification and the second number the diameter of the objective lens. Thus an 8x25 binocular has a magnification of eight times and an objective lens twenty-five millimetres in diameter. These are highly significant details.

MAGNIFICATION

While high magnification may seem desirable, it comes at the cost of stability. Stability, as we shall see, is vitally important. The higher the magnification, the harder it will be to hold the binoculars steady and the more difficult to use, a difficulty that will increase as light levels diminish. Unless you mostly intend to use a field glass in bright sunshine, fitted to a tripod, I would advise you to not reach beyond a magnifying power of eight; indeed, there is a great deal to recommend a 7x binocular.

OBJECTIVE LENS DIAMETER

The larger the objective lens, the more light the binocular can gather and the better it can be used in low-light conditions. However, the size of the objective lens will also determine the size and weight of the binocular. Small-diameter lenses, such as twenty-five millimetres, are considered pocket binoculars. Many people justifiably love their highly portable pocket field glass; after all, any binocular is better than none. However, as soon as we attempt to use such a binocular for serious fieldcraft, we will find ourselves struggling, as it is just too small. At the other end of the scale, a fifty-six-millimetre lens, for example, is amazing – the 8x56 is often referred to as a night owl. But now we are dealing with a large, heavy binocular, really only suited to specialised use or transportation by vehicle. That leaves us the midsized binoculars, with objective lenses between thirty to forty-two millimetres in diameter. It is in this range that we will most likely find the versatile binocular needed for our fieldcraft.

EXIT PUPIL

Exit pupil

When you hold a binocular up to the light and look at the ocular (rear) lenses, you will see a circle of light. This is the light that leaves the binocular, called the exit pupil, and its diameter is an important consideration when choosing a binocular. The diameter of the exit pupil is easily established by dividing the diameter of the objective lens by the magnification. Thus a 10x50 binocular exit pupil is five millimetres in diameter and a 10x25 binocular exit pupil is

2.5 millimetres in diameter. To properly integrate the binocular with our eyesight, we need to match the exit pupil to the pupil of our eye. As we have seen, in bright light human pupils contract, and in low light they dilate. The amount by which they adjust will vary according to a number of factors but most relevantly with age. As we advance in years, our pupils will contract and dilate less. When choosing a field glass, we look to a choice which matches our pupil dilation so that we can optimise its use in low light.

While individual pupillary responses to light vary, the results of a paper by Jay Bradley, published in the *Journal of Refractive Surgery* in 2010, provides a useful understanding of how our pupil dilation changes with age. In a study of 263 individuals, the following results were recorded.

Age range	Mean dark-adapted pupil diameter (millimetres)	Range (millimetres)
18–19	6.85	5.6–7.5
20–29	7.33	5.7–8.8
30–39	6.64	5.3–8.7
40–49	6.15	4.5–8.2
50–59	5.77	4.4–7.2
60–69	5.58	3.5–7.5
70–79	5.17	4.6–6.0
80+	4.85	4.1–5.3

From this we can see that the old recommendation of choosing a binocular with a five-millimetre-diameter exit pupil or larger as a good night-viewing binocular holds up very well. It is also apparent that the most popular binocular, the 8x42, with its exit pupil of 5.25 millimetres in diameter, is a very good fit for exit-pupil dilation over a wide range of ages and that the 7x42, with a six-millimetre-diameter exit pupil, deserves better consideration than it receives today.

SIZE AND WEIGHT

When purchasing a binocular, the consideration most neglected is the size and weight. This is as critical as the magnification and exit pupil. Holding two binoculars side by side in a shop is not the same as having worn one around your neck all day, every day, for a week, as you will on a safari, for instance, let alone having carried it on a trek in the high mountains. Size and weight matter.

My experience has taught me the value of the wonderful 8x32 binocular. With an exit pupil four millimetres in diameter, it is a compromise, but it is never left behind due to its weight and is never a burden. It is also less tiring to hold, easy to carry in hand luggage when flying and so long as it is of the highest quality performs fabulously. Having used all sizes of binocular, I have never once wished I was carrying anything larger or smaller, but I have several times cursed myself for using a larger binocular. The only other binocular that challenges for my attention is the 7x42, which is always a joy to use and the king in low light.

But we each must make up our own minds in these matters. Here is a list of my top choice of binocular types for fieldcraft.

6x30 A little under powered for birding but wonderfully light and good in the dark

7x35 A great all round binocular good for everything

7x42 One of the very best binocular configurations, superb at night, a joy to use

8x30 The classic lightweight mountain binocular

8x32 The perfect all round bino, compact, light and always to hand, perfect for expeditions

8x42 The birders favourite, great all-round performance

CLOSE FOCUS

The top brands engineer their field glasses so that they can focus closely. If you are keen on watching butterflies, dragon flies and other similar creatures, this a wonderful feature worth taking into consideration.

FIXTURES AND FITTINGS

Last of all, check the fixtures and fittings. These should be well made, and moving features should do so with precision and a slight firmness so that there is a tangible feel of quality. Avoid binoculars with loose-fitting eyepieces or rattling fittings, as these hint at poor engineering. Unfortunately, it is all too easy for a cheaply engineered binocular to be dressed up in rubber armouring in an attempt to emulate the top brands. As a guide, I have encountered many issues with my guest's optics, to say nothing of the hard use I give to my own. Someone once remarked that my equipment receives a lifetime of use in one year; that is not far from being true.

Our binoculars are precision instruments, and things can go wrong, particularly when using them in very hot or cold climates. Carrying some double-sided adhesive tape and some gaffer tape can fix many minor issues. Across most brands, the fixture that most often fails is the adjustable eye-relief cup; on major trips, I carry spares of these. Major binocular repairs are best carried out by the manufacturer. All the top brands are very helpful in this regard, the cheaper brands less so, a factor that reveals how highly, or not, they value their own products.

I would carefully consider to whom you choose to lend your binocular. It is a precision instrument, fragile and easily damaged. I treat the lenses of my optical tools with the same care a samurai would his sword. The last thing I wish to see is a smudgy fingerprint on a lens. One year, when I was filming in Australia, the director working with me had loaned his shiny, new binocular to a small Aboriginal boy who was fascinated by it. A few minutes later, I sat interviewing the boy's mother in the shade of a tree with the boy sitting beside her. A trifle bored with the interview, the boy started to pound the binocular onto the sand to make nice ring patterns with the lenses. With the interview in full flow, I watched with horror that the boy was now burying the binocular in the sand. He then excavated it and repeated the whole operation several times more. The patience of the director was a marvel. He retrieved the binocular and never gave it a second glance; well, not until later, at which point he probably howled in anguish. Deep respect to him.

Adjusting a binocular to your eyesight

To make a binocular perform correctly, it must be perfectly adjusted to our eyesight. We are all individuals: the shape of our faces differ, our eyesight varies and some of us need glasses. Binocular design takes all of this into account, allowing us to adjust our binocular to ensure we each achieve the optimal viewing experience. Learning how to set up a binocular, a process which takes only a few moments, is an essential skill.

INTER-OCULAR ADJUSTMENT

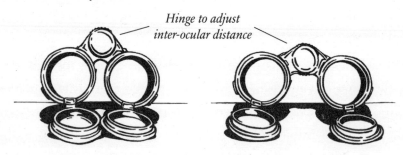

Hinge to adjust
inter-ocular distance

The hinge in the design of the binocular allows the lenses to be swung closer together or wider apart to suit the separation of our eyes. The aim is to centre our eyes over their respective exit pupils, at which point viewing is comfortable. Without worrying about focus, close the binocular hinge and then gradually open it while looking through it towards a daylight landscape. As you do so, you will see the view alter – we are aiming to only see a single clear circular image, not a squeezed vertical oval (eyepieces too close together) or a figure-of-eight image (eyepieces too far apart). The latter is so often wrongly depicted in the movies. Once set, it should be comfortable to look through the binocular, although we may need to return to this setting for fine tuning after we have adjusted the other settings.

EYE-RELIEF ADJUSTMENT

The light rays we observed forming the exit pupil reach their optimum focus a few centimetres behind the ocular lens. We need to adjust the binocular eyecup height so that our pupil is held at that focal point when looking through the binocular. This distance is called the eye relief. Consult your instruction manual to learn how to adjust your binocular eyepieces. Never force this adjustment: some eye cups must be turned, some pushed in or pulled out, while in some older models a rubber eye cup is rolled up or down. If you wear spectacles, it is normal to set the eyecups retracted to their lowest or near-lowest setting. Some spectacle wearers, though, prefer to set their binocular to their eyes, rather than their glasses, as this makes it easier to control distracting side light. Set too close and you will observe a shadow at the edge of the circular view; set too far out and you will observe a wide, well-defined black border surrounding a narrow circular view. Set correctly, your vision will be filled with a clear circular view with a narrow indistinct black border and you will feel the binocular to be a natural extension of your vision.

FOCUS

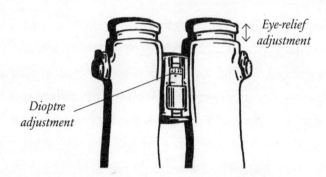

Eye-relief adjustment

Dioptre adjustment

The ideal design of a field binocular has a central focusing adjustment that simultaneously focuses both lenses. This is usually a wheel operation on the central column. This enables us to keep the subject in precise focus at whatever range we are observing from. However, few people have identical vision in each eye. To accommodate these differences, binoculars are designed so that one of the telescopes can be set with an independent focal adjustment. This is a very important setting to make that is often not achieved correctly. Here again we must consult the instruction manual, as modern binoculars often have cleverly designed means of dioptre adjustment. In general, establish which lens can be adjusted independently and then perform the following steps.

1. Select a subject that is well lit and sharply defined to focus on. A fence wire or thin branch in the mid distance (20–30 metres) is ideal.
2. Close your eye that looks through the adjustable eyepiece.
3. Using the central/main focusing wheel, adjust the focus for your open eye so that the subject is perfectly sharp.

4. Locate and, if necessary, unlock the dioptre-adjustment mechanism.

5. Close the eye that was open and open the eye that was closed.

6. Using only the independent dioptre-focus adjustment, focus on the subject until it is perfectly sharp. If necessary, lock down the adjustment mechanism.

7. Look through the binocular with both eyes open. You should now see a perfectly crisp, circular image, focused on the subject.

8. Try focusing on a different object. If you have correctly adjusted the binocular, it should focus perfectly for both eyes – there should be no feeling of eye strain or discomfort.

With experience, you will sense when a binocular is perfectly balanced for your vision; do not hesitate to repeat the process or make minor adjustments until you are perfectly satisfied. Once set, you will not need to repeat this adjustment, unless your eyesight alters or the setting is changed; for example, if you loan your binocular to some-one else, although we have examined that risk.

Using your binocular

Now the fun begins. Like all tools, there are techniques we must learn to make full use of our field glass.

FINDING THE SUBJECT

When we are searching for wildlife, if we hear a disturbance, we turn towards it, allowing our peripheral vision to detect movement, and once found we focus in on the subject. Now we must add our field glass into the process. To do this, there are two useful techniques: the first is to maintain our watch on the subject and simply raise our binoculars to our eyes. Done correctly, the subject will be in our field of view, and we need only focus the binocular. The second method is to look for other identifiable features that can, like a handrail, be followed with the binocular to the subject – perhaps up the trunk of a tree to a branch that leads to the subject, for example. It all sounds so obvious, but experience has taught me that in the excitement of trying to observe something rare, sight of it is often lost at this moment. Practise, practise and practise again until it becomes second nature.

The same can be said of focusing. Practise focusing on subjects moving towards and away from you until you instinctively turn the focus wheel in the correct direction. A binocular is only as good as the person operating it – our aim is to totally master its function.

When I get the chance to escape for a few hours, I like to head to a birdwatching reserve and the peace of a hide. I was sitting quietly in the corner of a hide last year, and, as normal, there were only a few other visitors. They would come in and scout the scene through the narrow viewing window for a few minutes and then move on. I was about to leave myself when a movement caught my eye – it was a merlin (*Falco columbarius*) darting across the far side of the water in front of the hide. In the hope of another view, I waited and was rewarded by a marsh harrier (*Circus aeruginosus*) gliding in to perch on a dead willow branch. Its position was quite low and concealed from the skyline, revealing how well its camouflage works. Enjoying the close view of such a stunning bird was made even more amazing with the aid of my spotting scope, and I drank in the experience.

As I was watching, a husband and wife entered the hide and sat down to watch. I thought how lucky they were to be here now and expectantly awaited their discovery of the nearby harrier. But despite aiming an expensive pair of excellent binoculars straight at it, they said there was nothing much happening here – just a few pintails (*Anas acuta*) and a great crested grebe (*Podiceps cristatus*) – and they left. I was shocked. They had looked but failed to see.

A few minutes later, after I'd left the hide, I encountered a grandfather and his grandson. The boy was about nine years old, with some ancient hand-me-down binos around his neck on a tatty leather strap that looked as though it would snap at any moment. Wearing an everlasting smile, he was positively bubbling over at the excitement of having just spotted the merlin. He was looking and seeing – what an amazing difference.

There is a skill to spotting wildlife – it is not as simple as just buying a good binocular. We need to actively engage our curiosity, using our eyesight skills to the maximum when looking through a telescope or a binocular. Critically, we must remain open to the possibility of encountering things when and where we least expect them.

CARRYING A FIELD GLASS

To be of any value, our field glass must be with us when we need it. As a tracker, my binocular is *always* with me. While the most common way to carry a binocular is around the neck, it is uncomfortable over prolonged periods. The problem can be alleviated to some degree by bearing the load of the binocular in the outer kangaroo pocket of a windproof jacket. Some binocular manufacturers provide extra wide straps in soft springy neoprene to help, but in hot climates these are sweaty, uncomfortable and generally bulky.

There are several better alternatives, the simplest of which is to use a binocular strap adjusted so that it can be worn across the body with one arm, usually the least dominant one, through the strap. This

is my preferred method of carrying a field glass, and instead of a strap that can become twisted, I use a round plaited nylon cord strap, which serves the purpose elegantly. I attach it by using two small lockable S-shaped karabiners. The binocular can be protected from damage and rain under my arm or slid forwards onto my chest, where it remains by friction to be instantly ready when needed. If crawling up on wildlife, it can alternatively be slid backwards to rest on my back out of harm's way. If I am wearing a rucksack, I unclip the strap and instead fasten the binocular to two short loops of nylon cord attached to the ruck-sack shoulder straps, so that it sits on my chest. Carried in this way, there is no perception of the binocular weight at all.

Finally, there are now binocular harnesses that cross between the shoulder blades and transfer the binocular weight to the body and shoulders. Some are simple straps, others protective binocular cases designed for the rigours of hunting. I have used both types, and the case style in particular is excellent, providing superb protection for the binocular. However, despite their advantages, my preference remains for the simple, less fussy cross-body-strap approach.

When travelling by vehicle wearing a binocular around our neck – for example, in a safari game-viewing truck – neck strain is often worsened by the constant jolting on uneven road surfaces causing the weight of the binocular to jerk on the neck. After a few days, this can begin to cause a repetitive-strain injury. I notice when leading safaris that the game viewers often leave their binoculars on the seats of the truck at rest stops. I can guarantee that at some point on every trip there will be a moment of excitement when an unattended binocular is knocked onto the floor and potentially damaged. Equally, any binocular laid to rest in a vehicle is at risk of lens damage unless the protective lens covers are being used. I never used to use covers on the objective lenses of my binocular, but after seeing a binocular objective lens become engraved by a ballpoint pen that it was resting against in a cubby box for a few miles, my opinion changed.

STABILISING YOUR FIELD GLASS

While the function and operation of a binocular may seem obvious and straightforward, I need to reiterate that mastering this tool is an art and that there is a gulf between the observations made by the casual user and the seasoned professional. When important visual determinations must be made, nothing can be left to chance.

To achieve the best possible vision through a field glass, it must be held still. Achieving stability is therefore a critical consideration. When holding a binocular, do so firmly, anchoring your elbows to your chest. In a vehicle, try to support your head against the seat. I also carry a bean bag that can be attached to a car window for binocular support – simple and versatile, it can make a huge difference, turning your car into a mobile observation hide. In woodland, look for a tree trunk or branch to anchor yourself against for support. As soon as the binocular is stabilised, your view will be measurably improved. I even control my breathing when making detailed observations.

When we hold the binocular to our eyes, we often need to shade one eyepiece from bright side light. This is easily achieved by using a crooked thumb. If you prefer, specialised eyecups with extended wings to provide better eyeshade can be purchased as an accessory. Shading the ocular lens greatly improves vision.

In cold weather, avoid breathing out when the binocular is at your eyes or near your face, otherwise your breath will condense on the lenses and fog your vision.

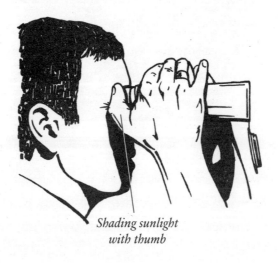

*Shading sunlight
with thumb*

My favourite method to achieve stability is using a tripod. Some binoculars can be tricked out with a clamp for attachment to a tripod; others can be easily attached using a universal mounting bracket with a rubber strap. Fitting a binocular to a tripod is the gold standard in observation, massively improving our vision. The joy of using a binocular in this way is the much wider field of view it provides compared to a spotting scope. Incidentally, if you fit your binocular to a tripod and repeat your dioptre adjustment, you may achieve even greater accuracy.

Should you have forgotten your loupe, you can turn your binocular around and look into the objective lens, offering your subject up to the ocular lens. It is not as good as a loupe but can be a useful hack, to use the modern parlance.

CARING FOR YOUR FIELD GLASS

A field glass is a total joy to use, but it must be cared for. Follow your manufacturer's instructions for cleaning. A cleaning kit should contain: a soft lens brush; a stiffer body-cleaning brush; a microfibre cloth; and some lens-cleaning fluid in a dustproof pouch for the purpose. A lipstick-style foundation make-up brush makes a good lens brush, and a toothbrush is good for body cleaning. I use a lapis bouldering brush, which is like a giant toothbrush designed for cleaning climbing holds, dedicated solely to optics cleaning.

Clean the binocular by brushing grime away from the exterior surfaces but not the lenses. Next, clean the lenses by blowing, brushing, washing and wiping, in that order. Holding the lenses upside down so that gravity assists the cleaning process, use a lens blower to clear dust and grit from the lenses, then delicately brush dust off them with a dedicated soft lens brush. With lens fluid and a clean micro-fibre cloth, remove any grease, smears and stains. In the field, I carry a small microfibre cloth and a tiny dropper bottle of lens-cleaning fluid on a fly fisherman's auto-retracting zinger attached to the zip or pocket of my jacket. If the lenses become wet in the rain, I can use this to clear them.

Never store your valuable binocular damp or mould might damage the lenses, and never leave it in direct sunlight or close to a heat source.

Special Optical Tools

Spotting scopes

Taking a holiday is rather a rare event for me, but a few years ago my wife and I enjoyed a week looking for wildlife in France. It was a great trip spent watching wild boar (*Sus scrofa*), honey buzzards (*Pernis apivorus*) and a special morning watching two montagu's harriers (*Circus pygargus*) hunting over the luscious sward of an organically managed field. In the Vanoise Alps, summer storms prevented us climbing to the peaks in search of marmot (*Marmota marmotai*) and lammergeier (*Gypaetus barbatus*), so we had to content ourselves glassing from the valley floor. As I set out our camp chairs and put the kettle on in antic-ipation of a very French repast of bread, tomato and the best local cheese, my wife scanned the mountainside for an ibex (*Capra ibex*). 'There's one,' she announced, directing me to a rocky outcrop high on the mountainside. She is an amazing spotter whose enthusiasm knows no bounds, and she regularly observes things at extreme range, but this was ridiculous even for her. I grabbed my field glass and scrutinised the scene. I could see the movement of a tiny brown shape, but at that extreme range, even with a binocular, I could not discern what it was. However, my subconscious, interpreting the tiny brown blur, was telling me that it wasn't an Ibex.

I now reached for the super tool of nature observation: my spotting scope. Setting the tripod up quickly and reclining into the camp chair, I eventually located the shape and focused in on it. Even with the 70x magnification of the ninety-millimetre-diameter scope, the view was small. I let go of the scope to reduce all vibrations and maximise the stability. As the scope settled, I could now confirm that it wasn't an Ibex. Instead, I could see a golden eagle (*Aquila chrysaetos*). It was standing on the prostrate form of a female kestrel (*Falco tinnunculus*), plucking flesh from its breast. The kestrel's mate was repeatedly swooping down, mobbing the eagle, but to no avail. As I watched, the male kestrel resigned itself to the loss and perched on a nearby rocky outcrop, looking on forlornly.

That my wife saw any movement at all at such a distance was astonishing and proves how effective glassing with a binocular can be. But this episode also demonstrated the power of the spotting scope. With a binocular, we detect and identify, and we can even read behaviour; with a scope, we do the same again at longer range, but we can also identify individual animals and see clearly what they are doing, even what they are eating. If you come to enjoy observing with a binocular, there may come a moment when you want to reach out further.

Like binoculars, there are many spotting scopes available, so rather than slow our journey by opening another can of optic soup, I will instead explain my choices and the reasoning behind them. My preferences fall between two types of telescope: the Gray & Co. draw telescope, still popular amongst highland stalkers, and the more complicated spotting scope, popular amongst the birding community.

Draw telescopes are extremely compact, lightweight, simple to use and designed for rugged field use. They are not waterproof; instead, they can be easily disassembled, without tools, for drying. Although they can be pressed into service to observe wildlife, their strength lies in initially spotting animals at a distance. They are not normally used with a tripod but rather stabilised against a walking stick or resting on a mossy bank or rucksack. They are ideal for scouting a landscape for wildlife. They also come equipped with a traditional leather protective case.

Birding scopes are the gold standard for wildlife observation. They come in many sizes and price categories. If your budget is limited, buy a good-quality binocular and a cheaper scope. There are some wonderful miniature spotting scopes available that are excellent for travelling with, but generally if I am going to carry a scope, I accept that I am signing up to its weight and size, in which case I might as well carry a full-sized large objective lens scope and benefit from the optical advantage it brings.

These scopes fall into two design categories: those with a viewfinder set at an angle and those that are straight. Birders often opt for the angled viewfinder as a shorter tripod can be used, but I prefer a straight view scope which I find quicker and more intuitive to use when responding quickly to a sighting of a bird or other animal. I carry a taller tripod, but which mounting a long-term observation, enables me to settle myself with my back resting against a tree or boulder and arrange the tripod so that it is easy to look through. When not observing through the scope, I simply look across it. Sometimes I turn the scope at ninety degrees to my direction of vision and observe with my binocular resting on top of it, switching to the scope once I have sighted a subject of interest. Always choose a tripod with legs that can be set at many angles so that the tripod can be adapted to the widest range of situations.

My favourite scope is made by Swarovski. It comes in modular sections, allowing the fitting, if necessary, of different objective lenses or eyepieces. Each module is weather sealed, and because it can be disassembled, it is easy to transport safely and comfortably in a rucksack.

Compared to a binocular, scopes are easy to set up. The only adjustment that is necessary is that of the eye relief. But just as with a binocular, practice is necessary to master the use of a field telescope.

Digiscoping

With the advent of the mobile-phone camera, it was only going to be a matter of time before it was used to take photos through a binocular or spotting scope. Today, all of the top brands produce clamps for mobile phones, or even digital single-lens reflex cameras (DSLR) and video cameras. Obviously, the lens of the device needs to be correctly centred on the exit pupil of the scope's lens. With a DSLR, the image projected onto the camera sensor will usually cover a DX (crop) sensor without vignetting but not a FX (full frame) sensor. While the optical quality of a scope is excellent, it is not a replacement for a camera. Inevitably, it is rather fiddly and cumbersome to operate once it has a camera or other recording device attached, which makes it difficult to respond to a moment, as can be done with a camera fitted with a telephoto lens, and there is no way to adjust aperture. In some ways, digiscoping is better suited to recording video rather than to still imagery. Proficiency with any digiscoping rig requires patience and practice; however, it has proved to be a valuable means of keeping a record of unusual sightings.

Night-vision devices

In terms of optical development, the new kid on the block is night-vision equipment. Once the sole domain of the military, civilian night-viewing devices of poor quality have been available for many years. But the quality now is truly amazing, with new offerings improving all the time. They fall largely into two categories: image-intensifying optics or thermal-vision optics. Image intensifiers work well with infrared illumination, while thermal imagers are totally passive, recording only images produced from heat signature. Thermal imagers work equally well for detecting wildlife in daylight, will function in zero-ambient-light conditions and allow for the detection of body heat at astonishing distances. I have spotted moths at 100 metres with such equipment. Most devices are of monocular design, and some have built-in camera and video-recording options. When using a monocular, use it with your non-dominant eye to preserve night vision in your dominant eye. Night-viewing binoculars have a far less disturbing influence on night vision.

The advantage of watching wildlife by night is that even animals struggle to see in the dark. If we are careful to stay down wind and quiet, we can use the cloak of darkness to approach very closely to

wildlife undetected, observing behaviour that would otherwise never be witnessed. Night-viewing binoculars are much less tiring to use than a monocular viewer, enabling comfortable prolonged observation. However, this technology, good as it is, does not replace the sensory awareness we have already examined.

Glassing the Grey Ghost

In late 2019, I was filming for ITV in Angsai near Yushu, Qinghai Province, in west central China. At that time, this area was set to become China's first national park. At over 4,000 metres in altitude, the air was thin, making climbing breath sapping. I was there to film any and all wildlife that we might encounter: yaks (*Bos grunniens*), blue sheep (*Pseudois nayaur*) and, most excitingly of all if lucky, the 'grey ghost', the snow leopard (*Panthera uncla*). Our hopes were high but not our expectations; the elusive snow leopard has earned its nickname with very good reason.

In China, the snow leopard is greatly respected. They are a Class A protected species, which has greatly reduced poaching. Anyone convicted of illegally killing a snow leopard faces a hefty fine, a custodial sentence or even the possibility of a life sentence. But they are still low in number and extremely difficult to spot.

With only a few days in the area and much to film, our schedule only provided for half a day to search for snow-leopard tracks and one day to find and film a snow leopard itself. Realising the enormity of the challenge, I was determined to give it my best shot, but I also accepted that my wishes were being accommodated by the crew. We all knew that those one and a half days could perhaps be better spent filming something easier to find, but equally we all knew this was a once-in-a-lifetime opportunity. Things weren't made any better by the fact that through a logistical foul-up, we hadn't been equipped with a telephoto lens for our wildlife camera. Finding snow leopards would be difficult enough; trying to film them with a wide-angle lens was an impossibility. Fortunately, after discussing the problem with Toby, the wildlife cameraman, we realised that it might be possible to attach my spotting scope to his camera, as it was configured for a Nikon mount. I had, quite by accident, brought my Nikon adapter with the scope. In a hotel room in Yushu, we tested the jury rig and concluded that it might just work.

Eventually, the morning came to search for snow-leopard tracks. With British naturalist Terry Townshend, our local expert, we climbed to a ridge where he had a trail camera set. Approaching the place with my lungs bursting, I spied a ten-metre-long exposure of rock, with a bare patch of sand in front of it. There on the sand, close to and pointing towards the low rock face, was a damp line. Could it be a scent marking? I carefully examined the ground – there, faintly, were the associated cat tracks, like a leopard's but slightly more tiger-like. It was a snow leopard. I followed the fresh tracks and saw that they were leading to the very ridge trail where, just twenty metres ahead of us, the camera was located. With anticipation, we examined the footage. There was a pika (*Ochotona himalayana*) doing a jig, and a common leopard (*Panthera pardus*) had also slid past the lens, but the memory card had run out of space some weeks before. It was frustrating but equally encouraging, a feeling every wildlife filmmaker will relate to.

That evening back in the Yak herder huts where we were staying, we discussed our options for the following day. We agreed not to return to the ridge; if we had disturbed any unseen snow leopards, they would be unlikely to return, and Terry and I both knew that fresh tracks almost certainly meant that the snow leopard that had left them would now be elsewhere. The decision was made to explore a different valley.

We were ready to leave well before first light. It was mountain cold, and snow had fallen across the surrounding peaks, but not enough to hinder us. We were instead delayed while our drivers tried to repair a breakdown. With accommodation in the valley limited, we were divided between three different yak-herding families. The valley we were heading to lay an hour's drive away, but the good news was that the wildlife cameraman and wildlife producer were accommodated at the entrance to that valley. They would go ahead and try to locate any snow leopards prior to our arrival. It wasn't ideal, but it was what it was.

Eventually, stifling my frustration at the delay, we managed to get going. The sun was already well up when we pulled into the entrance of the large Y-shaped valley, with a stream running towards us through the middle. To the left of the stream was a small ridge-like hill, with a commanding view of the surrounding hillsides. There on top of the snowclad hill was a group of yak herders and our colleagues; they stood out like a sore thumb. My heart sank. I looked at Terry – the expression on his face betrayed the very same thought: the forward party were too conspicuous. I could feel the possibility at least of success slipping away.

At the foot of the hill, we gathered our thoughts. Our wildlife producer looked frustrated. He is a brilliant field naturalist and knew as well as I that more stealth was required, but he explained that the locals had said that they saw leopards all the time, just walking about. I pointed out that they only see what they see; they don't realise what they haven't seen. Nonetheless, the news was that no snow leopards had been spotted that day.

Experience has taught me time and again that a good long look will often reveal an animal that has been missed. I recced the shadowy side of the hill and realised I could set up a blind in some low juniper trees. Although the ground was steep, it would be a good spot to glass from, and I would be able to conceal myself and the camera crew. So, I set to: blind up, tripod up and my binocular mounted to the tripod. I would have preferred to use my scope, but that was now attached to the wildlife camera. Eventually, despite the steep gradient trying to slide me into the valley, I settled myself and started to glass the opposing hillside in earnest. In the meantime, Terry headed further down the valley to glass the next hillside. As he scrambled away with his scope, the identical model as mine, over his shoulder, I envied him that advantage.

Glassing is an art. Every part of the landscape must be meticulously investigated with the utmost care and diligence, constantly using peripheral vision through the optic to detect any tell-tale movement of an otherwise camouflaged subject. That day, any anomalous shapes and colours received extra scrutiny as I searched for the presence of the abnormal or the absence of the normal. As I scanned the hill face, I was searching for places which might particularly favour a snow leopard, places where it might feel comfortable and secure, where it might enjoy the warmth of the sun. I noticed a large herd of blue sheep grazing on an opposing hillside. They are the principal prey species for the local snow leopards, and they were utterly relaxed, which was not a good indicator.

With practice, it is possible to thoroughly scan a landscape quite quickly, and after twenty minutes I was certain that there was not a leopard on the hillside I was observing. If there was, it was not visible. A decision had to be made: to sit and wait concealed for a snow leopard to arrive or to move to a new location. Now filming pressure raised its ugly head. Our Chinese producer suggested that we didn't really need to succeed; there were plenty of library clips we could cut in. I said to him that this wasn't an option; if we were not successful, that is how the story would be told. He looked disgruntled, and I sensed a later discussion brewing. He was saved by the walkie-talkie crackling into life. Terry had located a snow leopard in the very next fold in the hill.

Hurrying to him in the dead ground cut by the river, I found him set up in front of a large boulder; it was an artful place of conceal-ment that testified to his field experience. He was beaming. Setting up next to his scope, we could see, just shy of a kilometre away, a tiny cliff-like scar in the hillside. At its foot was a small, level space, partially obscured by a large boulder. On the level ground to the right of the boulder was another rock – but then it moved. Setting up my binocu-lar on a tripod, I was able to see the rear end of a snow leopard and its tail. Borrowing Terry's scope, I could also see the ignominious sight of the testicles of a male snow leopard. It was an amazing opportunity. We immediately deployed the wildlife film team to a closer position offered by an intervening finger of land. It would be a tough climb of forty minutes, and the only cover would be a break in the slope where there had been a minor landslip. Hardly easy ground, but the wind was at least in their favour.

The footage we recorded was with the aid of my spotting scope. Using my humble 8x Swarovski EL binoculars, with the gold stan-dard stabilisation of a camera tripod, I was able to follow the action, discerning that we were watching a female with a male cub and that the mother had an injured left forefoot. It was brilliant. We watched the snow leopards for several hours before they eventually stood up, revealing their long, thick tails and their stocky bodies. They departed gently, making their way over onto the hillside I had first glassed. I have rarely seen such amazing camouflage. When a snow leopard stops moving, if you even blink, you lose sight of it until it moves again.

When the wildlife team returned to our position, our Chinese producer was ecstatic. I simply said to him, 'It is better to film it for real.' Breathless and emotional with the exertion, excitement and success, he just beamed back acknowledgement in the form of an massive smile. It was a marvellous sighting of one of our planet's most enigmatic species. Of all the many rare animals I have seen, this was without a doubt the most memorable.

CAMOUFLAGE
The Octopus

I went to buy some camouflage trousers the other day but couldn't find any.

Tommy Cooper

Standing with my dive buddy in the bright spotlight on the deck space at the stern of the boat, we are ungainly, encumbered by heavy lead weights and air tanks, festooned in the essential but ridiculous paraphernalia of diving. Fortunately, the Red Sea off the coast of Egypt is calm today, with only the gentlest of breezes, warmed by the sun-heated rocks of the surrounding desert, blowing across us. Stooping slightly forwards, with our legs more spaced to maintain balance under our loads, we do our safety checks, diligently running through the well-established drill. It is a ritual that precedes every subaquatic adventure, one which reminds us that we are about to enter an environment that is totally alien to human beings.

We check that our buoyancy jackets are functioning, and that our weight belts are sufficiently tight and correctly fastened. We carefully inspect all our equipment releases are functioning and that we know where they are located, taking breaths from our regulators and octopuses (emergency regulators) whilst watching the air gauges to establish that our life-sustaining air supply is functioning correctly. Lastly, our fins in hand and our masks around our necks, we check our dive computers are working and that we have functioning lights, for this will be a night dive.

Checks done, we shuffle to the dive platform at the very stern of the boat. It is crowded with a party of less experienced divers excitedly and nervously doing their own safety checks. We will keep out of their way and let them go first. As they stride off the dive platform, I spot a pair of fins sitting on a bench. I pick them up just in time to hand them to a diver floundering in the water without them. 'Thank you,' he says, with embarrassment in his voice.

'No problem. We have all done it,' I reply, smiling, although my smile is lost as he struggles to put his fins on quickly.

At last, shepherded by their dive leader, the melee of divers drifts far enough from the boat for us to enter the water. Masks on, we smile, give the OK, put our regulators in and stride into the water. It only lasts for a moment, but I love it so, as surrounded in bubbles the water embraces me and my weight settles into the snug caress of my safety equipment. Floating at the surface, we turn to face each other, and with composure and practised signals we raise our deflator hoses and vent air from our stab jackets. Gracefully, we begin our descent into the dark ocean.

Night dives are one of the most fascinating experiences in the natural world, providing the opportunity to witness the hidden life of one of our planet's most diverse ecosystems. We have planned our dive carefully. The dive boat is moored beside a small reef comprising several modestly sized coral heads interspersed with a sandy seabed. The deepest part of the reef is twenty-two metres. We dived the reef in the late afternoon so had the opportunity to spot areas to investigate at night. We intend to stay shallow, for most reef life is to be found there. As we descend to the nearest coral head, I can see a confusing mass of divers' fins and flashing torches above and still close to the boat. Like all divers, I have lived through that phase of learning. I am happy on this occasion to be well clear of the confusion. I calmly turn away from it, Beethoven's piano concertos playing in my mind.

As we approach the coral head, my senses attune to the mood of the reef. The atmosphere is quite different at night than during the day. I spot a large snail near the base of the coral, a partridge tun venturing out, hunting for sea cucumbers. Now the reef's night shift is out in force. A school of flashlight fish hangs off the reef. They are named for the special organs beneath their eyes that contain bioluminescent bacteria and emit a blue-green light. Able to control the output from these 'flashlights', they use them to confuse their predators, to attract their prey in the darkness, to repel intruders and for communication. An old Bedouin fisherman once told me that his father would follow the light from schools of flashlight fish to safely navigate a passage through reefs in darkness. In the daytime, they shelter in cave-like recesses in the coral. Now those same crannies will be occupied by sleeping day fish. We circuit a coral head from its base and find a coral grouper facing outwards from a miniature coral cave that looks impossibly small for its occupant. I wonder how it ever managed to back into such a tight space. A little further and we see one of the coral's most bizarre sights, a turquoise-and-orange parrot fish tucked under a sheltering fold of coral, enveloped in a cocoon of mucus. Each night the parrot fish makes this cocoon to protect itself from the unwelcome attention of biting parasites called gnathiids; it is the aquatic equivalent of a mosquito net.

Completing our circuit of the coral head, which can only be five metres in diameter, we ascend gently to explore its top. One of the great joys of diving is the sense of weightlessness. Once you have mastered your buoyancy control, it is possible to hover effortlessly, inching backwards and forwards or side to side, exploring the extraordinary life of a reef close-up without ever touching anything. In fact, cradling our gauges, we are at pains to avoid touching the coral, mindful that damage to the mucus membrane of a coral can lead to its infection and demise.

In just this way, we begin a stealthy glide over the top of the coral head when a movement catches both our eyes. We turn simultaneously to better see the disturbance. At first, we can see nothing, then there is another movement and the shape of an octopus is discernible. Now with a point of focus, the current that has thus far been so gentle as to be unnoticeable suddenly flows in opposition to our goal, posing the momentary problem of how best to position ourselves to hold station and observe the octopus without exertion. Turning our heads into the current provides the solution – only gentle finning will be needed to allow us to remain stationary. I check my dive computer: we are at fifteen metres, which is perfect. At such shallow depth, the physics of diving are in our favour, as our air consumption will be minimal, our dive long in duration. Now, almost as if waiting for the audience to be seated, the octopus delivers its virtuoso masterclass in camouflage.

From its demeanour and behaviour, we realise that the octopus is hunting but cannot yet see what. Slowly and with deliberation, the octopus pours its gelatinous form from one coral outcrop to the next, its body instantly changing colour in a perfect assimilation of the colour of its surroundings. Occasionally, it pauses motionless to allay any suspicion in its yet invisible prey.

Watching an octopus's skin change colour is mesmerising. While the chameleon has won notoriety for its ability to change its body colour to match its surroundings, a process which takes it several seconds, it is the cephalopods, the squid, cuttlefish and octopuses, that are the true masters of colour change. They use their astonishing ability for concealment from and to startle predators, to communicate, and to attract a mate. They can dramatically change their body colour and patternation, to all practical purposes, instantaneously.

How they achieve this is a miracle of evolution. The outer layer of octopus skin is translucent. Beneath it are a variety of specialised cells responsible for the astonishing colour changes. Close to the skin surface are chromatophore cells that appear as millions of tiny dots. Each chromatophore cell is filled with a colour pigment and controlled by muscles. Occurring in black, brown, orange, red and yellow pigments, these cells are elastic and can be expanded or contracted at will in less than a second to dramatically alter the skin colour and pattern. Beneath these cells is a layer of iridophore cells that reflect light back at differing wavelengths, providing blues, greens, silvers and golds. Underlying these, are leucophore cells that reflect the full spectrum of light, providing white to reinforce the chromatophore colour transformations. These cells can also reflect the environmental colours, assisting precise local colour matching. But more than just changing colour, octopuses can also alter the surface of their skin. They have a network of muscles under their epidermis that can raise three-dimensional bumps at will. These papillae can be shaped into lumps, ridges and spikes to convincingly transform their external appearance, akin to mythological shapeshifting

After a few minutes, the octopus once again starts to move, gently raising itself. Now I understand why: in a fold in the coral is a crab hidden from easy sight. The octopus is carefully looking over the lip of intervening coral. Then, as if by magic, the surface of the octopus's skin erupts into wart-like growths that closely resemble the coral – perfect three-dimensional camouflage. I realise that had we not spotted this octopus when we did it would now be invisible to us. Almost imperceptibly, with just a slight quivering, the cephalopod oozes closer to its prey. Then with a rush it falls like a curtain of death upon the crab, doomed to the deadly bite from the octopus's beak oozing venomous saliva. It is all over in a moment, the octopus carrying the crab away into the cavernous darkness of the coral head, well beyond the reach of our dive torches and prying eyes. What an incredible event to witness at such close quarter.

Back on the dive boat, we graciously accept a hot chocolate fortified with a shot of rum. The dive platform is clear and tidy; the other divers have been back for some time. It appears that they never managed to untangle themselves from the frenzied start of their dive and saw nothing. That is how it is sometimes, but I know that in time they will relax into the experience of night diving and will be able to sit above deck, as we do, under the myriad bejewelled desert sky, recalling the aquatic wonders just witnessed.

More than most, I have had the opportunity to marvel at nature's experts in camouflage, but even now, I think that octopus delivered the finest masterclass in camouflage I have ever witnessed, perfectly blending its body colour and pattern to the surroundings, even mimicking the shape and texture of the coral. But most important of all was its demonstration of intelligence. Octopuses are believed to be the most intelligent of all the invertebrates. Here we saw this very much in action, the octopus patiently inching its way to its prey, using cover and the dead ground in the broken coral landscape to its advantage. Even the timing and direction of its pounce, delivered to achieve total surprise, mitigated the risk from the crab's claws and prevented any chance of resistance.

Octopuses are the most charismatic of creatures. I once saw one walk across open sand on two tentacles, the others held aloft, its whole body deformed to mimic the crenelated surface of coral. So effective was this camouflage that even when looking directly at it I could not distinguish what it was. I had to follow it for some way before, disbelievingly, I recognised that it was an octopus. Researchers have even suggested that octopuses can dream. Watching them hunt certainly demonstrate their boldness, imagination and sense of how other creatures might perceive them. Other divers I know have observed octopuses carrying shells as part of their disguise or mimicking the spiny form of a venomous lionfish. There seems to be no limit to their cunning.

I must admit to camouflage envy when watching an octopus, for camouflage is an essential skill of fieldcraft that greatly enhances our opportunities to observe wildlife candidly, safely and without causing disturbance. Being able to witness natural behaviour at close quarters is an essential part of better understanding the natural world and is immensely rewarding. While researchers are developing adaptive camouflage systems for the military, we cannot yet come close to imitating the active camouflage of the octopus. But we can learn from its masterclass, even its mistakes. The octopus I spotted walking was so clearly out of place that it aroused my curiosity and thereby my pursuit. Had I been a predator, that could have proven to be a fatal error.

Dependent upon its camouflage to avoid its predators and to outwit its prey, the octopus teaches us the first fundamental principle of camouflage.

Camouflage Fundamental Principle No. 1

Where we cannot be hidden, we must use our intelligence, imagination and inventiveness to become unrecognisable by disguise, blending invisibly into our surroundings, concealed in plain sight, without arousing curiosity.

The octopus has in my opinion the best camouflage in the natural world (unless there is a creature hiding from us that we have yet to discover), but it is not alone. Throughout nature, there are many stunning examples of camouflage, such as the extraordinary markings of the nightjar (*Caprimulgus europaeus*), which enable it to masquerade as a lichen-covered branch, or the buff-tip moth (*Phalera bucephala*), which perfectly resembles the broken tip of a dead silver-birch branch.

Camouflage adaptations enable both predators and prey to outwit their foes, the latter mostly relying on stillness and cryptic colouration that blends perfectly to a local habitat. Outside of the setting it is camouflaged for, such disguises are far less effective and may even be counterproductive.

Predators that ambush their prey, such as the puff adder (*Bitis arietans*), can vanish in a wide range of settings. Dependent on their camouflage to hunt and to defend themselves from predators, they are frequently accidentally stepped on, resulting in their reputation for inflicting the most venomous snakebites to people in Africa. The greatest start I have ever had in the wild was from a horned adder (*Bitis caudalis*) in Namibia. Laying perfectly concealed, with most of its body buried in the sand beside a Nara melon, it was so well camouflaged that even if I had been looking directly at it, I am sure I would not have seen it – it was, in effect, invisible. As I reached out to pick up the melon, the little snake exploded from the sand. Fortunately, it made no attempt to bite me and instead fled. I do not mind admitting that its lightning movement made my heart skip a beat, as did the fascinating way it vanished from sight once at a safe distance from me. I have never forgotten that moment, a salutary lesson from a master in camouflage to never become complacent. Patience combined with camouflage is one of nature's most deadly predatory strategies, as we shall explore later.

> **Camouflage Fundamental Principle No. 2**
>
> Even the best camouflage is improved when combined with patience, stillness and slow movement.

Predators that are more mobile, actively stalking their prey, have evolved more versatile camouflage suited to a wider range of circumstances. If we compare, for instance, the pelage of a lion (*Panthera leo*) to that of a cheetah (*Acinonyx jubatus*), we see how camouflage is closely linked with the animal's behaviour and lifestyle.

The cheetah is a highly specialised hunter, vulnerable to the unwelcome attention of larger predatory mammal species such as leopard, lion and hyena. Its beautiful spotted pelage must provide safe concealment from predators when it is resting in dappled shade, and camouflage while stalking prey and when guarding a kill. With a night-vision capability similar to our own, cheetahs prefer to hunt in daylight. Able to accelerate in their charge from zero to seventy-five kilometres per hour in two seconds and reaching top speeds of around ninety kilometres per hour, they hunt most efficiently during the cool hours of the early morning and early evening when it is easier to avoid overheating. Fast and fleet of foot, the cheetah relies upon this ability to outmanoeuvre its prey.

But despite these remarkable attributes, the cheetah is unable to maintain a full-speed charge for further than 250 to 500 metres. For this reason, it must approach its prey closely enough to maximise the chance of success before launching its attack, usually stalking it to within fifty to one hundred metres. Launching its charge from a longer distance risks the loss of surprise, creating an opportunity for the prey to flee and perhaps escape by outdistancing it.

Being tall and slender, a cheetah has a good field of view and a small body profile to conceal, particularly when seen head on. Its disruptive markings break up its outline, enabling it to blend incredibly well into grassland. But cheetahs do not only hunt in open savannah; they also hunt in thorn scrub and open woodland, where they can use natural cover to stalk closely to their prey. I have observed in these circumstances how they choose to use the available shadows and cover for concealment whilst maintaining access to a clear field for mounting their swift charge.

It is estimated that cheetahs are successful in 50 per cent of their stalks. But even when successful, the cheetah is by no means certain of a meal. After exerting so much energy, it requires thirty minutes to regain its breath before it can effectively feed. During this time, it can easily be displaced from its kill by other predators or scavengers. I have even watched in dismay as a pregnant cheetah, hunting alone, was driven from her kill by a martial eagle.

Sadly, in some well-known conservation reserves, the pressure from viewing buses has become so relentless that the local cheetahs have adapted their hunting routine, choosing to stalk in the unfavourable warmer hours of the day when the tourists have retreated to the shady verandas and pool sides of their game lodges – a reminder that we have a responsibility when observing wildlife not to interfere with the natural behaviour of the animals we observe.

In contrast to the cheetah, the lion is a heavy, powerful cat that does not usually run its prey down in a prolonged chase, preferring to make a short charge from as close as possible, relying upon its camouflage, the group effort of the pride and ultimately its enormous strength to overpower the prey once contact is made. The lion's ability to stalk is largely underappreciated, but lone lions, particularly lone males, can be incredibly daring and stealthy hunters.

Right: The sweet fragrance of honeysuckle fills woodland on summer nights. Locating the flowers in darkness by following the scent plume without the use of a torch can sharpen our awareness of the nuances and strengths of odours more generally, awakening and enhancing a powerful sensory ability that we rarely make full use of.

Left: A field loupe can reveal the inspirational natural architecture which surrounds us but mostly passes unnoticed. A classic example of this is the fusilli-shaped anthers of common centaury. Becoming alert to the fine details in nature greatly improves our overall awareness and observation.

Right: Robins are friendly birds, loved for their habit of following gardeners in the hope of securing a worm cast up by a garden fork. But we should not pass up the lessons to be learned by observing them at close quarters, without the need for an optic. They have taught me many things: most importantly, to always look beyond the identification of an animal and to ask 'what is it doing?' and 'why is it doing it?'

Above: The portable blind is lightweight and quickly rigged. It is ideal for observation of shy wildlife or when it will be necessary to wait for a long time. The concealment it provides allows the observer to move around discreetly to maintain comfort. The secret to its use lies in reading a landscape and identifying the optimal location for its deployment. I look for natural shadows or similarly toned and textured vegetation to join onto so that it does not appear as a contrast to the overall scene.

Below: A bag hide is lightweight and compact, and it can be deployed at a moment's notice, completely disguising the human outline and tripod. Even when set up in the open, as here, animals pay it little regard, making it a great option for wildlife photography. Positioned to blend into the background, it is astonishing how closely otherwise shy wildlife can be observed.

Above: A spotting scope provides an astonishing view of wildlife, enabling us to watch it at a significant distance, or better still to observe it at closer range in great detail. When close to wildlife, gloves and a camouflage buff conceal the bright shine of bare flesh that might otherwise betray our presence.

Below: Thermal scopes and binoculars transform the night, enabling easy detection of heat sources and the observation of wildlife in total darkness. Here the antlers of a fallow buck barely show, as cleaned of velvet they provide no heat signature.

>100

A   5.0x   08:52 PM

Above: When using a loupe, stabilise it against your cheek and bring the object you are examining up to the focal point of the lens. An illuminating loupe is very helpful.

Below: A simple hand loupe suitable for field use, it is the first tool of the naturalist and can reveal the most astonishing details in nature that would otherwise pass unnoticed. Most importantly, it encourages us to look more closely at the world around us.

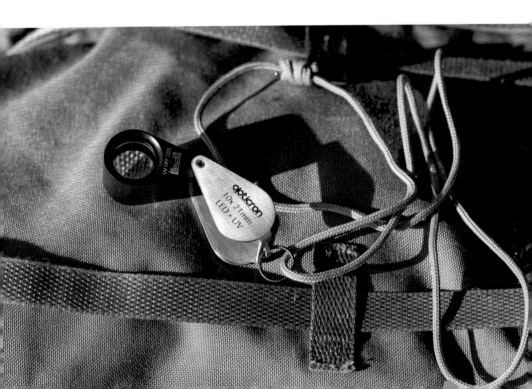

Above: The insulated Jerven Bag can be used as a warm, weatherproof bag hide. The extraordinary mountain camouflage blends perfectly with the environment, making it particularly good camouflage for those engaged in detecting wildlife crime.

Below: A professional tent hide set up in Scotland while filming a capercaillie lek for ITV. Despite its strange appearance, wildlife quickly come to accept the presence of such a hide, so long, that is, as the occupants remain silent. Enter and leave such a hide discreetly at times when wildlife activity is at its minimum.

Above: Four of my preferred stalking shoes. Left to right: Salomon Forces Speed Assault Boot, Russell Moccasin, Courtney Boot, Rogue RB2. All quiet and comfortable with a good tread. In wet conditions, my favourites are the extraordinary Russell Moccasins – made to measure, they fit like a glove and are incredibly silent. The Courtneys are great all-rounders, particularly in thorn country. The Rogues take a drink in every puddle but are really tough and great to live in. The Salomons are featherweight and quick drying.

Below: This simple brew kit (water bottle, steel mug with lid, stove base, and a Trangia spirit burner and extra fuel) makes a huge difference to comfort in the field and most importantly enables me to stay out longer, remaining hydrated and thereby alert. At its most basic, it contains some coffee sachets, tea bags, stock cubes, hot chocolate, snack bars and sachets of instant oats. For longer excursions, I add military-style ration packs.

Above: The joy of watching wildlife. This roe kid was born only shortly before this photo was taken. The mother is coaxing her newborn to stand. As a tracker, a moment like this is so exciting, with a new trail joining the other stories that are written on the ground.

Below: Always look carefully. The tiny kid can be seen sheltering beneath its mother's chest.

Above: Sometimes the simplest fieldcraft is the most effective. Here I am sitting so that my silhouette is attached to a tree and my movements are obscured by shadow. Wearing a *sissitakki*, a warm, lightweight jacket designed for Finnish long-range reconnaissance troops, it is possible to sit quietly in the coldest weather.

Below: As our observation skills are honed, we seem to trip over wildlife encounters, such as this one-day-old fallow buck. His defence is his camouflage and his stillness. During the day, his mother will leave him and only call him to her side at dusk. If you encounter a young deer like this, do not pick it up or handle it – it has not been abandoned. If you can do so without causing alarm, take a photo and then quietly move away.

Although not confined to hunting by night, lions are mostly nocturnal hunters. Their light, dusky pelage, often with spots so faint as to be barely perceivable, enables them to vanish into long grass when stalking their prey, creating the optical illusion of translucency in open savannah. The size of lions requires them to maintain a very low profile when stalking in the open, flattening their bellies to the ground when stalking. The tops of their heads are flattened to present a less visible profile, minimising the risk of their silhouette being seen when looking across the top of long grass. Even when you can see a lion's head as it tries to improve its field of vision, it is bewildering how the rest of its huge body seems to have vanished from sight. This effect is even more pronounced at night, when the lion becomes, for all practical purposes, invisible to its prey.

When resting, the lion has few concerns from other predators, its greatest threat being that posed by rival lions. Even so, lying up in thorn scrub, lions blend so well with the land that they can be virtually impossible to see. In the African bush, it is all too easy to inadvertently walk up on a lion by mistake.

One thing that is common to both cheetahs and lions, as well as to other predators, is that when resting, particularly through the heat either side of midday, they choose a lying-up position that provides shade and cover but also the possibility to spot and ambush passing game. Camouflaged as well as they are, they remain alert in case an unwitting victim should blunder within their reach.

Camouflage Fundamental Principle No. 3

When resting, choose an unlikely place to stop, maintain a low profile, stay quiet, remaining alert to unsuspecting wildlife passing by.

The more I encounter camouflage in nature, the more in awe I am of the process of natural selection. I have often wished I could invite Alfred Russel Wallace and Charles Darwin, the great champions of the theory of evolution, to sit beside my campfire. If I could, I would discuss with them how humanity might learn from natural selection to live in better harmony with nature. If we explore the delicate relationship between a predator and its prey, it is apparent that each ultimately depends upon the other for survival. In simplistic terms, too many predators results in a decline of the prey and the predator's starvation, while too little predation, on the other hand, leads to loss of food by overexploitation by too many prey and the prey's starvation. Does this hold true for human society as well?

Working in Tanzania with Hadza hunter-gatherers, who live more closely to nature than most of humanity, I have witnessed that even with their superb fieldcraft and skill with the bow and arrow, they are not always successful when hunting. Anthropologists who have studied their hunting claim a success rate of one success in every ten hunts. I wonder if the limit of the Hadza's hunting technology is what enables them to live in harmony with their prey. The way nature manages to set a fine balance between predator and prey is mysterious and I believe warrants much closer investigation. Watching fishermen in boats with outboard motors employing sonar devices to locate large pike in quiet corners of remote Canadian lakes causes me to wonder. Would it not be better for the fish if the fisherman had no sonar and was less successful? Would it not be better for the health of the fisherman if he had to paddle to those quiet corners, rather than use an engine? Would it not be better for the environment if the canoe was made of ephemeral materials like wood and canvas rather than plastic or aluminium? I fish those same lakes with limited tackle and no special gadgetry. It makes me thankful and respectful of the fish that sustain me.

'Why am I thinking of these things now?' you might ask. Well, employing camouflage is an essential skill in our fieldcraft, one that does not come without responsibility. Camouflage will enable us to approach wildlife very closely indeed, and the enlightened naturalist acts always to minimise the disturbance of the wildlife they observe. In employing camouflage, we have a responsibility to behave in a way that does not interfere with the wildlife we wish to observe.

One of the most common tales I have heard from wildlife-conservation rangers around the world is that rare and endangered bird species are increasingly being disturbed during the nesting season by overzealous bird photographers. Approaching too closely to take an impressive photo to post on social media, they unintentionally cause distress to species that are already struggling to find suitable nesting habitat. It is easy to underestimate how vulnerable a nesting bird feels. Unwelcome human attention can and will trigger their survival instinct, causing them to flee and abandon their clutch.

Fortunately, modern optics mean that we need not approach wildlife so closely as to cause it anxiety, and naturally not all wildlife is necessarily disturbed by our close proximity. When I think of some of the really close encounters I have had with wildlife, I realise that it is those close observations that make it possible to perceive the personality of individual animals, experiences which have opened my heart to the wildlife that I share my life with.

When I set out to watch wildlife, I dress to facilitate my concealment in the natural landscape. That does not mean that I reach for camouflage-pattern clothing. Camouflage requires some careful thought. My main consideration as always is to employ a 'less is more' approach, packing a light and simple outfit. The less encumbered I am, the more alert I remain, and the more willing and able to respond swiftly to opportunities and to changing circumstances.

My main criterion when choosing what to wear has little to do with concealment by appearance and everything to do with concealment by stillness. Watching wildlife demands that I remain motionless for long periods while exposed to the elements, be they cold, wind, rain, scorching sunlight or the unwelcome attention of biting insects. My clothing choices must enable me to counteract these influences, otherwise it will be impossible to remain still and maintain concentration.

The best times of day to observe wildlife are mostly the early morning or at last light, which means it is the cold that poses the greatest challenge to my comfort. Even in countries where the daytime temperature can soar into the high forties Celsius, warm and windproof clothing remains a necessity. I prefer layers of clothing that can be combined in different ways to suit many temperature conditions, particularly layers that can be compressed into a small space in my daypack, although in very cold conditions the benefit of a long, warm coat is undeniable. Jackets for protection from wind and cold should have comfortable handwarmer pockets and a hood. The hood provides both warmth and provides wonderful shade for the face.

The colour of the clothing is my next consideration; it absolutely must blend with the landscape. My priorities are to choose clothing for its colour and its surface texture, only occasionally for its pattern. Disruptive patterns are most valuable when approaching wildlife very closely or for rangers involved in counter-poaching operations who need to conceal themselves from human observation. In truth, plain, drab colours are all that are needed, and besides, animals with the best visual acuity will most likely detect our movements even when we are wearing camouflage clothing, in which case it is better to resort to the use of a blind or hide, but more of these later.

The colours I choose are natural, earthy and soft in hue, such as fawns, light browns and light greens, as these blend well in many landscapes. In tone, it is important that the colour does not contrast with the landscape. Colours that are too bright will appear luminous as the sun goes down; colours that are too dark will appear black at dusk, particularly obvious to view in an open landscape. If I could pick one colour for my clothing, it would lie somewhere between the light-olive green grey of an ash tree's bark and the green of a green woodpecker's breast feathers. These lighter hues blend well into a wide range of open landscapes and become disruptively patterned when shadows fall on them in woodland. At dusk, they harmonise so well with their surroundings as to appear almost transparent. If you are going to be solely in shadowy woodland in the late evening – for example, when watching badgers – a dark-green wool jacket provides wonderful concealment, but in open country remember that it becomes a visibly contrasting black.

In snowy landscapes, we should emulate the willow grouse and don white camouflage. When both the ground and trees are laden in snow, use a white camouflage oversuit – ex-military white nylon camouflage suits are easily obtained from surplus stores. When the trees have no snow but the ground does, just use the snow-suit trousers and a green jacket.

The texture of your clothing's fabric is also very important, a factor which usually receives only scant regard. Smooth cottons and nylons reflect light unnaturally. This reflectivity creates an unwelcome contrast with the natural landscape and can negate the most effective disruptive patterns. Softer surfaced fabrics are less reflective, absorbing light like moss and consequently melding more seamlessly with the landscape. Soft fabrics are also generally quieter. I cannot count the number of times I have read that a fabric is silent only to be astonished by how noisy it is in when worn. Try to choose fabrics that are not prone to snag on thorny vegetation and that do not rustle as you walk. Most importantly, never trust the sales pitch. When choosing colours, be sure to test their effectiveness by hanging your garments on a tree or fence and stepping back to view them from a range of distances and in a range of light conditions so that you learn their effectiveness and discover any weaknesses.

What about camouflage patterns? As we can observe in nature, patterns that break up the outline of a body form are a great way to become invisible, and disruptive-pattern materials do this admirably. There are even some that now have a leaf-like surface texture to improve their camouflage in a more three-dimensional way, while other patterns have been designed specifically to confuse the light wavelength perception of deer. Most of these camouflage garments are made for the hunting market, which has become big business in some parts of the world. However, rather like the adage 'fishing lures are mostly designed to catch anglers', so too camouflage appeals mainly to the whims and enthusiasms of the purchaser. The wildlife we intend to observe is rather less discerning, so most of the time simply choosing suitably coloured and textured clothing is more than sufficient. If we are concealing ourselves from humans, as wildlife rangers and anti-poacher patrols must, or attempting to remain undetected in very close proximity to wildlife, then, as we have seen, camouflage patterns are essential. However, if I do need to employ camouflage clothing, my preference is for clothing in military patterns that are cheaply available from surplus stores. It should also be noted that in some countries it is illegal for civilians and tourists to wear camouflage clothing.

There are some clothing colours that should be avoided. Blues and yellows are particularly visible to the eyesight of many mammal species. Blue and white can attract the attention of biting flies, particularly tsetse fly in Africa.

When you launder your outdoor clothing, use a natural soap such as Nickwax Techwash. Normal household detergent will impart scent to your clothing, and the brighteners in the detergent will give your clothing a glow that is very visible to many mammals. It is important that the clothing you use for watching wildlife is kept clean to avoid developing the strong human odours that are recognised by wildlife as the scents of the most dangerous creature on the planet. Standing in the smoke from a campfire for a few moments will help mask unnatural odours in your clothing, as woodsmoke is a natural odour that raises no alarm in wildlife. Avoid using scents such as aftershave, perfume and deodorants; simply washing with soap and water is the best solution. For many years, I have used pine-tar soap before heading out in search of wildlife. Like woodsmoke, the pine scent creates little contrast with natural outdoor aromas. It is also brilliant for washing away sticky pine resin from skin and clothing. Strongly scented shampoo also often attracts biting insects.

As I mentioned, my outer clothing layer needs to be equipped with deep handwarmer style pockets. These are excellent for keeping my hands warm but also reduce their visibility. In my waterproof jacket pockets, I permanently keep a waterproof peaked cap that can be worn comfortably under the hood of the jacket, as well as a pair of Sealskinz waterproof gloves, again for warmth and for camouflage. In my daypack, I stash a small pouch containing ex- military camouflage leather gloves, a Tilley hat, a camouflage Buff neck wrap, a mosquito head net, insect repellent, sunscreen, lip salve and a head torch. With these few items, it is possible to vanish into the landscape and to watch without distraction from weather or biting flies. Footwear is also critically important, but I shall leave discussing this until later.

It is easy to become fixated with clothing choices, and I would also caution against buying high-price garments. It is quite possible that we shall need to wade streams and slither through peat to achieve a closer view of wildlife. Clothing that can be abused is very much the order of the day and will remove any hesitation in such circumstances.

While wearing suitably unobtrusive clothing is a real aid to our disguise, it is just the starting point of our adventure in concealment. Strange as it may seem, the best camouflage is not camouflage at all; of far greater importance is the way in which we read terrain and thereby determine where to position ourselves. Every landscape we explore will have features that can help or hinder us in our concealment. Learning to recognise these is critical for our success.

My aim is to observe wildlife without myself being observed. To achieve this can be very difficult. Not all landscapes provide equal opportunities for concealment, and many of the species I am searching for are gifted with extraordinary powers of sensory awareness, coupled with an alertness honed in the daily struggle for survival. To gain the edge, I employ a well-practised process that may seem complicated as I explain it, but which is incredibly straightforward to employ, so much so that it becomes second nature. The key thing here is not to blunder into a landscape without a plan. Thinking back to some of the situations I have faced where there seemed to be no available cover at all, I would say you also need to be a little crazy, imbued with a predator's boldness to relish such challenges and to succeed regardless.

As is so often the case, our success will be built on early preparations. Before setting foot on a trail, I clean my optics, consult a reliable weather forecast and pack the appropriate clothing that I am likely to need. I also include a small first-aid kit, my head torch with spare batteries, and enough rations and water for my excursion. Being well fed and watered is not just important for safety, it also enables me to remain comfortable and, more importantly, to stay alert. I might also need to pack a blind or portable hide; I will make this choice having completed my research.

The next step in my preparation is to study the nature and habits of my quarry, memorising all of the information that I shall need. To do this, I read as many reliable field and behaviour guides as are available. I also try to canvass the opinions of local experts, allowing them to share their experiences with me. This sort of intelligence is critically important – field researchers, rangers and even on occasion poachers have often provided me with highly significant information that cannot be found in books.

Personal experiences transform my quarry from a two-dimensional book illustration into a dynamic three-dimensional creature. Before deploying to the field, I will challenge myself to write down all the relevant information from memory and, as mentioned previously, sketch rough drawings of any key identifying features. You do not need to be an artist for this; it is simply a process of preparing the memory to quickly register differentiating markings – I can't emphasise enough how useful a technique this is.

We each learn in different ways. For me, writing down facts in this way helps to cement them in my memory. You may prefer another method – do whatever works for you. The sort of information I need to acquire covers the physical characteristics and lifestyle of the animal, how to distinguish it from other similar wildlife, and how to differentiate between the male and female, where this is possible: feeding habits; daily routine; behavioural traits that I might be able to observe and interpret; calls and signals and, vitally important, its tracks; feeding signs, droppings and other traces by which its presence can be established; and its sensory strengths and weaknesses. But be careful here: the way information is shared can be misleading – for example, the assertion that a rhinoceros has poor eyesight. Compared to its sense of hearing and smell, its eyesight certainly seems to take second place. However, I can assure you from personal experience that you will not think its eyesight is poor during an unexpected close encounter. A rhinoceros's eyesight is perfectly adequate to its needs; it is more the case that its other senses are more developed.

With a growing knowledge of my quarry, I can begin to turn my attention to the ground I shall be exploring. My aim is to gain a general appreciation of the area. I start by doing a risk assessment, identifying any danger areas such as rivers, cliffs and caves. I consider any dangerous animals that might inhabit the area, from malarial mosquitoes up to polar bears, and take appropriate countermeasures. Are the local population friendly or hostile? What is the detailed weather forecast? How might this impact my expedition? For example, flash flooding resulting from rainfall in a distant catchment region. If I am in a coastal area, is there dangerous mud? What are the tides forecast to be?

If possible, I always prefer to study a survey map of the area at this point. I will consider the approach routes, methods of access and possible escape routes. A key factor is the prevailing wind direction. I need to be able to approach the area by walking into the wind, otherwise my presence will be carried to the noses of my quarry, which will remain invisible to me. This isn't necessarily the end of the story; it depends on the animal. There is a chance that even when my scent is detected, if I find a place to sit where the wind is in my favour and if I am early on the scene, my quarry may choose to disregard the scent alert and relax again. But that is a lot of ifs – it is far better to avoid my scent travelling ahead of me, even if that means having to take a long circuitous route into the area. Some animals, such as wild giant pandas, always respond strongly to a scent alert, making them next to impossible to watch in the wild.

On my map, I will highlight the danger zones, the access points and the locations of recent sightings along with their timings. This will seed my mind with an understanding of the layout of the landscape. Now I can start to concentrate on how my subject moves within this landscape. This is not as good as actually laying eyes on the ground, of course, but it is surprising how often judgements made by a map recce prove to be correct. I might now also be able to decide whether a blind or hide is going to be needed and update the contents of my pack as necessary. And I will be able to estimate the likely timing of any encounter, although my plan is always the same: I will arrive early and stay late.

There remains one last consideration before putting my feet on the ground: checking the wind direction on the day. This will determine the direction I actually make my approach from. If arriving by vehicle, I will take special care not to slam doors or make unnecessary noise.

One question that is always in my mind is whether or not to do a ground reconnaissance in advance. Logic would suggest that this is a good idea; however, as soon as I am in the field, there is a possibility that I will unexpectedly encounter my quarry. For this reason, when searching for a rare or shy subject, a ground recce is often best avoided or kept to the absolute minimum.

On your home ground, where you can easily and frequently go in search of wildlife, you should certainly carry out a ground recce. For animals which emerge at dusk, this is best carried out in the late morning to midday period when your subject is resting in cover, as this will provide ample time for your disturbance to be forgotten.

Look for the tracks and signs that indicate harbours, those areas where your subject lies up and areas where your quarry likes to feed. In those circumstances where I cannot risk a ground recce, I will look for an opportunity to glass the area from an overlooking vantage point with my spotting scope. Otherwise, my assessment of the ground must be made immediately on arrival in the field.

Whether the recce is made prior to your visit or on arrival, it always aims to establish the same things:

~ Where are the hot spots, the places where I am most likely to observe my quarry?
~ Are there any black spots, those places the quarry will watch with the greatest vigilance for signs of danger? For example, gates and styles, or gullies used by predators.
~ Where are the cold spots, the places of least concern to my quarry where I can conceal myself most easily?

I am looking for potential places to observe from that are close enough to provide the view I desire without my presence being detected. With wildlife, this ultimately means without my scent being detected. It's worth considering the slope of the ground – as the sun sets, the air cools and the wind direction usually changes. At dusk, cold air begins to flow downhill like an invisible river finding the quickest route to sea level. For this reason, I prefer to be down-hill of my quarry at dusk.

Having identified some potential observation places, I prioritise them and establish whether or not there is dead ground that will make it possible for me to move between them whilst remaining hidden from view. The last factor on the recce is to decide if I shall need to use a blind or a hide.

Without a planned course of action, I might see wildlife, but mostly it will be fleeing from me, because, as you might well have realised, what I have been describing thus far is aimed at animals that are prey species, such as deer or antelopes. Trying to predict the behaviour of predators is much more difficult. Many predators live almost entirely on the move and are capable of quickly traversing great distances. Usually the best option is to watch their prey species in anticipation of spotting them while hunting.

I use the landscape itself as part of my camouflage. Experience has taught me that it is possible to conceal myself in virtually no cover at all, particularly when I am wearing clothing of the correct colour. As the darkness of dusk grows stronger, so it will become possible to venture out of cover and move closer to the quarry for an improved view, a process that teaches me a great deal about the vulnerability of my quarry but also about the world of the predators. Such knowledge helps to keep me safe when there are dangerous animals to be avoided. Observing dangerous game should never be attempted by a novice without the company of an experienced or professional guide.

Ground Reconnaissance

1. Harbours (note entrances)
2. Hot spots (most likely places to see quarry)
3. Black spots (places of greatest concern to quarry)
4. Cold spots (places most likely to be ignored by quarry)
5. Dead ground (ground hidden from view)
6. Potential observation posts, or OPs (prioritise these)
7. Special camouflage gear required (blind, bag hide, hide)

Map Reconnaissance

1. General appreciation of the terrain
2. Dangers:
   - ~ Environmental
   - ~ Animal
   - ~ Vegetation
   - ~ Terrain
   - ~ People
   - ~ Weather
3. Access routes
4. Escape routes where necessary
5. Most common wind directions
6. Prior and recent sightings and times

As a naturalist, my most important consideration in terms of camouflage is to maintain the widest possible field of view whilst enabling me to remain mobile. There are, however, circumstances that will require me to compromise this concept to achieve success; for example, if I expect to have to maintain my observation for a prolonged period where there is little natural cover, when trying to observe particularly nervous wildlife or when, with special permission, I am observing an endangered species. To meet these and other similar circumstances, I have several specialised camouflage tools at my disposal.

Portable Blinds

When searching for a good observation position, I look for a thin screen of natural vegetation to shield my presence from view. When this is not available, I use a portable blind. These range in design from cunning mirror boards that angle slightly forwards and down to reflect the local vegetation to ex-military camouflage nets. My favourite blind is a camouflage net attached to a tight mesh backing, 2.7 x 1.5 metres. This compresses into a small space, is very lightweight and can be deployed in a few moments. To facilitate this, I have attached long two-millimetre guy lines to each corner. By attaching them at the corners via a loop of three-millimetre elastic cord, I need only tie out the ends to suitable branches with a quick-release knot, adequate guy-line tension being provided by the elastic cord. Backed with a tight mesh, this net is less liable to become tangled on spikey vegetation, as is the case with a conventional camouflage net.

I have two versions of this blind, one in a dark-pattern camouflage and the other in a much lighter pattern. The most versatile is the lighter pattern, but the dark net has proved useful in shadowy woodland. Large enough to conceal two people, blinds such as these allow me more leeway in terms of the movement that is inevitable when watching for a sustained period. However, it remains essential to use hat, gloves and some form of face covering. I always position the blind so that it fits naturally into the landscape, setting it up as an extension to an existing natural feature or within a natural shadow.

Bag Hides

My very favourite item for very close concealment, particularly when taking photographs of wildlife, is a bag hide. This is, as the name suggests, a large bag of camouflage material that I can place over myself, my optic and my tripod. They are equipped with an opening for the camera or scope lens.

There are a variety of different designs of bag hide. All work extremely well, but my favourites are either made entirely of camouflaged midge-proof netting for use in hot weather or made from fully waterproofed insulated camouflage fabric for cold windy conditions. The netting bag hide has the advantage of concealing me but allowing me to easily see out from inside. This enables me to maintain an excellent field of view and detect wildlife before it steps in front of my lens. The insulated hide I favour has a wonderful lichen-covered-rock pattern, which in use gives the appearance of a large boulder. Warm and snug in cold windy conditions, it is excellent for observing flighty animals such as wild otters. Sat in a boulder field, this hide blends in so well that you become immediately invisible.

The real advantage of a bag hide is that I am completely concealed from the view of both my subject and any other wildlife that might raise an alarm. This means that I can take up a position much closer to my subject than when using a blind, assuming that it is safe to do so. But just as with a portable blind, a bag hide is best positioned to fit within the landscape. In other words, find a reason for your hide to be where you position it. On one occasion, a wildlife cameraman whom I often work with set up his bag hide on a bare, open moor only to discover that he had become an impromptu perch for the very hen harrier he was trying to film.

In cold, exposed conditions, such as encountered in upland mountain terrain, I use a king-size Norwegian Jerven Bag as a bag hide. It is particularly well camouflaged, resembling a lichen-covered rock, weatherproof and well insulated. Cold makes it difficult to sustain the prolonged concentration necessary when watching wildlife. Overall, portable blinds and bag hides are light, incredibly compact and versatile. Really, I cannot recommend them highly enough. There are very few circumstances that they will not meet, particularly when employed with skill. They can even be combined for extra camouflage. What I like best is the mobility they allow me. Coupled with judicious and patient use of natural cover, they have provided me with unique opportunities to witness otherwise hidden moments in the lives of wild creatures without their knowledge of my presence.

However, the drawback of a bag hide or portable blind is that great care must be exercised to avoid being detected whilst setting one up. For this reason, I largely reserve their use to situations where I can wait in ambush in a place where my subject walks or feeds. They are certainly not suitable for watching over a nest or any place where my subject is anchored in the terrain and feeling vulnerable. For those circumstances, a full-blown hide is far better, as it can be positioned in such a way that I am not observed when entering or leaving.

Tent Hides

Tent hides are mostly available today as lightweight, highly portable designs in camouflage-pattern nylon, which is light and fast drying. Although I mentioned previously that nylon is not generally a good camouflage material because of its reflectivity, hides are semi-permanent features, so they are accepted into the natural order in a different way. Quite honestly, they could be bright orange if left in situ for long enough.

The best nylon tent hides I have seen are those designed by my old friend, the renowned wildlife cameraman Simon King. However, many professional wildlife filmmakers prefer more cumbersome, sturdier designs in heavyweight canvas. These have the advantage of not flapping in a strong breeze, the noise and movement of which can disturb the wildlife you seek to observe.

Setting up a hide is not as simple as pitching a tent. It requires considerably more care. In an ideal world, the hide will be positioned well in advance and given time to weather in, and to be accepted by the wildlife as a natural feature in the landscape. Adding some natural camouflage to the exterior to break up the hide's contrasting shape also helps. Ideally, the hide will be located so that the route in and out is hidden from view of the subject. A portable blind may be pitched to help in this regard. The advantage of a hide is that while totally screening me from view, it also provides me protection from the weather. Depending on the design, it can also accommodate more than one observer, enabling shifts to be kept. The great drawback of a hide is its reduced field of vision. Even with multiple viewing windows, there is no guarantee of being able to see the subject. Despite some advertisements showing a naturalist reclining in a fishing chair whilst photographing out of a window, the truth is somewhat different. Tent hides are rarely comfortable, and the best shots are often those made at eye level to the wildlife. Much of the space is taken up with the necessary equipment of filming, and there remains the constant need for silence.

I experienced a great example of the limitations of a tent hide's field of view when filming lekking capercaillie (*Tetrao urogallus*) in Scotland. A lek is a gathering of males that display and compete to attract the favourable attention of visiting females in search of a suitable mate. These often occur year after year in the same location and are a special moment in the wildlife calendar. However, capercaillie receive special protection within the UK, and it is an offence to disturb them while lekking. Consequently, special permission and a suitable licence had to be obtained. Despite this, we still had to employ the greatest possible care. If capercaillie are disturbed while lekking, particularly during the peak season (April to May), they might not breed that year.

With the assistance of local experts, our hide was positioned well in advance of the lek and well camouflaged. Along with my wildlife cameraman, we entered the hide silently under the cover of darkness. Our plan was to film the lekking behaviour and, if possible, to exit the hide sometime in the quiet midday period of the following day. But as is so often the case when working with wildlife, things did not go exactly as planned.

We were certainly in the right spot and at the right time. It was just that the competing males were preoccupied with a female in a pine branch directly above our hide. Whilst we could hear the full excitement of the display and filmed brief glimpses of a parading male in all his magnificent splendour, the action was frustratingly taking place behind our hide, out of sight of our viewing ports. The birds were highly active, and remained so throughout the day, meaning that we could not leave the hide until well into the following night, a stay of eighteen hours – a very familiar story, no doubt, to the wildlife cameramen and women who spend many weeks staking out such scenes for blue-chip wildlife documentaries.

Sadly, we only had a budget for one day of filming. But what a privilege it was to be so close to capercaillie at such an intimate moment in their year, and, most importantly, we had not disturbed them in any way. Capercaillie became extinct in the UK late in the eighteenth century. From 1837 onwards, they were reintroduced in Scotland, but they remain a marginal and threatened species. There are many contributing causes to their continuing struggle, but the single greatest problem is the loss of suitable habitat, which has resulted from the fragmentation of native woodland.

This is a real example of where rewilding of landscapes may be the solution. Allowing healthy native woodland to regenerate on a suitable scale has the real possibility to swing the balance back in the favour of the capercaillie. It is my fervent hope that in years to come we may see these wonderful birds more easily and know that they represent the wellbeing of dynamic ecosystems from which we benefit as much as they do. For this to happen, wisdom must replace the insanity that currently lays waste to the biodiversity of our world.

Motor Vehicles

One of the best viewing hides of all is a motor vehicle, and watching wildlife from a car can be amazing. Wildlife is very accustomed to the presence of motor cars and relaxed in their presence, although they might react to visible movement or sound emanating from the vehicle.

If I am going to watch wildlife from a car, I follow a set routine. Firstly, I pack a large flask of coffee or hot chocolate for cold weather and ice-cold lemon barley water for hot weather, along with some small snacks. I keep a warm jacket in the car so that I can watch with the windows open. A bag of suitable field guides is kept within arm's reach in the rear footwell. Before I arrive at the place I intend to observe from, I stop in a safe layby and clean all the windows. I then park without causing any obstruction to other traffic or pedestrians, no closer than 100 metres from the subject, turn off the engine and remain quiet, making no sudden or exaggerated movements. You can observe using your binocular or spotting scope. A bean bag can be used on the car door to stabilise a camera or scope, or there are many clamps that can be easily affixed to a car window for the same purpose.

Permanent Hides

Many nature and wildlife reserves maintain networks of permanent viewing hides. A step beyond field camouflage, they nevertheless provide exceptional opportunities to observe wildlife whilst remaining hidden. When using these hides, employ common sense, follow the local rules and avoid making noise or disturbing movements. Take your time to tune in to what is happening, making certain you scrutinise the nearby vegetation as well as the distant scene.

Public hides are also a wonderful place to make the acquaintance of other nature lovers. Be certain to close the windows and shutters before departing, and always leave the hide in a better condition than you found it. As you will discover, nature lovers cherish these hides, testimony to the wonderful sights that have been and remain to be witnessed from them.

• • •

Whilst I wish I had the camouflage capacity of the octopus, the crude human camouflage I have employed, in all its forms, from the luxury of a public hide to the damp shadow of a bush, has transformed my understanding of nature. Being able to closely observe wildlife from concealment is more than just a thrill – it provides me with the opportunity to answer nature's riddles for myself by close personal observation. I see camouflage as more than just a fundamental skill of the naturalist's fieldcraft. Camouflage is the key to a hidden world that surrounds us, yet is otherwise invisible to us. It is the first step on a journey that can strengthen within us the value of life itself.

PATIENCE AND STILLNESS
The Saltwater Crocodile

For three or four minutes I had stood perfectly still with no
thought of danger and then all at once I became aware that
the tiger was looking at me from a very short range. The same
sense that had conveyed the feeling of impending danger to
me had evidently operated in the same way on the tiger and
awakened him from his sleep.

Jim Corbett, *Man-Eaters of Kumaon*

Northeastern Arnhem Land, Australia. We had been loading boats in
and out of the river for two days. It was a difficult task, for there was
no proper boat ramp. Instead, a deep gulley 100 metres long had, at
some time past, been cut into the bank of the river, angling downwards to the water's low-tide level. Using this, it was possible at high
tide, when the launching gully was semi-filled, to back a trailer down
and reverse the boats out onto the water.

The river was our highway to the remote coast. It was muddy, fifty
metres wide with steep banks lined with an impenetrable fringe of
pandanus palms. Typical for the region, it was tidal for many miles
inland. Returning down the river at the end of the first day, we were
late, and the low-tide mud banks were exposed on either side of the

river, revealing tracks of huge saltwater crocodiles. Every fifty metres, a crocodile had hauled itself out of the water to warm itself in the sun, and they were now lying above us on the banks, like menacing gargoyles on a state building. It was an unnerving experience.

Being late back on the tide made getting the boats out of the water a real trial, as the low-water level was now just a bit lower than the lip of the gully. A run at the gully would bump our boats up onto the slimy river mud from where they could be winched onboard each of our trailers. Inevitably, the last boat stuck on the lip, out of reach of the winch cable, the still falling tide setting it tight in a vice-like suction with the mud.

A rope was hastily found to bridge the gap, requiring the boat driver to slither down into the sticky ooze to attach it. I watched him in fascinated terror, only too aware of his vulnerability to a crocodile attack. Several times the rope snapped and had to be reattached. With each attempt, the boatman's frustration grew, and his regard for the ever-present danger diminished. We all breathed a sigh of relief when the boat finally slid up the mud to the trailer.

The next day, we made a determined effort to be back while there was enough water to make the loading easier. Sitting in the first boat, we turned and accelerated towards the boat ramp. Just on the brink of lip, the whole boat jumped, and the propeller struck a solid, submerged object. One of my team-mates said, 'You hit a log.'

The boatman replied, 'That wasn't a log.' The look on his face expressed what wasn't spoken … it was a croc. Sure enough, when the second boat made its run, the log was gone. There is a saying in Australia's Northern Territory, 'Never walk the same way to a river to fetch water twice.' It is good advice. That crocodile had responded to our difficulties of the day before and had decided to lie in wait for someone to make a slip.

With an evolutionary lineage that can be traced back 200 million years to the Triassic period, the saltwater crocodile (*Crocodylus porosus*) is the undisputed master of ambush hunting. It is the wild animal I most respect, and the one I never underestimate. But it was not always the case. In my early travels in the top end of Australia, like most people, I talked my understanding of the saltwater crocodile more than I walked it. On one visit, I came perilously close to discovering at first hand how dangerous these creatures are, while many years later I made a television documentary about them and really learned to respect them.

These incredibly powerful creatures can grow to seven metres in length and a weight of one tonne. Any saltwater crocodile three metres in length or larger is likely to consider a human being a potential food item.

When you see crocodiles lying in the open, it is difficult to appreciate how perfectly camouflaged they are. If it was not so dangerous, I would suggest you take a close look at their skin, which has an amazingly subtle range of tones, shapes and colours. In the dappled shade of a stream, they can remain motionless, undetected within a few centimetres of their prey, appearing as a piece of fully or semi-submerged vegetation. In open areas devoid of dappled shade, they play a game of deceit, giving the impression that they are slow and sluggish, when they are actually capable of an incredibly explosive, lightning-like strikes, either directly forwards or with a raking sideways bite from their long powerful jaws. They can even erupt upwards from the water to two thirds of their body length or more. Sensing an opportunity, crocodiles will move slowly towards their prey, so carefully and slowly, in fact, that their movement often passes unnoticed, centimetre by centimetre, gradually stacking the odds in their favour: slowly, slowly, catchee monkey.

> Saltwater crocodiles have extraordinary camouflage. Close up it is possible to see how complex the pattern is.

A few days after the boat-ramp experience, I was camped on a remote Arnhem Land beach. I was filming a story of wartime survival. For several days, we had noticed a huge crocodile cruising up and down the beach, watching it with curious fascination. I now realise that it was checking us out, an incredibly dangerous indication that is often the overlooked precursor to a fatal crocodile attack. We all, local guides included, had thought little of it. On the third day, we discovered that same huge crocodile in the shade of a creek just below our campsite. Although it raised a discussion, it remained yet another warning that went unheeded. Consider also that we were on spring tides, with extreme low water, hence the difficulties at the boat ramp, and extreme high water, reducing our beach campsite to a strand of just ten metres between the dense forest and the water's edge.

The next day, with Aboriginal guides, I went spear fishing in the crystal-clear shallows at low tide, bringing back a ray and a huge mud crab to the campfire. It was my intention to cook the food in the shady forest well away from the water's edge. But the director, always keen on an artistic frame, insisted that the fire should be on the open beach so that we could film the scene with the sun setting behind us. So it was that I cooked the meal in the embers of the fire, serving it on leaves from the shady dinner-plate trees lining the beach.

That night, as I lay on my swag under a mosquito-net dome tent, I heard a sound and watched in horror as that huge crocodile walked slowly past me to help itself to the remains from the campfire. I kept a machete in hand in case of an attack, reasoning that I could swipe it on the snout and make my escape. I now know that I was kidding myself. That crocodile was every centimetre of five metres in length – I would not have stood a chance. No one to my knowledge has ever survived the bite of a salty over four metres in length. Apart from the aforementioned behavioural warning signs that had gone unheeded, what I also did not appreciate is that crocodiles have an acute sense of smell and a passion for shark and ray meat. Fortunately, there was a different ray available for it to dine on that night.

The documentary which provided me with the opportunity to really understand these fascinating creatures was in 2013. It was only after going out to collect trapped saltwater crocodiles with the Darwin Harbour Problem Crocodile Management Team and the wildlife rangers in Kakadu National Park that I truly became immune to the crocodile's extraordinary skills of misdirection.

Most memorable was the moment a four-metre crocodile broke the duct tape securing its rear feet whilst in the five-metre management team patrol boat. I was asked to stand on its head to provide restraint while it was resecured – an interesting moment for me that is all in a day's work for the courageous harbour patrol. Whilst the cameraman faffed around with the wrong lens on his camera, I discovered just how powerful an animal it is. Pure muscle, that croc easily lifted me off of my feet – it was immediately apparent that in a fair competition no human is a match for the ferocious strength of a saltwater crocodile.

A few days later, I watched with macabre fascination as fishermen ignored the signs at Cahill's Crossing in Kakadu National Park and waded the causeway at night, oblivious to the presence of numerous large saltwater crocodiles. No one died that night, but plenty have. It is astonishing how we as a species disregard good advice regarding crocodiles.

Not many years later, I was again filming wildlife in Arnhem Land. We were in a small billabong as it was shrinking after the commencement of the dry season. This causes the local crocodiles to become concentrated in a small area. To try to swim in that water would mean certain death. Our local guide was in a tin boat. I was in another and the film crew in a third. I had briefed the crew, to the best of my ability, about the risks of being so close to crocodiles. As I watched a comb-crested jacana walking across lotus lily pads, the crew's engine suddenly gunned and they sped to the shore. They had spotted a water buffalo on the surrounding flood plain and were seeking dry land to stabilise the long lens and film it. I watched in horror as without a cursory glance they hurriedly beached the boat and scrambled up the shore to the left of a large tree. A moment later a huge crocodile, perhaps three and a half metres long, slid startled into the water from the right of the tree. I looked at our guide who had gone pale watching the events play out. The crew were oblivious that they had been within two metres of a croc or even that they had disturbed it. They were lucky. Had they gone to the right-hand side of the tree, as they might easily have done, this story would, as they say, have a different ending.

The following day, in my small tin boat, I intercepted a huge crocodile making off to a quiet recess in the same billabong. In its mouth it held the body of a 350-kilogram wild pig with the same ease that a Labrador retrieves a pheasant. With my boat temporarily blocking its way, it made a valiant attempt to submerge with the pig and swim beneath me. But even this reptilian's strength was no match for the laws of physics. Archimedes would have been pleased to see his principle in action as the pig's body stubbornly refused to be submerged, although he might for a moment have wondered if he was about to be proven wrong by that crocodile.

The crocodile did not give up. It halted with irritation one metre from my port gunwale, looked me in the eye and bellowed a hiss of chilling menace. The sentiment was clear: this was his terrain. I was being warned off. In the back of my mind, there were the tales of small tin boats being overturned by large crocodiles, so with the message received, I motored out of the way. Now with a few supine whips of its tail, the giant reptile re-established forwards motion, then, seamlessly switching to a slower stealth mode, vanished with practiced ease to a dark and scary nook in the thickly overgrown bank where it could stash its prize and mount guard over it.

What intrigued me afterwards was the way in which the crocodile had communicated with me. This did not conform to the impression they normally convey. This was an encounter that revealed a much more calculating intelligence. I made a note never to forget that. Now, when you travel in crocodile country, I hope that you will be better informed than I first was, and do not say that I haven't warned you!

• • •

While many people fear or loathe crocodiles, they are in fact incredible creatures. The more I learn about them, the more impressive they seem.

The threats that they face today are largely as a result of a loss of habitat and illegal hunting. In northern Australia, their numbers were massively reduced by hunting up until the 1970s. But between 1970 and 1974, the northern states of Australia gradually brought the saltwater crocodile under protection. Since then, the numbers of crocodiles have increased, as has their physical size. Although we have still to see truly large crocodiles as reported from the past, this may be as a result of damage to the gene pool following the overexploitation of the largest crocodiles. Also, as the crocodile population has increased, large male crocodiles have pushed out smaller males into other riparian areas where crocodiles haven't been encountered for decades. This has led to an increased occurrence of negative human crocodile encounters.

It's worth considering that the crocodile has the strongest bite of any land creature, so strong that those who survive being bitten by a crocodile often suffer serious infections from necrosis at the tooth-mark sites, the pressure of the bite being so great as to literally destroy human cells. They can also live very long lives and are protected from infections by their blood, which has natural antibiotic properties. If you think you can outswim one, think again. They are known to be able to swim three times faster than the fastest human swimmer. All in all, they are a bit of a natural superstar.

Yet despite their ancient lineage, they are possessed of only a tiny brain, roughly equal in size to their largest tooth. This is no hindrance to their ability to learn, particularly recognising recurring patterns of behaviour in their prey. This fascinates me, in evolutionary terms. Saltwater crocodiles and their other crocodilian relatives are a success story, living affirmation of the triumph of their ancient hunting strategy. We are wise indeed to be cautious in crocodile country, but we can also learn from their techniques of stealth and concealment.

The crocodile's success is built upon its ability to ambush its prey. If there's one thing that a crocodile knows, it is that every creature is vulnerable to surprise, no matter how alert or how well gifted in sensory awareness. Even the strongest of its opponents is weak when taken by surprise and dragged into water and drowned. It is its mastery of ambush that to me characterises the crocodile. I can think of no other creature more gifted in this regard. When we're watching wildlife, we can employ the same skills the crocodile employs to ambush the animals we wish to observe with our eyes, binocular or camera.

By their nature, crocodiles are nocturnal predators. Under the cover of darkness, they have the greatest opportunity to ambush their prey, which is often using that same darkness for its own protection. In this there is nothing unusual; the majority of predators time their hunting activity to coincide with their prey's movement. We too will be searching for wildlife when they are most active. Putting yourself in the right place at the right time of day is half the battle when it comes to finding wildlife to observe.

What, for me, makes the crocodile stand out is its incredible willingness to adapt its behaviour without hesitation, to take advantage of any new perceived opportunity. Crocodiles are highly alert, even when they seem torpid, to the activity of wildlife around them. They are formidably capable of recognising and learning the behaviour patterns of potential prey species, just as that crocodile had recognised our pattern of behaviour at the boat ramp in Arnhem Land. They are masters of quietly repositioning themselves to take advantage of unwary animals behaving in the same way more than once. Mostly crocodiles are so stealthy that we do not see them going about this activity. But if you take the time to observe their hunting practice as I have, you will see that sometimes, as already mentioned, they will very gently ease their way into a place of ambush by tiny incremental movements that are so slow as to be virtually undetectable. At other times, when they feel they can, they will move much more dynamically, swimming swiftly to such a spot, usually submerged. Crocodiles in this way seem to suddenly appear where least expected. It is easy to write off this behaviour as purely instinctive, particularly when we see how small their brains are. However, I firmly believe from my experiences with crocodiles that they are more capable of calculated movement and more strategic in their method of ambush than we give them credit for.

We can learn from the way in which a crocodile is opportunistic and alert to patterns of behaviour to assist us in our search for otherwise difficult-to-approach wildlife. When I encounter wildlife without causing it alarm, I make a point of noting the time as well as the location of the encounter. Following the example set by the crocodile, I will position myself in concealment near to where I saw the wildlife at the same time on a following day. Just as the crocodile prefers to arrive early for his dinner, so I will arrive early for my viewing. So effective is this method that I caution you to use a camouflage blind to avoid causing any negative disturbance to the wildlife you may otherwise surprise. Of course, no method is successful all of the time, but experience has taught me that this process greatly improves my chances of success.

But crocodiles do more than just carefully put themselves in the right place at the right time. This is just the backdrop to their two most deadly stratagems.

Without any doubt, it is the crocodile's ability to remain absolutely motionless that is its greatest hunting advantage. By this process, it transmutes itself into a seemingly harmless inanimate object. Even when you can see a crocodile and you know it is there, its stillness enables it to slip from the focus of your conscious mind. It is a worrying weakness that a saltwater crocodile is all too willing to exploit. I have often wondered as I watch a bird land on a motionless crocodile if the crocodile is happy. For the bird's presence endorses the crocodiles camouflage, proclaiming it a natural unmoving object within the landscape.

Stillness is an art that takes a considerable time to learn but is a vital skill the naturalist must master.

When I guide people to watch wildlife, I have learned there is no point asking them to be quiet or silent, for each of us has a different perception of what silence is. Inevitably, someone will fidget, scratch and generally rustle, unaware of how such tiny sounds contrast sharply with the natural atmosphere, causing wildlife to be more alert to a potential threat and thereby decreasing our chance of success. Instead, I ask them to be still. This is a more certain request that bears fruit. But what is stillness and how still is still?

To my mind, there are two types of stillness: there is internal stillness and external stillness. External stillness is not moving, not scratching or fidgeting, not swatting away an annoying insect. In short, remaining as motionless and as immutable as a rock within the landscape. This is the easy aspect of stillness that just requires mental discipline and some focus. Much more difficult to achieve is inner stillness, and yet here lies one of the greatest attributes of a wildlife observer. When we are truly still within, we are by nature still without. Inner stillness enables us to detect the subtlest disturbances in the natural world, in both a conscious and a subconscious way, providing the mental space in which these disturbances become obvious, can be analysed and their meaning determined. This is nothing supernatural; quite the contrary. It is an ancient ability we each have within us, but one that is often eroded by the chaotic disturbances of our modern lives.

Achieving inner stillness is not difficult. We just have to value the benefit and make time for it. Almost inevitably when I travel to a landscape in search of wildlife, I arrive in a mental state that is anything but still within, particularly if I've driven there. The very act of driving requires alertness and searching, almost the polar opposites of inner stillness. Consequently, I unfailingly try to spend a few minutes allowing my spirit to catch up with me. I need to calm my inner being and tune into the natural rhythms of my location. I have several favourite ways to achieve this, but what they all have in common is sitting still and relaxing for a few moments. It may be that I light my hike stove and make a quick brew, or I might sit with my back to a tree and whittle on a piece of wood for a few moments. In both cases, I become a physically smaller presence in the landscape. My disturbance of the landscape is reduced, speeding my acceptance by the wildlife and allowing my senses to attune to the local subtleties. With each minute that passes, the disruption of my arrival amongst the wildlife subsides. There comes a point when I'm able to step foot on my way within the curtain of silence that protects wildlife from outside intrusion.

This is what I'm ultimately trying to achieve. It's like a doorway to a secret world. When you are still within, you become hyperalert to the subtlest of changes in nature, and much more able to make associations between them and to recognise patterns. It forces you to slow down and reduces the exaggeration of your otherwise tell-tale movements. With experience, stillness itself teaches the value of stillness. It is always worth remembering that even if you are not camouflaged, by remaining perfectly still there is a very good chance that you will remain invisible to wildlife.

One year, I remember sitting in just this way in a small glade amongst a number of very large beech trees that had blown down in an autumnal storm. I chose the spot because the fallen trees afforded me concealment from the surrounding area. As I sat there, basking in the sunshine, carving a small piece of wood – I do not remember what I was carving – I heard an unusual rustling, scratching sound coming from beneath the trunk of the huge fallen beech just two metres in front of me. I stopped moving and sat absolutely motionless and watched with astonishment as first one and then another young roe-deer buck emerged from the tiny space beneath the tree. It was clearly a very awkward squeeze. They then shook themselves, looked around without even paying me a second glance and trotted off. It was an amazing moment, reinforcing the value of stillness.

So, as we walk the trail of the crocodile, we have learned to place ourselves in a position of opportunity, slightly earlier than the optimal time, and we have become as motionless as a rock. Our chance of success has greatly increased, but we still have one more crocodilian stratagem to employ. It is said that 'all will come to those who wait', and this may well be the mantra by which crocodiles live. For what is most chilling about crocodiles is their astonishing capacity to wait. They seem gifted with a super abundance of patience.

In a strange way, this is one of the hardest lessons for a human to learn. Perhaps it is the price we pay for our large brains that the long wait is anathema to us. We have active, stimulus-hungry minds that entice us to peer over the next horizon. We bore easily. We demand to know, 'How long will it take? Isn't there a better way?' As hunters, we devised traps and contrivances to do the waiting for us, but as naturalists wanting to witness wildlife behaviour at first hand, we must more than accept the long wait; we must learn to embrace it.

Sometimes waiting can seem dull and boring – nothing seems to be happening, when actually something is happening. There are natural patterns at work within the environment that are difficult for us to perceive, ranging from the vocal alarm calls of birds to the pattern of movement of fleeing wildlife. Some of these signs we will notice and read, some we will not. Like dominoes falling, these disturbances spread out, each triggering the next. Our intrusion into the environment is like a stone thrown into a pond, ripples spreading out in all directions, the disturbance reaching the attention of creatures we have no awareness of. Simply sitting still and being patient allows for that disturbance and its consequences to fade. Soon we are forgotten by the keen-eyed creatures that saw us arrive. In effect, we become invisible, and each passing moment is a deeper investment in our cloak of invisibility that increases our odds of success.

It is quite natural to reach a point when nothing seems to be happening and the nagging question has to be asked, 'Should I wait longer, or should I move on?' This question must not be asked prematurely, which is usually the case when we are not properly dressed for the cold, damp or biting insects. Assuming that I am not distracted by such discomforts, my way of dealing with this is always to wait longer – just ten more minutes, then another ten and so on. This method frequently pays off. However, if the inner voice of my subconscious is telling me otherwise, I must consider my options more carefully.

The battle between the conscious and subconscious mind is a difficult thing to read. Our subconscious mind is a powerful adjunct to our decision-making, excellent at detecting the faintest clues that the conscious mind has overlooked. It is also good at drawing attention to factors that we might have noticed but ignored, because we are overly focused on a particular course of action. As a guide to managing these two thought processes, I look in the first instance for some conscious clue to support my subconscious appraisal, or I question why my subconscious is telling me something different. Only time and experience will allow you to balance and reconcile the contribution each has to make, a process that gradually teaches faith in the subconscious.

The laws of nature dictate that even the stealthiest crocodile cannot succeed every time. Watching crocodiles whose lengthy stalking has been flouted, we learn to accept failure stoically. While crocodiles show plenty of emotion at territorial encounters, I have never yet seen one show any at a failed stalk. They simply slide away and vanish, confident that there will be another opportunity. There will be many times when our patience does not bring reward but equally future occasions when it will. The impact of the successes will greatly outweigh the failures.

Just yesterday I noticed a roe-deer doe that had been lingering in the same coppiced area for several days. Her bulging belly revealed that she was heavily pregnant. In my area, roe deer usually give birth in the first two weeks of May, which meant she was very close to beginning her labour. Without causing her any alarm, although she had seen me, I moved quietly on out of her way. Perhaps an hour and a half had passed while I kept vigil with my camera in a location where I often see foxes. I intended to stay longer, but my subconscious mind was calling me. Trusting the voice, I headed home.

At a junction in my path – one way leading home, the other back to the doe – my subconscious called again. I responded and quietly made my way back towards the deer. She was still where I had seen her earlier, but her belly was no longer distended. Downwind of her and well concealed, I watched discreetly for twenty minutes, at which point she made a muted squeak and went over to a bump in the ground. Then I noticed the bump wasn't a bump at all but was actually moving. It was the head of her newborn kid. Tenderly, she licked her offspring's head, nuzzling it with maternal gentleness, encouraging it to stand. With the difficulty of unfamiliarity, the baby deer propped itself up on its pin-like legs, one by one, splayed wide and awkward. Gradually, it narrowed the space between its feet, until with great effort it stood for the first time in its life.

It was a magical thing to witness. The tenderness with which the mother cared for her young was beautiful, something that lives within you for ever. Fortunately, I have seen this event several times in my lifetime, but the magic never fails to move me.

As I write these words, that young deer is concealed in the thickets. Only this evening when the coast is clear will the mother call it from hiding to feed and to be with her. For its very survival, it depends upon its camouflage and its ability to remain perfectly motionless. Stillness, in many ways, is the ultimate camouflage.

STEALTH
The Leopard

Having tracked, located and stalked a leopard, far more pleasure is got from pressing the button of a camera than is ever got from pressing the trigger of a rifle.

Jim Corbett, *The Man-eating Leopard of Rudraprayag*

Our campsite was nestled amongst the smooth boulders of a beautiful *kopje* west of Namibia's wonderful Etosha National Park. We had reached the phase in the tracking course when we lay human trails of increasing difficulty for our students to follow. All life seemed to be arrested as the sun wrestled with us, holding us in the vice-like hold of its oppressive heat. Only the buzzing from the occasional crazy insect flying by at speed pierced the palpable silence of sufferance.

A short walk from the campsite was a permanent wildlife viewing hide. Perched above the precipitous side of a large *kopje* overlooking a tiny water hole, it provided better than average shade. From this lofty vantage point, I watched with a colleague as the daily visitors risked their lives to save their lives, running the gauntlet of predators to obtain a drink of water. Today, the waterhole was eerily quiet. The whole atmosphere was one of restrained menace, a gin-trap set, hidden and ready to be sprung. But at times like this you can never be certain. Were there predators lying in wait, or was it perhaps just our overactive imaginations?

With the sun at its highest point, the stillness was broken by a slight trail of dust in the distance. Through our binoculars we followed the progress of a warthog family running single file to the water hole. With their tails held upwards like radio antennas, and moving in perfect unison, they looked like a squadron of armoured cars. At the brink of the water hole, they lined up abreast of each other and drank in synchrony, before turning with their mission accomplished and, still maintaining their original formation, retreating to the thorny scrub of the Namibian bush veldt. The sun having just passed its zenith, we set off to lay two solo trails for our students to track.

The afternoon would be a difficult tracking exercise, but we knew the students were ready for it. After a hesitant start at tracking two days before, they were now starting to make real breakthroughs. Passing the group shade tent, all was quiet. We could see them huddled into the shade for comfort. They looked fatigued, the combined effect of the sun and the visual strain of searching for spoor was taking its toll. But I anticipated that as the sun dropped, their energy and enthusiasm would return, just as the lowering angle of light would make the spoor easier to spot – easy being a relative term when searching for the tiniest of disturbances. We walked up the track from the campsite for 200 metres and then off to the left along a game trail that joined it at a right angle. We did a radio check with our walkie-talkies and then separated ourselves by 100 metres.

I announced over the radio that I was ready to begin. 'Roger' was all that came back. My reliable colleague was never known for his flamboyant use of words. Leaving good starting footprints in the cocoa fine dust of the game trail, we each began walking as we had planned, two separate parallel trails up the hill through the thorn scrub to the top of a large smooth-crowned *kopje* ahead of us. Staying in touch by radio, we would be able to avoid our trails converging or crossing, a level of difficulty yet too challenging for our novice trackers.

The trick is to lay a trail hard enough to test the students' growing talents, yet not so hard as to be impossible. The challenge of these trails would be to find the sign at all, for once off the game trail the substrate was iron hard, sun-baked soil with tiny granite pebbles cemented together. Unable to push through the thorn scrub, the trails we laid braided their way around the spikey vegetation, utilising a maze of lesser game trails. Eventually, I could see another major game trail ahead of me that was across my axis. This would provide a well-defined halfway point on the trail. I knew my colleague would be making the same judgement.

As I reached the game trail, I could see a perfect set of leopard tracks in the dust. The edges of the depressions made by the toe pads were crisp and well defined, the base of the pad impressions perfectly smooth. These tracks were very fresh. I called up my colleague on the radio: 'Are you on the game trail yet? Over.'

'Roger, just on it now – over.'

'I have fresh leopard tracks, coming your way – over.'

'Oh … There are none here – over.'

'Wait – over.'

'Roger, standing by.'

I pressed my thumb into the dust beside the tracks to obtain an age comparison. In truth, I did not need to – I already knew the outcome, just as I knew that my compatriot would be carefully scanning the game trail for tracks and more importantly the bushes for rosettes of spots. As I lifted my thumb, the depression I had made matched the leopards identically. These tracks were literally moments old.

'They are *very* fresh. It must be between us. Take care – over.'

'Uh, yes will do. Thanks – out.'

The calm in his voice belied his obvious concern. Now the vicious thorn bushes seemed tame compared to the claws of one of the most stealthy and explosive predators on the planet. Leopards don't pick fights – in fact, they go out of their way to avoid them – but if they feel cornered, threatened or are wounded, watch out. Hesitation is not in the leopard's nature. They know that a lightning fast, furious assault, directly attacking their threat, will usually provide the opportunity to make their escape.

Very carefully, we completed our trails to the top of the *kopje* without incident. Relieved, we sat and glassed the scrub we had just traversed. But search as we did, there was no sign of that cat. When a leopard doesn't want to be seen, it simply vanishes. Part of its personality is to vanish like a ghost without giving away that it has been disturbed. It will often stop and look back to see whether it has been successful in its evasion, but otherwise it returns to cover to hatch a new plan of action.

Since that day, I have had many opportunities to track leopards, in many different locations. My fascination and respect for this animal is without limit. I love watching them, and I think that of all the animals that I have trailed it is the leopard that has the most perfect footprint of all. Following leopard trails has taken me into some quiet corners that I would never have otherwise found and into some that I would rather have avoided. One young male leopard's trail led me up a very small and tightly enclosed dried stream bed. Either side of me the vegetation was tall, thick, golden grass with acacia thickets behind. The leopard was typically keeping close to the edge of the stream. The sun was already warming the sand, causing the faint leopard tracks to lose their definition. Rounding a tight left bend in the stream, there in the middle of the bed, on top of a mound of sand, I could see a deep foot depression. It looked fresh. Taking care to remain silent, I moved forward to check it out. It wasn't a leopard's track but quite literally the largest lion track I have ever seen. What was worrying was that it was perfectly fresh and led across my path obliquely towards the bush over my right shoulder. That lion was now somewhere behind me.

Despite being armed with a suitable rifle for defence, my main source of protection is always early detection of a threat. That defence had already been breached. A flock of laughing doves sped past just overhead. I could hear every wing beat massively magnified. I realised my senses were already in overdrive, and I could feel sweat beading on my neck. I focused on maintaining a wide field of vision. Stress can cause perceptual narrowing, reducing our ability to detect nearby dangers that would otherwise be obvious.

Moving ever so slowly, I made the rifle ready to meet an imminent attack and turned to face the possible threat. This was essential. If a charge comes, it requires split-second responses. Action is quicker than reaction, so there is little time to waste realigning position. I was acutely aware that a lion can charge at more than twenty metres a second and estimated that the gully wasn't more than eight metres wide. I needed to keep my gaze upwards; my feet would now have to feel their way. As I headed back down the trail, my eyes were at ground level of the surrounding bush. I strained to see through the vegetation. Through a tiny hole, I spotted a flicking movement deep in the shadows beyond, and then again, another flick.

I froze and studied the movement; at first, I thought it was a bird, then my brain registered what it was. It was a tail tip, a lion's tail. The lion was lying down, rump towards me, about forty metres away. With each flick of its tail, I could now make out a perfect sight of its testicles poking out from behind its hind quarters. A comedic moment, perhaps, under other circumstances.

More carefully than ever, I retraced my steps down the stream, keeping my rifle up and at the ready, maintaining my wide field of vision in case the lion was not alone. I do not think that at any other time in my life I have ever moved more quietly than I did that day. But in a strange way I was protected by the very leopard I had been trailing, for like all leopards, it exhibited a genius for choosing a quiet path, well concealed from sight. Retracing its route afforded me some of that protection.

Leopards are true masters of stealth and provide the inspiration for the more advanced skills that I am now going to describe. Camouflage and stillness are coming with us, but we will now explore the landscape on the move and learn to approach wildlife closely without detection: the art of stalking.

To stalk well requires considerable skill, effort and practice. It is a perishable ability. If you do not exercise it, the skill will fade. Consequently, it remains today solely in the custody of the most dedicated. This has probably always been the case. Even in tribal societies, not every hunter is a top stalker. I remember meeting a Bayaka man in the Central African Republic who attempted to slip unnoticed into the shadow of a door inside a hut where I was having a conversation. Although my back was turned to him, I caught his tell-tale movement out of the corner of my eye. I asked my host if all the Bayaka men were as stealthy as him. Playing his game, I was careful to indicate his presence with a gesture of my thumb and without turning to look at him. I was told, 'No, this man has a reputation in the community for being able to make himself invisible.' As I left the hut, he was still standing there like a statue in the shadows.

Stalking is many things: it is a skill requiring consideration of technique and form; it is a way of thinking; and, perhaps most importantly, it is a heightened state of sensory awareness. Everything we have thus far explored will now be brought to a pinnacle of perfection, but this skill cannot be learned in an armchair. It absolutely must be lived.

Feet

When I am tracking, individual footprints can tell me a great deal about the animal that I am following. Experience has taught me to pay very close regard to the tiniest of details. Following human footprints is usually a case of recognising an ugly sole design and memorising the signs of damage or wear or tear that are specific to one person's shoe; following animal tracks is a much more subtle art. This is so intense that years later I can remember the tracks of creatures I have followed with great clarity. Ghostly images of these tracks live within my memory. When I recall them, in some strange way my brain can decipher them, enabling me to read the personality of the animal itself.

When I look at the track of a leopard, beyond its identity, the first thing that I read is its stealth ability. It shares a track feature that places it in the company of the other most stealthy cats: lions, mountain lions, snow leopards and tigers. This is the very large rear, or metacarpal, pad on its paws. When I see this, it is a warning that I am following an animal super-evolved to be stealthy and silent. A male tiger may weigh 300 kilograms and be three and a half metres long, but despite this, tigers are renowned for their ability to hunt silently. What I have learned from this is that when it comes to moving quietly, feet matter. I have particularly wide feet, which I like to think helps me to pad about softly, but for humans it really comes down to our choice of footwear. Thinking back to that dry stream bed, if I had been wearing noisy shoes, I might not be writing these words today.

Following four Ju/'hoansi bushmen hunting in 2004, I was surprised when they suddenly adopted a crouch and sloughed off their tyre-tread sandals. Their sharp eyes had spotted a steenbok (*Raphicerus campestris*) in the shade of a tree ahead, and they were beginning a stalk, bows ready, poison arrows fitted to the strings, making their final stalking approach barefoot for added stealth.

I asked them afterwards if they would have removed their sandals if they had been near a lion. They were adamant that under those circumstances they would need their sandals to be able to run into hiding because the ground is so thorny. This was their solution to the conflicting needs of protective footwear and stealth.

As a species, we evolved to walk bare foot. When we first added foot coverings for protection, they were simple moccasin-style coverings that preserved the toes' role in walking. Research has shown that when we walk barefoot, we experience as much as 12 per cent less knee impact. When we started to wear hard-soled shoes, our stride lengthened, and we began to walk more on our heels, rolling forward to the toes, which were no longer able to add significant push or spring to our stride.

This way of walking has greatly reduced our ability to move quietly. When we consider walking techniques to improve our ability to spot wildlife, we are wise wherever possible to restore the role of our toes in our walking method. Just as those Ju/'hoansi bushmen cast off their sandals when stalking, we need to try to break free of stiff-soled footwear.

I have lost count of the different designs and brands of footwear I have used and worn out stalking. The fact is that the perfect footwear for stalking has yet to be made, although there are a few good contenders. It is equally true that one shoe type is never going to suit all possible circumstances. Inevitably, we will need a variety of shoes to suit different environments.

When I choose stalking footwear, I look for a design that will provide safety and protection from the local environmental threats. The shoe must fit correctly. I prefer to try on potential new shoes late in the afternoon when my feet are at their most swollen and always with the type of sock I intend to use. Socks are equally important as the shoes; I use wool 99.9 per cent of the time and fast-drying socks the rest.

No matter how good a shoe's reputation for stalking, it must be appropriate to the conditions. There is no point wearing a legendary African *veldschoen* on a Scottish peat bog. The poor old 'vellie' will end up taking a drink from every puddle. Much better to use a local boot or rubber wellington for peat moors.

The tread pattern is very important. Smooth-soled designs without a stepped heel are the quietest. But some degree of compromise may need to be made here, as grip is also important. More than once whilst trying to approach closely to wildlife by traversing the slippery inside slope of a gully, I have taken a tumble when my shoes lost traction – more damaging to my pride as a stalker than to my body, fortunately. In rocky terrain in warm climates, I like my soles to be fashioned from a compound sufficiently soft to provide good adhesion to the rock so that I can walk up and down steep surfaces without slipping. In muddy conditions, there needs to be a good tread to bite into the soft earth. Although chunky treads can be noisier, experience has taught me that I can always walk more carefully to achieve quietness, but it is impossible to be silent when crashing to the bottom of a gully on my posterior.

Ultimately, my most important criteria for quietness is the flexibility of the sole. When I am wearing the shoe or boot, the sole should flex upwards with my toes when I lift them. Every shoe I have ever used that does this has proven to be a quiet design, even those with a heavy tread pattern.

Some shoes may squeak when walking. This is maddening, and I have no idea why it is the case. When this occurs, I try soaking them and walking in them until they are dry. Sometimes this works. In specialised environments such as mountains, rainforests or the arctic, the most important consideration is always to choose footwear that provides the appropriate environmental protection over how loud it is. We have no choice but to learn to walk quietly in such footwear or carry special stalking shoes for when needed.

My biggest dislikes are footwear that is too hot, too cold or, most importantly, too heavy. My needs as a tracker are the greatest influence in my choice of footwear. I demand light footwear. The lighter my feet, the more alert and less fatigued I will be. This alone can make the difference between success and failure. For this reason, I will sometimes compromise in my choice of footwear, choosing in favour of lightness and fleetness of foot.

Of the many boots and shoes that I have used over the years, the following are my favourites.

Footwear for general wear

WELLINGTON BOOTS

Essential for very wet conditions. Choose high-quality boots such as Chameau, Percussion Rambouillet or Nokian. Look for models that meet the toe-raising test. It is surprising how quiet such boots can be. When wearing them for long periods in cold weather, I wear a compostable plastic bag next to my skin under my socks. This prevents perspiration dampening my socks and reducing their insulation properties, keeping my feet warm all day.

MILITARY/HIKING BOOTS

General mountain-walking boots are essential for steep, high country. I prefer military-style boots, particularly above the ankle, for the added protection they afford. After searching for many years, I have come to favour those made by Altberg Boots. This small British company based in Richmond in Yorkshire has won the respect of their customers through their uncompromising pursuit of excellence. They make a wide range of boots to suit many different climatic conditions and can make pairs to order if you have difficulty finding off-the-shelf footwear to fit.

Footwear specifically for stalking

MOCCASINS

I have used many different traditional moccasins, even making my own, but I find their smooth sole can lack sufficient grip. Perhaps my absolute favourite stalking boots for temperate conditions is a moccasin made by the Russell Moccasin Company. These are bespoke moccasins with a bespoke price, but they are wonderful and hard-wearing. I use a minimalist Thula Thula seven inch in all-weather Tuff leather with a Vibram Newporter sole and no heel lift. If you are not used to moccasins, have yours made with the heel lift. They are astonishingly good, even in very muddy conditions. In the wettest weather, I use them with waterproof socks but have never yet actually needed the socks, as they function so well without them. These are comfortable, hard-wearing and silent boots. I take these on canoe trips to wear ashore and cannot recommend them highly enough.

VELDSCHOEN

Veldschoen are the classic low boots and shoes of the South African bush, long favoured by professional hunters for their stealth and incredible durability. The reputation of this time-honoured design is well earned. I would steer you towards the excellent boots made by Courteney in Zimbabwe or Rogue Outdoor Gear in South Africa.

. . .

Footwear choice makes a significant contribution to our stealth but is not the whole story. More important than footwear is how we move. Leopards learn the skills of stalking in their play as cubs, pouncing on their siblings and the tips of their mothers' tails. We shall have to play catch-up.

Stalking

In 2010, I was tasked with finding a particularly elusive leopard in a Namibian game reserve for ITV. Although there is a high-voltage electric fence around the reserve, it is 250 kilometres long, which meant that each day I was setting out to search an area the same size as Greater London. No easy task, and one that would have been impossible without the assistance and support of the expert local guides.

Each morning, I would cut for sign in the soft ground of dried watercourses and gullies where they intersected the reserve's extensive network of roads. Over the course of a week, this began to provide me with a detailed picture of how many different leopards were moving in the area. Over several days, I repeatedly cut the spoor of a small male leopard circuiting through the area. Following the trail of that young leopard was fascinating and enabled me to understand how it was using the ground to its advantage. I was even able to describe its personality and pattern of behaviour, something we were later able to confirm when we managed to capture him on a trail camera. What I learned from that leopard has proven to be invaluable ever since.

Leopards, particularly young males lacking a territory, live in a very tough neighbourhood. Until they are large and strong enough to challenge the status quo, they must avoid contact with other male leopards, particularly the dominant territorial male who defends a large territory encompassing the smaller territories of several female mates. The resulting conflict would almost certainly result in injury and could prove to be fatal.

Lions are also a threat to a leopard. Feline predators routinely kill other species of cat, most likely to reduce competition. Despite a male leopard's extraordinary strength to size ratio, it is no equal to the much larger lion, particularly when faced by a coalition of young male lions or a pride.

Outside of reserves, leopards also fall victim to traffic and to illegal poisoning, snaring or shooting. Interestingly, research seems to indicate that it is female leopards living in the wild, rather than in nature reserves, that are most often the victims of illegal hunting. This may be due to their presence being more detectable, as they hold smaller territories and divest some of their attention and energy to raising their cubs. Equally, the need to provide food for their young can bring them into conflict with local farmers should they prey upon livestock.

The complexity of these hazards was well reflected in the young leopard's trail. Following his spoor, a picture of stealth and caution was revealed. By estimating the age of the spoor and comparing it to the position of the moon, I was able to establish that the leopard was moving as much as was possible within the moon shadow cast by the lip of the gully. At bends in streams, he would forgo the shadow, cutting across to the inside bend, where it afforded him the best chance of ambushing potential prey immediately around the corner.

With the sandy stream bed recording his tracks well, I was able to pick up this behaviour pattern several times. Each time he had checked around the bend, he would again resume his patrol in the security of the shadows.

That he knew the ground was also well recorded. Occasionally, he would leave the sanctuary of the gully and cut a corner overland. Why he did this is a mystery. Perhaps he was trying to cover more ground in less time. Perhaps the wind had changed, blowing his scent forwards. Or perhaps some other unidentified player in the scene had barked an alarm.

Out of the riverbed, following his trail was painfully slow on the very hard ground and through the dense, dry vegetation, but taking a compass bearing on his axis of movement proved a useful guide to relocating his tracks several hundred metres further down the riverbed where he had re-entered it. It was absorbing tracking.

That young leopard was living a life in huge contrast to that of the dominant male, who was old, large and wise. We nicknamed that larger leopard Houdini for his ability to avoid cage traps and trail cameras. He walked self-confidently down the stream beds, but also along the side of the reserve roads, more akin to the behaviour of a lion. When we eventually managed to film him with night-vision camera equipment, he walked boldly up to the edge of a waterhole, his head drooped slightly with age and sporting a well-developed dewlap. Despite a gathering of lions on the opposing side, Houdini appeared totally unphased. He looked the lions in the eye with attitude, as if to say, 'I am going to drink, what of it?' and proceeded to sup his fill. Then, just as calmly, he walked away again. From his body movement, had we not had the luxury of night-vision gear but only moonlight, I would have assumed he was a lion from his self-assured swagger.

Piecing together the nocturnal wanderings of those leopards was a unique experience, one which provided me with a glimpse of their dangerous lives. This also reinforced for me several fundamental principles of stalking.

1. **Know the ground**
    Knowing where dead ground is to be found, where the game trails lead, where a stream can or cannot be crossed, all provide the opportunity to move ahead of a subject and lie in wait or to change an angle of approach to better match the wind conditions.

2. **Read the ground and create a plan**
    Although rarely captured on film, tracking leopards clearly revealed that they read the ground, stalking with a clear method and plan of purpose.

3. **Use dead ground**
    I try constantly to be guided by how much leopards favour dead ground. Every leopard I have ever tracked prefers to patrol using dead ground. In dead ground, you cannot be seen, but equally it is difficult to see out. This has the effect of encouraging human stalkers to mistakenly choose to walk in more open conditions, where the visibility seems better.

4. **Cling to the shadows**
    Wherever possible, avoid places of bright illumination where movement is obvious and differences in colour tone with the surrounding landscape are more obvious. This is a

critical lesson in stalking – using shadows to conceal colour, form and movement.

5. **Choose easy paths**

   Leopards generally make extensive use of game trails and trackways. This does not mean that they are incapable of moving quietly through vegetation, where they can be just as stealthy. But why take a difficult route when there is an easy one? Game trails are softer and mostly clear of vegetation, enabling them to move silently to close the distance and surprise their prey.

Leopards are, of course, renowned for their ability to climb trees, often hoisting their victims up into the branches out of the reach of other predators and scavengers. I believe tree climbing is also important and have been climbing trees since my childhood. Walking across a fallen tree as a natural bridge has proven incredibly useful and is an everyday reality when hiking in many jungle regions. This is something which needs good balance and plenty of practice. I was lucky my judo instructor encouraged me to look for narrow features to walk along from an early age. Later, I'd wear a heavy rucksack when practising. A good way to start is to walk along fallen trees that you find in woodland. With experience, your self-confidence will follow along.

Whether leopard or human, the process of stalking can be broken down into several distinct natural stages. There is no need to learn these, but they will serve to explain the overall process on paper. Always remember that stalking is very straightforward: our aim is to approach our subject closely enough to make detailed observations without being detected. To achieve this, we must not let our movements, scent or sounds move ahead of the range of our vision.

The arrival

Arrival is all about tuning and blending into the landscape. For this, I like to walk a short distance into the area I intend to search. Find a quiet spot away from the tracks to make a brew. At first, I will not notice that I have caused a disturbance to the wildlife, as my mind is still filled with the logistics of getting there. After a few minutes, normally when my water begins to boil, birds who had fled return and peer down at me with suspicion. I will make my beverage, and while it cools a little I simply relax. By now those birds have decided I am not a threat and are back to their usual business, flying low over me. After a leisurely drink, I pack my kit and set off. By now I am part of the scene, but most importantly my senses have tuned into the mood of the location, and I have slowed down, ready to receive stimulus to my senses.

The patrol

I follow a game trail if possible, and I walk alertly in a calm manner, slowly allowing my senses to reach well ahead of any disturbance that I am causing locally. I will stop often to watch and to listen. I pay attention to everything. Even if I am looking for a roe buck, for example, I allow insects, birds, mice, squirrels, and really anything and everything to attract my attention. In nature, all things within the web of life are connected. I want my subconscious mind to have access to the fullest range of stimuli. I very much enjoy this phase; it is critical to my success.

The discovery

I proceed reading the ground, walking as much into the wind as possible, taking advantage of the dead ground, searching for hot spots and detouring around black spots. Eventually, I will discover my subject – perhaps the shoulders of a roe buck just visible over the long grass behind some tall, flowering hogweed. If its head is down grazing, I will subside into the long grass, step into a nearby shadow or place my body alongside a tree trunk to become an extension of it.

I watch to see whether there are any signs that I have been detected. If there are, I will approach no closer, instead backing away discreetly to look for a new direction from which to approach. It is important to remain relaxed and casual in your movement in this situation. Moving from a relaxed and casual but attentive state to a stealthy one may trigger the flight of your prey. Animals are incredibly alert to posture and body language – if you look like a threat, you will be a threat. I once watched a young leopard that was stalking a ground squirrel manage his body language. He had approached from the nearby woodland but now had fifty metres of clear ground to cover. Instead of a full-on stalking approach, the leopard ambled very slowly forwards, straight towards the ground squirrel. Every now and then the ground squirrel would sit upright and scrutinise the leopard, who would sit up straight, projecting the most innocent look imaginable. I swear that if that leopard could have whistled a casual tune, he would have done so. Watching only from the corner of his eye, as soon as the ground squirrel's head went down again, he would regain his focus, his blue eyes locked onto his prey as he moved forwards. So, this little entertaining but deadly game played out. On this occasion, the ground squirrel eventually recognised the ploy, bolting into the safety of a burrow.

Planning the stalk

Once I am happy that there is no sign of disturbance, I plan my stalk. I am looking for features in the landscape, trees, rocks, termite mounds, ant hills, anything that I can make for that will provide some cover and break the overall distance to my subject into manageable stages. I also establish where I am ultimately heading; in fact, planning backwards from the preferred end point is often the best way to formulate this plan.

Closing the gap

Ideally, I will find dead ground to shield my movement from view as I move between the features I have chosen. Depending on the nature of the terrain, I may need to crouch or crawl for part or even all of the approach. If I am out of sight, I need not watch my subject at this phase; instead, I will focus on the feature I am making for. If I am only partially concealed, I will not take my eyes off my subject whilst moving. Looking down to check the ground for obstructions whilst moving forwards will guarantee I will be spotted, with the very great probability that when I stop and look up the subject will simply have vanished, having fled whilst I was looking down. I must remain constantly mindful to the possibility of being heard or of the wind changing direction. In the latter case, I may need to retrace my steps and try again from a new direction, like the saltwater crocodile – softly, softly ...

As I reach each feature in turn, I carefully observe the subject, not allowing my face to be seen, sometimes using a piece of bark or a dead branch as a temporary mask.

Final stalk

The final stalk is usually the most difficult, and here we must remember that we only succeed if the subject remains unaware of us. If I am in any doubt, I will stay where I am and observe from there. Moving forwards, we must now keep our eyes on the subject; if it spots us, it may fix us with a suspicious gaze. The only solution to this is to freeze. Caught in a creature's unexpected gaze, I have many times had to remain balanced on one leg like a broken Roman statue for fifteen minutes or more.

Observation

Observing is the real purpose, and now that the opportunity presents itself, drink in the experience – you have earned it. No wildlife documentary comes close to the thrill of personal field observations. These are memories that are never forgotten.

Withdrawal

In many cases, the subject will simply leave before you do, which is ideal, but otherwise you must be able to exit undetected. Remember that it is far more difficult to crawl backwards whilst watching a subject in front of you.

Stalking Techniques

Walking techniques

For over a million years, we humans have been performing a miracle with every step we take, the miracle of walking upright. This unique ability tells us a great deal about our earliest ancestors. Standing upright enabled them to see well ahead in the landscape, allowing them to detect the presence of threats and potential prey with their excellent human vision. Walking upright is also an incredibly efficient, agile form of locomotion, well adapted to long-distance endurance travel; in short, we evolved to be mobile. Walking is good for us.

Once we establish a good walking rhythm, our gait is relatively fast – sufficiently fast when walking through open woodland to surprise game species. One of the ancient hunting strategies I have witnessed employed by the Hadza in Tanzania is to spread out widely spaced, line abreast and with the assistance of hunting dogs, and to walk swiftly through savannah woodland as a human dragnet. Game species taking flight, panicked by the surprise appearance of a hunter or his dog, run in error into the arrow range of another yet undetected member of the hunting party. When you are out for a country ramble, you might well have unwittingly roused a deer from cover in a similar way. When we wish to observe wildlife more closely, we must avoid such disturbances, adjusting our walking technique so that we are able to see the subject well before it sees us.

ALERT WALKING

Walking alertly is less efficient than normal walking and not suitable for swiftly travelling long distances. It is a mode of walking that is adopted when we wish to investigate a landscape. It is a slower, less visible, quieter way of moving. Begin by stopping and deciding to walk more alertly. As you will discover, changing the way you move will change the alertness of your mental state as well – quite literally, we are switching into stealth mode.

This way of walking has a profound calming effect on the mind – we become more passively receptive to the sights, sounds and scents around us, more attuned to the environment. This change in our mental alertness is a powerful tool. To walk in this way we take slower, shorter steps. This will allow us to pay more attention to the environment around us and to the nearby obstructions. Branches and twigs that we would normally barge past when walking normally, we will now delicately avoid. When I am walking in this way, the distance between the toe of my rear foot and the heel of my front foot reduces to between ten to fifteen centimetres, and my front foot lands nearly in line with my rear foot. My feet still meet the ground with the heel, predominantly the outside of the heel rolling inwards and forwards with each step. This change in speed has a dramatic effect on posture, causing a more upright shift in stance, which in turn raises our eyes from the ground, increasing our field of view further and wider, and subsequently improving the use of our peripheral vision. This, as we have learned, increases our ability to detect movement.

When you first practise this method of moving, you may find that your body becomes rigid, unbalanced and zombie-like. Try instead to be very relaxed, flex your knees to allow your centre of gravity to drop slightly and allow your arms to hang freely from your shoulders. This way of moving should feel light, nimble, well balanced and responsive. Avoid overthinking the process. Look out into the world and focus on finding wildlife – it will all gradually fall into place. Once you get the hang of it, you will be surprised how often you come across the more common mammals without their being aware of your presence. Even when they do spot you, it is normally at enough distance that you are within their sight zone (more on which later), and they do not feel so threatened as to cause their immediate alarm or flight. This way of walking has enabled me to feel a true kinship with the wildlife I share my lifetime with. It is the first step on the path of stalking, and I would argue the most important and rewarding.

STALKING STEP

If we wish to walk up on an animal more closely, we shall need to employ a stalking step. This is a tiring method of moving. Even stalking leopards will occasionally pause for a momentary rest during long stalks. And just as with the alert walk, shifting into stalking mode has a psychological effect, sharpening our senses even further.

Now we shall maintain our weight on our rear foot whilst placing our front foot ever so carefully immediately in front of it. As I place my foot, I lift my toes and contact the ground with the outer portion of the ball of my foot, rolling it carefully inwards followed by the heel and toe. Throughout, I feel the ground for obstacles with my foot, without ever taking my eyes from my subject. Only once the foot is properly placed do I shift my body weight over it, which releases my rear foot to be moved forwards. In this way, it is possible to move very slowly, freeze if necessary and make virtually no visible movement. The upper body should remain relaxed but with as little movement as possible. Use this method to stalk from one piece of cover to another. Watch a cat stalking to see this method of foot placement in action. Balance is again the secret, this method requiring slightly more knee flex. It is also possible to move swiftly using this method if the opportunity arises; for example, if your subject drops its head to graze and you need to swiftly cross a small distance of open ground. If I am able, I will glance down to the ground occasionally, without moving my head, and memorise a clear path forwards for the next few paces.

. . .

Employing these walking techniques takes us on a journey into our distant past when our very survival depended upon our skills as predators. Today, using them can transform our appreciation and understanding of nature. When I gaze upon the astonishing French Palaeolithic cave paintings found in the Grotte Chauvet or at Lascaux, I know that these detailed depictions of the fauna could only have been made with the close observation that results from stalking prowess.

Crawling techniques

Alert walking and stalking are the most versatile of the ways in which we may need to move, and they are particularly well suited to movement among trees where our upright silhouette blends in. In more open country, we will need to lower our body profile. People do this quite naturally, willingly stooping into a crouch when necessary. But when is this necessary? Some animals will take flight if they read the body language of a crouching approach, while they might pay little regard to a walker. This is often the case where wildlife has regular contact with people walking. The purpose of lowering our profile, therefore, is to remain concealed from view behind some natural cover or dead ground.

BEAR STALK OR MONKEY RUN

The largest land predator on Earth is the polar bear (*Ursus maritimus*). While they regard humans as dangerous, they nonetheless see us as potential prey as well. When they have the opportunity or need, they can, and sometimes do, hunt people. Despite their size – a male polar bear can weigh 500 kilograms or more and stand upright to a height of three metres – they are adroit stalkers. I once watched alertly as a polar bear disappeared behind an iceberg 500 metres away, only to suddenly reappear again at 100 metres – time to start the snowmobile engines and put some distance between us and the bear. Later, I was able to return to the location and follow its tracks. I found that the bear had slipped into a hidden fold in the ice flow behind the iceberg that led towards my former position at an oblique angle. Using the dead ground of this gully, it had crawled carefully towards me, occasionally taking advantage of patches of virtually frictionless glare ice to slide on its belly. Crawling is fatiguing, every advantage of circumstance should be employed. By these means that bear had crawled for hundreds of metres, completely unseen, attempting to close the distance on me. Watching a polar bear stalking a seal, we receive a masterclass in this method of crawling.

This is the most comfortable crawl on all fours. Crawling on our hands and knees, we place our hands carefully, feeling for noisy objects such as dead sticks or for sharp items such as thorns. Then as we move forwards, alternately moving our opposing arms and legs, we place our knees where our hands have already been. (The British army uses a similar technique for rapid movement behind cover called the monkey run.) Just as the bear teaches us, this is an effective low-profile method of slowly stalking close, particularly after dusk.

LEOPARD CRAWL

A leopard is the absolute master of concealing itself in the shallowest of depressions. To achieve this, it lowers itself onto its elbows, which are tucked beneath its body, and quietly and quite swiftly crawls forwards. We can emulate this, but it isn't easy. To do so, we can simply bear stalk with a more lowered body, or we can crawl on our forearms and elbows rather than our hands, thus dropping our shoulder height. It is difficult without consistent training to maintain this crawl for long distances. So, it is only used for short-distance approach through vegetation or in low light. The advantage of this difficult crawl is that it is quiet and permits us to thread our way through tangled vegetation.

CROCODILE CRAWL

A more comfortable very-low-profile crawl is the crocodile crawl. Here we flatten our body to the ground and crawl forwards using our feet and hands alternately. We can do this either by slightly raising our body from the ground as we move forwards or when the ground is smooth enough by sliding our torso. This is a difficult crawl to employ in dense vegetation but excellent for moving through the shallowest defile or dead ground in more open country. (The British army call this the leopard crawl.)

KITTEN CRAWL

The kitten crawl is the stealthiest of all crawls but only usually used for the very final approach. Here we flatten our whole body to the ground, including our chin, so that we are as flat and low as is humanly possible. Then with our hands at our shoulders and our feet together we inch our way forwards a few centimetres at a time. This crawl produces the least visible movement of all the crawls and is excellent for easing into a very close place of observation. (The British army teach this crawl using the same name.)

ROLL

Sometimes the easiest way to move in dead ground is to roll over. This is particularly the case when traversing a slope. Rolling is easy,

Above: This lion demonstrates his adaptation for predation: when stalking, his nose will rise, providing excellent scenting ability, and his eyes will scan for prey, particularly in darkness – the light fur beneath his eye sockets helps to improve his already superb night vision. The lion's head shape is also significant: the flat top barely rises above the vegetation when hunting, and the tufty fur blends with long grass and serves to soften his outline.

Below: If you want to find a predator, watch the prey. Search for prey species lining up looking in one direction, like these impala ewes watching an African wild dog.

Above: Bat-eared foxes are insectivorous, mostly consuming termites. Their characteristic ears are important for their thermo regulation. But they also have astonishing hearing, which they use to locate subterranean food sources such as dung-beetle larvae in dung balls buried several inches underground.

Below: Dik-dik are fascinating. Tiny antelope, well adapted to arid conditions, their large snouts enable them to cool their breath in extreme conditions, while their upper lips are prehensile, allowing them to pick vegetation from between thorns. Long eyelashes provide touch warning of thorns to protect their eyes, which are all-important for detecting predators. The dark patches in front of their eyes are preorbital scent glands for territorial scent marking.

Right: Without good peripheral vision, it would have been impossible to react fast enough to capture an image such as this: two lanner falcons pouncing on a dove.

Below: Filming a wildlife documentary for ITV on Kangaroo Island, South Australia, with wildlife cameraman Martin Hayward-Smith, using the advantage of high ground to observe wildlife undetected. Here we are observing a seal colony, but I know that Martin will also be alert to the possibility of sighting sharks, a passing pod of whales or a peregrine falcon.

Right: Mounting a binocular on a tripod is the gold standard for binocular stabilisation. Used in this way, the performance of the binocular is greatly enhanced. The binocular's wide field of vision makes such an arrangement the ideal method to scan a landscape for wildlife. I often carry an ultralight tripod for this purpose. Here I am using my camera tripod to scan a distant *kopje* for leopards as the sun sets.

Above: The puff adder relies upon its astonishing cryptic camouflage for both predation and self-defence. While not regarded as the most venomous African snake, it is responsible for the most human envenomation because it is often not seen and accidentally encountered.

Below: The lion's camouflage is hardly ever commented on, but it must not be underestimated. At night, a lion's dusky pelage appears to be translucent, while in daylight lions sitting or lying down can vanish from sight in even the wispiest grass cover. It is all too easy to walk into a pride of resting lions.

Above: A huge saltwater crocodile trying to make off with a dead feral pig in its mouth. Finding me in its path, it tried to submerge with the pig, demonstrating its immense strength. It then announced its anger by hissing at me, a chilling threat. Looking at this photo, I realise that it could easily have upset my boat if it had wished.

Below: High in the Flinders Mountains, Australia, a simple swag base camp. This provides a pretty typical example of my gear: bino, scope, day pack, field guide, loupe, etc., along with a Peli case for transporting the scope and other optics by helicopter. But the most important things are experience and know-how, which are invisible.

Above: Ju/'hoansi, San, bushmen demonstrate their exceptional stalking skills. Traditionally relying on short-range poisoned arrows, stalking was a fundamental life skill. Today, they maintain these skills as an enduring part of their cultural identity. Notice how they keep their heads up, eyes fixed on their quarry. Strictly single file, they are leaving the cover of the thorn scrub and moving forwards towards a tree twenty metres ahead, using it for cover as they move. In this way they will move from one point of cover to another, gradually closing the distance to their quarry.

Below: A thrilling and extremely rare encounter with a resting leopard. Mostly leopards detect humans first and vanish from sight, relying on their amazing camouflage for invisibility.

Above: The mischievous antics of confident young predators like this lion cub are always wonderful to watch, but it is wise to maintain a good distance. Young animals are apt to approach people out of curiosity, unwittingly raising the threat of a negative encounter with their parents.

Below: When attacked by a predator, a ground pangolin curls into a ball and relies on its armour of scales for protection. It is a unique defence that has protected these otherwise gentle animals for millennia. Sadly, it provides no protection at all from poachers who sell them for their meat and their scales, which are used in Chinese medicine. A tragedy in the making, pangolin species are freefalling to extinction.

Right: Lined up in the horns of a black rhino, the message is clear. I have a passion for rhinoceros. They are actually gentle, charismatic animals, and I never tire of watching them.

Below: Three white rhinoceros create an all-round defensive position to protect two young calves hidden from view. While their thick hides, horns, temperament and tactics protect them from their natural predators, they fall easy victims to the firearms of poachers.

Below: A sight I dread seeing, the remains of a rhino slaughtered by poachers for its horn, a victim of human greed, stupidity and callousness. When I saw this, I wondered what future is there for the species that is responsible for such wanton destruction? Unless we find a solution, we will bear witness to the extinction of these and so many other wonderful creatures.

efficient and quiet. If carrying a camera or daypack, cradle it to your chest, so that you can protect it from damage.

· · ·

With all the crawling techniques, it is vital to ensure that the backside does not rise above the shoulders or that an untidy foot waggles upwards either. Such simple errors will certainly spoil the stalk. Crawling is also energetic and something which should be practised. It is not surprising that there is a reluctance to crawl when observing wildlife, but for those who are willing, the rewards are waiting.

Stealthy movement requires good technique, practice and agility. Youngsters will manage just fine; for those of us a little further down life's path, natural discretion will determine the extent of our capability, and we may have to find alternatives. Generally, I find that there is an unwillingness today to do more than just walk up to wildlife on easy ground. This is a real shame, as it greatly limits both the observations that can be made and the feeling of immersion within nature.

As a tracker, I have no choice but to follow where my subject leads me. Consequently, I am always willing to traverse rough country, crawl, climb and, if necessary, wade through bogs and swim rivers to improve my point of observation. This willingness to go the extra mile has massively rewarded me in terms of the natural wonders that I have been able to witness. If you are willing to accept a little discomfort, there is a world of unforgettable experiences waiting to be accessed.

One cold February day, I went out to watch goldcrests (*Regulus regulus*) in the woods. Weighing about six grams, it is the smallest of our native birds. I first became a fan of the goldcrest when I found one hovering in front of the wing mirror of my Land Rover. It looked as though it was vainly admiring itself. Moving closer for a better view, I discovered that it was stealing insects caught in a spider's web stretched between the mirror and the door frame.

Winter is a good time to watch them, as they are more visible once the leaves have fallen and the domestic population is bolstered by goldcrests migrating from Scandinavia. It was once thought that these tiny birds were too small for such a journey; with their arrival coinciding with that of woodcock (*Scolopax rusticola*), also visiting from Scandinavia, the belief arose that goldcrests rode on the backs of woodcocks, and they were given the name woodcock pilots – a great idea, perhaps, but sadly not true. A similar false claim used to be made of humming birds riding on the backs of geese to migrate. There is an insect that catches a ride on the back of a bee, but that is another story.

I headed out into an old hornbeam coppice, and finding a spot just inside the wood where there is a badger's set with many elder trees and some hazel all with low branches, I sat quietly with my back against a tree and waited patiently. Sometimes, when I go out like this, I see nothing; at other times it is amazing. This cold morning was the latter. After a few minutes, I was graced with a flock of long-tailed tits babbling around me – only close-up does the delicate pink in their plumage really show. Then, eventually, I was rewarded with a solitary goldcrest. Normally, they resemble a cross between a warbler and a blue tit, but not today. It was bitterly cold, and that little goldcrest had puffed up all its plumage for warmth to the point that as it dangled on the tip of a hazel branch, causing the branch to droop and bounce under its body weight, it resembled a tiny, furry, Christmas bauble. Satisfied and in need of movement to restore warm circulation to my extremities, I headed deeper into the woods. I hadn't gone far, maybe twenty metres, when, glassing with my bino, I spotted a fox asleep at the base of a tall hornbeam 100 metres ahead of me.

February is the height of the fox-mating season, and it is not uncommon to find exhausted foxes, mostly dog foxes, sleeping off the night's activities like teenage revellers after a hard night on the town. The fox was curled up snug, nestled between the buttresses of the tree, with his nose tucked under his tail. I wondered how close I might be able to stalk up to him. Foxes possess the full package of senses: good eyesight, a very keen sense of smell and extraordinary hearing. They are also highly alert and very intelligent, and this was no town fox used to handouts and bin raiding. This was a country fox who lived totally by his wits under the permanent sentence of death from every gamekeeper in the country. With good reason, I might add – foxes wreak havoc with livestock, poultry and game birds. All my gamekeeper friends, though, have confided in me their admiration for these worthy canine adversaries.

Carefully, I laid my daypack on the ground and began my approach. I broke the stalk down by first moving to an old boundary mound in the wood. For this, there was plenty of cover and relatively clear ground. By avoiding any fallen branches, I was able to quickly reach the spot. The fox never stirred, so I continued to a large standard oak tree via a silent well-trodden deer rack. (Rack is the old hunting and tracking term for a deer trail; many of these ancient words are still in use in Britain today.) Then, moving very slowly, I closed the gap to fifteen metres, where there was a straggly, dead hornbeam, long shaded out by the oak's canopy. Here I waited, watching carefully. Now I could see the fox was stunning, his coat a beautiful red. He was in the peak of health and only half asleep; his ears were still mobile, responding every now and then to the natural sounds of the woodland.

Between me and the fox, there was no cover, no deer racks, just a mustard-yellow layer of fallen hornbeam leaves. Fortunately, the leaves were wet and would not rustle. With no detectable wind and being slightly up hill of the fox (it was late morning and the weak winter sun was doing its best to raise thermal drafts), I decided to see how close I could get. I pulled my scarf up over my face, then, just as I was about to make my move, he raised his head and took a look around, as though his internal alarm had registered my presence. I of course froze. After a moment, he seemed satisfied – he shuffled and tucked his nose back under his tail.

I began now to stalk very carefully towards him. The only way to move quietly was to walk like a leopard. Every time I placed my foot, I lifted my toe and felt for any tell-tale snappy twigs in the leaf litter, oh so carefully compressing the leaves beneath my foot before transferring my weight to it. There was absolutely no cover between me and the fox; it was a crazy competition between his senses and my ability to move silently. I made it five metres closer. I couldn't believe it. To relax and catch my breath, I paused. Suddenly, the fox's eyes opened. He was looking straight at me, but I was a crocodile. After a long, penetrating gaze, he decided to go back to dreams of his vixen. I again moved closer, even more carefully. It was exhausting. My whole body was as taught as a bow string – another three metres, then four, then five. 'This is insane,' I thought. The fox's ears swivelled, and he opened his eyes again, but I was squinting. This close, my eyes would be a dead giveaway. Animals are hypersensitive to the image of a predator's eyes, so much so that some have markings resembling eyes to deter predators; for example, the peacock butterfly, which can also hiss to support its deception.

Squinting worked. The fox looked at me for a long while, trying to remember if I had been there earlier, then decided I was OK. Glancing carefully to the left and right, something clearly felt awry but back to his dreams he went. If I had not been wearing camouflage clothing, I am certain that he would have recognised me then, if not earlier.

I began to crouch, praying my old knees would not creek or my clothes rustle. Expecting him to bolt any instant, in a crouch I made it closer until my face was just two metres from the fox. Still he lay there unaware. Now I know I should have backed off again, but in truth it would have been impossible to retreat as quietly as I had arrived. So, breaking all my own rules, I gently said, 'Hello.' Instantly, the fox was alert, the shock of my proximity dawned on him, and for the briefest moment we made eye contact. The look of surprise he wore at that moment was unforgettable, and in a trice he was gone, darting right and swiftly into a thick tangle of mature brambles, where he knew that I could not follow. I am sure that fox took more care in his choice of resting place from that day forward. For me, it was an unforgettable experience that provided a tangible connection to the life of a wild animal that would have otherwise seemed distant and otherworldly.

ONLY A JOURNEY

Wilderness is a necessity ... there must be places for human beings to satisfy their souls.

John Muir

It is in remote wilderness that I really come alive. In fact, the more remote it is, the more I like it. I want to immerse myself completely. I am impatient dipping my toe into wild country while clinging to the hem of civilisation's skirt. My enthusiasm can be off-putting to those who do not share my passion.

Perhaps because of these factors, I found myself staring at the accommodation of a luxury eco lodge in Costa Rica. Along with the film crew, I was there to make a documentary about jungle survival, and we were on the fringe of a beautiful area of rainforest in the Corcovado National Park. However, no one had told me that we would be accommodated in this lodge. In fact, I had been led to believe that we would be camping in the rainforest. Consequently, I had only brought my rucksack, packed for rainforest hiking. Heading to the dining area for dinner, wearing my best jungle greens, I felt like the guest who turns up to a suave soirée dressed for a fancy dress.

After the meal, the team and I retired to the outdoor bar, a little whitewashed, thatched cabana with a string of dim lightbulbs providing jungle mood lighting. This could not have been further from what I had been anticipating. As I stood there coming to terms with the realisation that I would be the party clown for the whole trip, two American tourists came to the bar in pressed white tropical attire and, with heavy New York accents, asked me where I had left my M16 rifle. It was the final straw. Realising that I wasn't in keeping with their holiday expectations, I headed back to the accommodation building, picked up my pack and headed out into the jungle alone.

Without the luxury of daylight, I scanned the dark forest with the puny beam of a small head torch. It is never wise to walk in rainforest after dark, for that is when snakes are most active. Central America has an abundance of pit vipers, such as the dangerous fer-de-lance (*Bothrops asper*), which certainly have the advantage at night. Behind their nostrils and in front of their eyes, they are equipped with depressions called loreal pits. These are openings to sensitive heat-sensing organs that enable them to detect infrared. Equipped with these organs, they can track their prey and strike with flawless accuracy in total darkness.

I walked slowly, taking double care not to unwittingly step on a snake. Over the years, I have had numerous close encounters with fer-de-lances, all of which have taught me to be wary in their presence. My herpetologist friends would frown if I described any snake as aggressive, so I shall compromise by saying that in my experience the fer-de-lance is a snake with a hair-trigger personality.

Looking for a good campsite in rainforest is also best done in daylight when it is easy to see hazards such as ant nests, wasp nests and 'widow-makers', the dead branches that get hung up in the canopy and which can drop unexpectedly with deadly force. When I eventually found a promising place, I went into autopilot, stretching my tarp, suspending my hammock with mosquito net and lighting a small fire to one side. I set my small billycan over the flames on a sharp stick pushed into the ground at an angle, and while the water came to the boil, I finished my preparations for the night. Now that I had come away from the frippery of the pseudo-rainforest camp, I was happy and relaxed. Besides, I would not now have to suffer the snoring of my colleagues in the stifling dormitory block. Even a chilled gin and tonic could not lure me back. I love camping in jungle.

After a comforting brew, I retired, relaxing into the cooling cradle of my hammock. I was tired. It had been a long day, and despite the strange sounds of the jungle night, I immediately slipped into a light sleep, with my head torch, which I normally suspend from a cord overhead, still around my neck. I did not know how long I had been dozing when the sound of footsteps in the leaf litter brought me to alertness. I was listening in my half sleep, all sounds entrusted to my subconscious for processing. Eventually, my inner voice roused me: 'Wake up, wake up. Take a look. This is unusual.'

Stirring, I realised that the footsteps were coming straight towards me. I dozily reached for my head torch and slipped it onto my head. Then, lifting the hem of my mosquito net, I leaned over to peer out. I switched on the light just as the creature stepped on the end of one of the sticks of firewood, causing it to flick up a small cascade of sparks from the ash-covered embers. I could not believe my eyes. There passing at an angle right beneath the far end of my hammock was a slender marten-like cat, about twice the size of a domestic cat. The last thing I saw was its strong puma-like tail before it vanished, along with its owner, darting away spooked by the sudden illumination from my torch.

I felt blessed. It was one of the most invisible of all rainforest creatures, a jaguarundi (*Herpailurus yagouaroundi*), the chimerical hunter of jungle shadows, found but rarely seen throughout Central and South America. Secure in the knowledge that my decision to decamp to the jungle had been rewarded, I drifted back to sleep and dreamed vivid dreams of stalking like a cat in the rainforest.

If you want to see rainforest wildlife, Costa Rica is without a doubt one of the best countries in which to do so. Generally, though, observing wildlife in rainforest is difficult, with the majority of jungle life found in the canopy and the unbroken shrouding of dense vegetation, where it is concealed from view. This is particularly so when hiking through remote rainforest, where the constant evergreen twilight makes you feel forgotten and remote from the world. On journeys such as these, even the most fleeting sightings take on greater meaning – perhaps the tantalising glimpse overhead through a gap in the canopy of a pair of scarlet macaws flying on morning patrol, or the beautiful streaming tail tips of a swallow-tailed kite seen from a dugout canoe while travelling up river with forest Indians.

These memories are hard won and live for ever in one's heart. Hiking up slippery limestone ridges, I once followed the tracks of a female jaguar and her cub for two days. As far I could discern from the age of the tracks, she was always ahead of me, maintaining just enough distance to remain discreetly out of sight. At one point, I could see where she had detoured, carefully leading her cub past a jumping viper (*Atropoides nummifer*) coiled in the middle of the track. This venomous snake relies on its camouflage for concealment and will often feign death if approached. But beware: it is renowned for its high-powered strike, which can lift its whole body off the ground, creating the impression that it is leaping. It is said that the bite of this snake poses little threat to a healthy adult human, but when you are remote from civilisation, risk is measured on a different, more cautious scale. I followed the jaguar's example, passing by and maintaining a safe distance.

That the jaguar was ahead of me for two days suggests that she was as curious of me as I was of her. I have often wondered if she stalked close to my camp in the night for a closer look. When at last her tracks angled off to the right of the knife-like ridge we were walking, taking with her all chance of a sighting, I felt the vacuum of sadness that comes when a trusted trail companion departs.

It is the fundamental truth of fishing: a hook doesn't catch a fish unless it is in the water. Nature walks and countryside rambles are good, but if we want to improve our chances of significant wildlife encounters, we must plunge ourselves into the environment for longer, embarking on multi-day wilderness adventures. More than just providing more opportunities to see wildlife, the whole experience of being on trail will heighten our sensory awareness and sharpen our intuitive response to nature.

All modes of wilderness travel can provide the necessary immersion: long 4x4 expeditions, horseback treks, or voyages in small boats and yachts. But without any doubt it is when we ourselves are providing the motive power that the deepest rewards are achieved, travelling on foot, by canoe, by kayak, on skis or by bicycle.

My favourite way to travel in nature is by open canoe. The whole experience of floating offers a deeper connection to nature. Simply to make progress, the canoeist must use their paddle skill and feeling for the elements to balance the demands of the water current with the demands of the wind. A canoe provides the most unique and tranquil access to otherwise inaccessible locations. When the skill has been learned, a canoe can be paddled slowly and silently. As such, canoes are not perceived as a threat by wildlife, their presence raising no more concern than a drifting log. Even when not searching for wildlife, in a canoe wildlife comes to me: crane flies and dragon flies hitch a ride on the gunwale; in foggy weather, loons surface beside me out of curiosity; and sometimes otters, wolves and even lynx stand on the shore and watch with fascination as I pass by. It is in a canoe I have had some of my most amazing wildlife encounters, floating alongside a grizzly-bear mother swimming across an inlet with her cub on her back, drifting up to within four feet of a bald eagle feeding a fledgling on a lakeshore and one morning paddling for hours with a playful porpoise.

By canoe I have been able to explore remote corners of the mighty boreal forest, journeys which have taught me the value and profound nature of large contiguous wilderness. There is a palpable energy in such places; the very ecosystem itself seems sentient. To survive, all life must live by the rules that the forest dispassionately enforces.

When storm clouds gather and the air around me scintillates with electricity, I instinctively know that I am doomed in a canoe if I remain out on the open water. Instead, I paddle swiftly to the safety of the shore and pitch my tarp in the forest to wait out the lightning storm. Sitting there under a postage stamp of nylon sheeting in the gloom of the deluge, I am bodily rocked by the booms and cracks of thunder, momentarily illuminated by the coruscations. Yet I feel no fear, simply awe at the puissant magnitude of nature. Sitting with my back against a canoe pack, with a mug of hot cocoa in my hand, I stare out under the eaves of the low-pitched tarp, now cascading with rain and feel purified, charged with the greatest joy that comes from the certain knowledge that I am alive and able to witness such a marvel.

Travel a thousand miles by train and you are a brute;
pedal five hundred on a bicycle and you remain basically a
bourgeois; paddle a hundred in a canoe and you are already
a child of nature.

Pierre Elliott Trudeau,
'Exhaustion and Fulfilment: The Ascetic in a Canoe'

Being close to water is good for the soul, and canoeing is a poetic, inspiring way to travel, but it is a special skill that takes time to master. If you are able, I urge you to give it a try.

Even if you are not able to go canoeing, nature can still be experienced to the full, particularly when we travel on foot. Walking is our most ancient way of traversing wilderness, which alone gives it special status. As our feet eat up the miles, walking hardens our bodies and strengthens our minds. When it is safe to do so, we can walk in a meditative state, unconscious of the distance we are clocking up. Looking back from a high vantage point over the terrain already covered is uniquely satisfying and immediately rewards any hardships experienced along the way. Looking forwards from that same prospect, our tired legs gain renewed strength from the miles already walked, and the horizon beckons with a palpable attraction and anticipation of the new experiences ahead. Recalling some of my most memorable walks, I realise that walking the land brings a knowledge of the terrain that is unrivalled by any other means of travel. Letting my finger walk back along the route on a map, I remember places and wildlife encounters with astonishing clarity.

When I hike through wild country, I feel liberated, able to go wherever I desire without dependence upon the support of nearby civilisation. At these times, I feel as though I am stepping back in time, exposing myself to nature in a way that was once the daily reality of our distant hunter-gatherer ancestors. Over the course of many millennia, they explored our planet, walking in small self-reliant family groups, depending upon their sensory awareness, intuition, memory and creative intellect to solve the problems they faced along the way. Walking in their footsteps awakens within me the dormant, vestigial abilities that are a gift from our forebears, qualities once essential to survival that have been honed over the long history of our species.

It is widely believed that a distant precursor of our species lived by hunting and gathering somewhere around 1.8 million years ago, employing the most rudimentary of tools. Like a relay runner's baton, hunting and digging sticks passed through a succession of hominin hands, each species adding their own refinements to the methods and technology employed.

Our species, too, was part of this long chain. We only abandoned hunting and gathering for farming approximately 12,000 years ago, a process which is still in progress today, with a handful of communities continuing to live by hunting and gathering. In short, we evolved as hunter-gatherers, and we lived by that means alone for more than 99 per cent of our history. It should come as no surprise that we remain highly adapted for such a lifestyle. Indeed, there is plenty of evidence to support the assertion that many of the physical and psychological maladies we suffer today result from our rapid change to a farming lifestyle and diet. Tramping, hiking, bush walking, trail hiking, yomping, bashing – call it what you will: walking teaches us what it is to be human, sharpens our extrasensory perception and provides purification from the toxic effects of modern living.

As I am writing, I have beside me a trusty rucksack – I have a love-hate relationship with it. While I love the freedom that it provides me, when it is fully loaded and I first put it on my body groans at the load and my brain rebels. But having long ago traded our fur for the ability to cool ourselves, I have no choice but to carry warm clothing to protect myself from the cold and bad weather, food for nourishment, and water to drink. In those places where fires are prohibited, I must also encumber myself with a stove and fuel.

It always takes a few days to settle into a strong walking rhythm, at which point my body will have grown accustomed to the pack and that sense of liberation will take over. My aim is to achieve a state of consciousness whereby my mind empties of distractive thoughts and emotions, enabling me to find synchrony with the flow of nature and the encounters of the trail – a state of consciousness known in Zen Buddhism as *mushin*. Long experience of climbing hills with a pack on my back, though, has taught me that while sweating up a hill, my mind will not empty until it has ferreted out every superfluous item in my accoutrement and questioned my reasoning for its inclusion.

When we walk in the bush, we absolutely must travel lightly, carrying only essential items. Excess weight not only slows us down, it also acts to limit our aspirations and our desire to reach a distant peak. We should feel capable of reaching any goal supported by our equipment not fettered by it. Every item in my pack must earn its right to be there, and wherever possible it should have more than one function. I am often asked what luxury item I carry with me, and the answer is always the same – it is the thing that I left behind.

In many ways, this is an art of compromise that favours lightweight compactness. Today, there has never been a better time to find ultra-lightweight hiking equipment, although I offer a word of caution: real wilderness travel will place extraordinary demands on us and even harder demands on our equipment. I could have created a rucksack graveyard with the many packs I have used to destruction. Ultra-lightweight is good but not if it comes at the cost of strength and durability.

Seen in this way, many of the technological gadgets we so delight are totally without purpose on the trail. Unburdening ourselves of their distraction is a wise first step. I know from my experiences guiding that while many people find this a little unnerving at first, after only a few days they feel emancipated and more able to engage with nature. On the trail, the magic is found in our encounters with the landscape, the wildlife and the support of human company, experiences that also serve to realign our moral and spiritual values.

If you are new to trail hiking, stay close to home while you learn how. It will take time to work out your equipment needs and to become accustomed to carrying a pack. Try not to become too bogged down in the world of 'kit'. There are myriad people who do little more than talk about equipment and write endless online reviews. It is always better to walk rather than to talk.

Inevitably, our choice of equipment is very personal. We each have different physical needs, strengths and weaknesses. My own preferences reflect my long experience of trail walking. I offer here a list of my outfit for summer travel in a temperate climate in the hope that it will provide a useful starting point for you to develop your own outfit. (I have removed the specialist equipment I carry as a guide.)

Rucksack

I can accommodate seven days' food and my essential outfit in a rucksack of between fifty to sixty litres volume capacity. This size also makes a good daypack in winter when more bulky items of clothing need to be carried. I like several large external pockets to live from on the trail. I do not favour zip closures, as they tend to fail and wear out, my preference being clip closures. Larger rucksacks may be more comfortable when heavily loaded and suit longer hikes, but a large rucksack is like a hungry dog: it just keeps swallowing equipment. The smaller pack provides useful resistance to overenthusiastic packing.

If I am hiking for more than a week, my preference is for a pack with an external frame. In my experience, these support a heavy load better. I never use a waterproof rucksack cover – the only reliable way to ensure gear stays dry is to contain it within a drybag inside the pack. Anything that must be kept dry, such as my sleeping bag and warm clothing, is packed in a separate lightweight drybag inside the liner. Packed in this way, a rucksack also provides significant emergency buoyancy should I fall into water. This system must be tested frequently. To do this, I tie a tethering cord to my pack and cast it into a lake for half an hour. Any leaks are quickly revealed and can be addressed.

Once we start to look at the kind of equipment that we need to carry with us, it becomes apparent that we are embarking on a serious excursion. This is good, for walking in remote country is a serious business, one that requires a sober attitude. Travelling remotely from the normal back-up of civilisation is exciting, but it is also inherently more dangerous than travelling close to home. We need to manage this risk, a process that starts with our attitude. It is often said that 'we'll prepare for the worst and hope for the best'. To be safe in wild country needs a different mantra: hope has no place in our preparation. We shall instead throw our heart and soul into training, as we simply prepare for the worst.

Preparation requires more than just a pack loaded with appropriate equipment. Knowledge and training are essential to safe and rewarding hiking. The good news is that this sort of training is fun, highly enjoyable and adds no weight to the rucksack. In fact, it might even help to lighten the load.

Wilderness First Aid

Any first-aid training is preferable to none. But when we consider travelling in remote country, our first-aid skills must reflect our distance from normal emergency support and communication.

Multi-day Walking Load – Temperate – Summer – Lowland

Lid Outer Pocket
- Head Torch
- Spare Batteries
- First Aid Kit (small)
- Waterproof Notebook
- Pencil*
- Compass*
- Map in Map Case
- Binocular*

Lid Inner Pocket
- Sharpening Kit
- Fishing Kit (tiny handline rig)
- Nylon Cord (ten-mitre paracord)
- Mosquito Head Net
- Insect Repellent
- Sunscreen

Under Lid
- Waterproof Clothing

Left Outer Pocket
- Army Water Bottle (one litre)
- Army Mug (stainless steel)
- Lid for Mug
- Brew Kit
- Spoon
- Lightweight Stove
- Fuel

Right Outer Pocket
- Army Water Bottle (one litre)
- Billycan Set (twelve centimetre)
- Mini Little Bug Stove
- Lunch Ration

Mid Outer Pocket
- Tarp (tracker's tarp)
- Water Bag (ten litre)
- Water Filter
- Andy Handy (shower head, attached to drybag for hygiene)
- Belt knife*
- Whistle, Fireflash Ferrocerium Rod, Mini Compass, Microlite and Tweezers* (worn on cord around neck)

* = Items worn on body

Main Compartment

- Large Drybag Liner (with valve to reduce volume)
- Sleeping Bag (three season, in drybag)
- Therma Rest (three-quarter length + repair kit)
- Bivvi Bag
- Warm Clothing/Dry Clothing (in drybag)
- Wash Kit
- Cotton Bandannas (two)
- Rations
- Extra Maps (in waterproof Alok zip bag)
- InReach (satellite communication)
- Toilet Paper (in zip bag with gas lighter)

Alternative Shelter Options

- Hammock, Lightweight Tarp and Mosquito Net
- Lightweight One-person Tent (if travelling without bivvi bag)

My clothing is divided into the day or wet clothes on my back and my night or dry kit worn only at camp in the evening.

- The head torch should be of good quality. In recent years, many cheap plastic models have flooded the market, many of which break all too easily. I now prefer head torches with a metal body.

- The first-aid kit should reflect your experience and training as well as suiting specific environmental hazards.

- Waterproofs for remote country should be sturdy and totally reliable, my favourite being the Swazi Thar XP. I have used this garment in the worst weather in the remotest wilderness. It has never failed, and the tussock-green colour is perfect camouflage.

- The billycan must be equipped with a bail arm and reliable stainless-steel rivets so that it can be suspended over an open fire if necessary.

- The mini little bug stove can be used with a Trangia burner or fuelled with small twigs. Conveniently, it will collapse to nestle within my twelve-centimetre billycan.

- The tarp I carry is the Tracker's tarp of my own design, square and rigged to be incredibly versatile. It can be pitched in woodland in many ways and with the use of its pole pitched on open moorland or mountain.

- The dromedary ten-litre water bag is filled at the last opportunity before pitching camp, removing the need for repeated walks to the water source.

- The filter I carry can be screwed onto the water bag, which provides filtered water on tap. If viruses are a threat, the water will need the addition of a chemical disinfectant or boiling.

- In wild country, a sturdy knife is an essential tool of survival and rescue, as important as an ice axe in winter mountaineering. Folding knives are inherently weak. Where legislation permits, a knife should be carried at all times.

- Warm clothing is vitally important; nothing is more demoralising than constant cold. Even in the warmest weather, it can be surprisingly cold at night. I carry a warm fleece pullover and a lightweight down jacket that compresses very small. A neck warmer and warm hat are essential. If the weather is forecast to be cold, or I anticipate the need to sit quietly to observe wildlife, I carry a Finish *sissitakki* jacket.

- The wash kit should be kept very small.

- Cotton bandannas have many uses, from emergency bandages, slings and filtering water to keeping the sun off your neck. I always carry two, usually wearing a third. These are my preferred travel towels; they dry in no time and can be boil washed when necessary.

- The InReach is for emergency use and to maintain contact with base. It allows for limited two-way SMS and email communication, as well as an emergency signal. It relies upon the Iridium satellite network and is a brilliant wilderness communication device. Nearer to home, you might instead be able to rely on your normal mobile phone. Keep it turned off to preserve the battery for emergency use only and stow it in a reliable waterproof.

Training of this sort is by necessity more advanced than basic first aid; it is a serious undertaking that puts the risk of travelling in wilderness into proper context. This not only equips us with the skills to save a life but will also underpin a more conservative attitude to risk taking. This in turn can prevent a medical emergency, which is ultimately our overarching goal.

Do not be put off by the thought of this preparation. I have spent the larger part of my life travelling in the remotest and harshest conditions without incident. It is also worth considering that first-aid skills learned by wilderness travellers have seen most use saving the lives of loved ones at home.

Navigation

The compass is the key that unlocks the wilderness. Learning to use a map, compass and GPS is vital not only to our safety and enjoyment of a wilderness trip but also to the planning and safe execution of the journey. Learning to navigate is great fun, incredibly liberating and can provide inspiration for new areas to explore. Start by learning to read a map and to use a compass. GPS is a wonderful tool of navigation but depending upon batteries and functioning satellites, it is not a replacement for the trusty map and compass.

Survival or Bushcraft Training

In wild country, we need real-world, nuts-and-bolts training that will ensure that we can secure the fundamental components of life support for ourselves from shelter building to fire lighting. Start by learning the skills that relate to your home country and build on this foundation of knowledge as you encounter new environments. Properly conducted, such training can be life-changing, teaching you how to avoid becoming a victim, building your confidence, and providing a wonderful introduction to the flora and fauna of the environment. Most importantly, it should prepare you to step into the wild safely, understanding the dangers of cold, heat and other environmental hazards. Having started the first bushcraft school in Europe, it saddens me to say that aside from the real professionals there are many people teaching this subject today who have little genuine experience. Be careful to avoid esoteric, ego-driven survival or bushcraft classes. This is a serious study, not a game for dreamers.

Swimming

On expeditions, the greatest cause of deaths are road accidents; second to this are deaths by drowning. Water is hazardous, particularly when it is cold, deep, turbid, fast flowing or inhabited by dangerous wildlife. Swimming is only part of the solution to avoid water hazards but one which can certainly save a life. Being a strong swimmer is fundamental preparation for wilderness travel and works wonders for personal fitness. If you cannot swim – learn to swim. If you are a swimmer – become a strong swimmer. We should all swim regularly.

• • •

It is my fervent hope that in this process of learning you will derive pleasure from knowing that you have properly prepared for your walking adventures. This willingness to thoroughly prepare and to value training also paves the way for learning more specialised outdoor skills, such as canoeing, sailing, caving and diving. Training is the most significant step towards relaxing in true wilderness, and, as you will discover, knowledge dispels fear.

Footcare

We utterly depend upon our feet when walking. Traversing rough terrain carrying a loaded pack will place considerable strain on our feet. When I am hiking, I consider my feet to be my most important asset; they must be properly cared for every day. Blisters are debilitating beyond measure, affecting our ability to walk but more importantly eroding our morale. Foot problems are generally difficult to treat without enough rest to allow healing. For this reason, prevention is not just preferable to treatment; it is vital to our enjoyment of the journey. If you will pardon the pun, we can address this in three steps.

Step one

Our footwear must be well chosen to fit properly. This is not necessarily easy – our feet come in more shapes and sizes than can easily be accommodated by footwear manufacturers. It may be that you are able to find the perfect boot at your first attempt. Equally, it may be that you try many different options until you find the boot that fits perfectly. Your boot should provide comfort without tight spots causing sharp localised pain, without toes feeling cramped and without the heel sliding up and down or the foot sliding forwards within the boot. All these problems are guaranteed to result in blisters or shed toenails. Never rush your selection of footwear.

My preference is for a lightweight boot with good flex in the sole. As already stated, this makes for a silent boot but is also far more comfortable to wear when squatting around a fire at the bivouac. And again, for wilderness hiking, I prefer military-style boots that reach up above the ankle. These provide good support and greater protection from boggy ground, thorns, biting insects and loose stones. However, when conditions allow, I will often opt for a trail running shoe for its lightness and quick-drying qualities.

Boots must be tested wearing the socks you intend to use. Socks are our first point of contact with our feet; they must be cared for and replaced when worn out. Check them carefully for wool pilling or seeds trapped in the weave. Small inclusions of this sort can start a hot spot that will result in a painful blister.

All footwear needs to be properly worn in before hitting the trail in earnest. This is equally true for synthetic boots, despite claims to the contrary. Achieve this by wearing the boots and walking short distances in them on a regular basis without a heavy pack. Gradually, they will stretch and give, adapting to the shape of your feet and your walking style.

Step two

When walking, any foot discomfort, such as rubbing at the heel or hot spots developing on toes or under the ball of the foot, must be dealt with immediately. It is very often the case that these problems occur early in a walking journey and are ignored out of embarrassment at asking everyone else to stop while you make necessary adjustments. If you plan on halting for a few minutes every hour, there is ample time to address any discomfort issues. Prompt action will prevent painful blisters that can blight a hike, ruining the experience for both you and your trail mates. These problems can be caused by a variety of factors – grass seeds in socks, wool pilling in socks, incorrectly laced boots – but mostly they are caused by footwear that does not fit correctly or that has not been well enough worn in. To deal with these issues on the trail, you can try adjusting the lacing, apply a plaster or moleskin for protection of hot spots or apply surgical tape as a second skin. Greasing with Vaseline between rubbing toes can also help.

If a blister has already developed, leave it intact if possible and pad around it. In practice, however, once a blister has appeared, leaving it can often lead to it getting larger. In this case, it is best to drain the blister. To do this, clean the area with antiseptic, heat a needle to sterilise it and when it is cool puncture the blister near its edge at the part of the blister that is least vulnerable to chafing. Drain the blister by squeezing and then apply a sterile dressing on top. Keep the wound clean and free from infection. Blisters that have already burst must be cleaned and dressed and similarly monitored to remain free from infection.

Step three

At the end of the day's walking, take proper care of your feet. This is difficult to overstate and must become a daily ritual. It is all too easy after a long day walking to just slop down and succumb to tiredness ignoring one's feet. After changing into your dry kit, wash your feet with soap and water. Check for any problems, then massage your feet all over as they dry. This will loosen tight muscles, restore circulation and encourage improved nerve function. Allow your feet to air well if possible. If there are biting insects, put on some waterproof over-socks. Some very lightweight footwear suitable to wear in camp is well worth carrying as part of your dry kit.

Care for Boots

Good footwear must be cared for. On the trail, at the end of the day's walking, clean them by scraping away mud with a stick, remove the insole, open up the bellows tongue widely and allow them to air. Do not hang them upside down, as this will trap moisture in the boot, prolonging the drying process. In a base camp, they should receive the same care as at home. Equip yourself with a suitable boot-cleaning brush to wash away grime and a brush to apply polish or proofing wax. Scrub away all soil, sand and dust with a brush and water. This process can be improved by using an appropriate footwear cleaning agent. Leather boots should be proofed with a suitable treatment. I prefer Nikwax Waterproofing Wax for Leather in moist conditions. This can be applied while the leather is still wet from washing. (Nikwax also make a very good range of footwear treatments for synthetic boots.) In more arid climates, a leather-conditioning cream should be used to restore life to dry leather. Most boot manufacturers will supply or recommend a brand for their products. Use these leather balms sparingly, as they may damage the leather: if used too frequently, the leather can stretch; if used too infrequently, the leather will harden and crack.

The most important advice of all, however, is to never dry your boots close to a heat source. Doing so can shrink and crack leather and cause bonded soles to separate. Remember the old saying 'where butter melts, leather melts'. If your boots are saturated, they can be dried faster by stuffing them with old newspaper, which is then changed once soaked.

In the field, wet boots can be difficult to deal with, a problem compounded by the fact that wet leather becomes less breathable, effectively trapping in foot perspiration. There are a few strategies that can be employed to deal with this:

- **Wear footwear without socks.** In hot, arid countries, it is not uncommon to encounter local guides wearing *veldschoen* without socks, the reasoning being that our feet are naturally waterproof, and the leather will dry better without wet socks inside. Also, our feet will breathe better. This method works well but depends on the footwear having been chosen to fit feet without socks. The drawback comes in cold, damp conditions when extra insulation is required, or in tropical conditions when feet may be wet for most of the day. Wet feet soften and are prone to injury by chafing. The worst scars I have ever seen from poorly fitting footwear were caused by wearing jungle boots without socks.

- **Wear wet footwear but dry feet at the day's end.** In the moist tropics, it is not unusual to have to wade streams frequently when hiking. I once had to wade the same stream fifty times over the course of two days, sometimes ankle deep, at others chest deep. Under these conditions, our feet will be wet all day regardless. Even so, I prefer to use wool socks for the cushion and protection they provide against abrasion. At the end of the day, I clean and air my jungle boots, rinse and wring out my socks. I wash my feet and massage them well before donning Sealskinz waterproof, breathable oversocks. These warm and dry my feet wonderfully; after half an hour, they are fully restored. This system has served me incredibly well over many difficult rainforest journeys, including one trip during which my feet were in muddy swamp water every day for just short of a month.

- **Employ waterproof socks.** Sealskinz waterproof, breathable oversocks can be worn when boots become saturated. The drawback is that the boots' breathability is so compromised by moisture that the sock no longer breathes effectively, resulting in socks dampened from accumulated perspiration. To prevent this, I employ a vapour barrier next to my skin. A small compostable bag is ideal for this. Worn next to the skin under socks it prevents the sock becoming perspiration dampened. In fact, my foot does not perspire, as the humidity within the bag is at 100 per cent. Over my sock, I wear a waterproof oversock, which fits snuggly and well. This protects my sock from becoming wet from the damp boot. In this way, my sock remains totally dry and clean, retaining its insulative value. Because my foot stays warm, my footwear is dried by the gentle warmth of my foot. If a waterproof oversock is unavailable, a plastic bag can be used in its place.

Living Outdoors

Living outdoors is a joy. It provides wonderful opportunities to observe wildlife. Essentially, you have temporarily moved into a wild neighbourhood. Although our outfit is simple, without the conveniences of modern living, many tasks will take much longer than normal. Despite the long outdoor days, time passes quickly. To gain the most enjoyment from living out, it is best to be very organised. Every item of your outfit should have a specific home in your pack, where it will live unless it is in use. In this way, items do not become misplaced. Smaller items can also be tied in with thin cord to prevent loss.

This is my typical hiking routine in summer:

In midafternoon, I will start to search for a suitable campsite, one away from animal and insect threats, close to a water source and, if necessary, with a good supply of firewood. Very often I already have a designated place in mind or have determined a possible campsite by reference to my survey map. Shortly before reaching camp, I like to fill my large ten-litre water bag. In this way, all my water needs are taken care of for the rest of the day and night. Arriving at the camping place, I check for insect pests and potential animal problems; for example, an excess of bear scat. By searching for my campsite early, I can always walk on to find a better site if necessary, still with enough daylight for comfort.

Having chosen my campsite, I pitch my tarp, followed immediately by lighting my fire or stove and making a comforting, rehydrating brew. While this comes to the boil, I take a further look around, establishing the precise shape my camp is going to take.

After my brew, I attach my water filter to my water bag and suspend it from a convenient tree. I collect firewood for the night and prepare a cat-hole latrine. It is better to prepare this in daylight.

Under my tarp, I set out my sleeping gear. I have a wash, attend to my feet and don my dry kit. If needed and the weather allows, I may rinse my day shirt and hang it to dry. Now I wash my footwear. If daylight allows, it is a good time to maintain a journal or read. These tasks being completed, I can attend to my dinner, relax and socialise with my trail mates. Together, we shall cook and share bad jokes. Any so-called 'grey water' (water that has been used for washing) must be discarded well away from the camp and any nearby watercourses. A quarter of an hour before darkness, I find my head torch and place it around my neck. Generally, I minimise the use of my head torch to save battery power but also to minimise the effect on my night vision and other senses. Novice hikers will often walk around with their head torch on when it is not needed.

As darkness falls, we all retire to our bashas to rest and sleep.

I arise at daybreak and put on my day clothes, even if they are wet, pack away my dry kit securely and air my sleeping bag. Now I heat water for a wash and breakfast. I will usually use my stove for this to avoid relighting the fire; a cold fire is always easier to extinguish and to clear away. With experience, this becomes an efficient routine. I now pack my sleeping bag and other gear, leaving my tarp till last. The fire is cleared away carefully to leave no obvious trace. Once all is done, we assemble and set out for the day.

When I walk in my favourite wild places, I often pass through anonymous, pristine clearings, where on nights long past I have sat with friends around a campfire. I am haunted by such recollections, for although some of these friends have now gone ahead to walk the trails in the next life, the shadow of their spirit lingers there still, triggering emotions and vivid memories of those firelit evenings. I have learned that sitting around a campfire we come closer in understanding of each other; flickering firelight has a way of revealing a person's true identity.

The Cat-hole Latrine

Carelessly disposed of human waste poses a risk to health. Our aim in creating a latrine is to minimise this risk, to prevent the waste affecting the local water supply and to maximise its rate of decay. In the process, we also protect the aesthetics of the wild and remove the possibility of providing other hikers with an unwelcome surprise.

The process is very simple: we bury excrement in a small hole, sometimes called a cat hole or scrape. This needs to be sited well away from watercourses, tracks and any campsite – no nearer than fifty metres and ideally 100 metres away. Look for a location with good exposure to sunlight, ideally with rich soil, and try to avoid ground full of rocks or roots that will hinder the excavation of a good latrine hole.

The hole itself should be fifteen centimetres in diameter and fifteen centimetres in depth. Fifteen centimetres equates roughly to the width of your fist with outstretched thumb. Some hikers carry very lightweight trowels for this purpose. I mostly improvise a digging stick. A cheaper alternative trowel is a tent snow peg, which can also be used to provide more secure tarp or tent anchorage in very soft ground.

Having made your deposit, if it is possible and safe to do so, burn the paper to ash. In moist, temperate ground, standard biodegradable toilet paper can simply be buried. Refill the hole and wash your hands. It is a good idea to transport your toilet paper in a zip-lock bag, along with a small gas lighter and some hand gel all ready for action if you are caught short.

Multi-day hiking is a big departure from day hiking. Just describing the nitty-gritty details, it becomes apparent that there are many distractions to the awareness we have been developing. At first, it will be difficult to remain hyperalert, but gradually we will relax into the flow of trail life. Simply by being present at those times of day when we are most likely to encounter wildlife, we will have magical experiences to encourage us. Coping with the physical demands of the trail is also rewarding, and the accompanying tiredness forces us to depend on our senses in a more natural, intuitive way, just as our ancestors once did. This prolonged exposure to wild stimulus is also deeply satisfying. It enhances our alertness to tiny disturbances, makes us more willing to investigate them and encourages us to question their significance in the larger scheme of things. With each step we take, we cleanse ourselves of the frenzy and concerns of modern life, becoming more sharply attuned to the natural rhythms of the moment, of the day and of the season. Immersing ourselves in the wilderness in this way, we expose ourselves to the greatest teacher of all: mother nature. No longer does our destination matter; it is only a journey. What matters is the present moment and the fellow humans whom we share it with.

Just as on that night in Costa Rica, if we are willing and able to sleep out in the wild, we walk in graceful harmony with the natural world, casting our hook into the richest water.

The Stove and the Campfire

Good hiking stoves are wonderful things. Lightweight and convenient, they rouse enthusiastic fascination in the same way that a train set can, generating endless debate. Some favour the Primus stove, a marvel of engineering that has been the mountaineer's companion since 1892; others prefer the silent Trangia, an essay in elegant simplicity. The Jetboil is the new kid on the block, and the Solo Stove is the hipster's friend. Hiking stoves heat our rations, boil our water and in the draughty vestibule of a mountain tent in a storm provide a reassuring sense of control. Many is the time I have heard the roar of a pressure burner described as comforting. Stove designs continue to improve year on year, and as a consequence we are blessed with many excellent ones to select from. The choice will largely be dictated by the fuel available in the place where we intend to travel. My preference is for simple designs, such as spirit burners or Solo Stoves, which have few moving parts. Pressure stoves are excellent at altitude where fuel volume and weight must be minimised, as they burn more energy-rich fuels.

A campfire is a primal thing. It calls to the ancient wilderness hiker within us, drawing us near, like moths to a flame. When the cooking is done, the billycan can be swung high to provide an endless supply of hot water. It is then that the fire comes into its own, warming us bodily and inspiring us spiritually. When we camp in country that is home to dangerous game, our fire repels threats and dispels fear. It is humanity's unique and most important tool, and as such the campfire is essential for re-establishing our bond with nature.

It is not always possible to make a fire. In the many national parks, where human traffic is heavy or when there is a high fire risk, we must instead rely on our hike stove.

When we make a fire, we are wrangling an elemental force, and it must be handled in such a way that we protect the wilderness we cherish from harm. Where an existing campfire site already exists, use it. If there isn't one, search for a good location. A campfire should only be kindled where there is no risk of igniting the surrounding vegetation, so ideally away from any undergrowth. Also, it should not be lit atop grass or other living vegetation where it will leave a lasting fire scar.

The substrate on which the fire is laid is critical. Never ignite a fire on peat soil or organic soil that itself is combustible. Such fires are difficult to extinguish and failure to do so can result in the fire smouldering underground where it is out of sight, only to surface later, igniting a forest fire. In such country, it is usually possible to find a gravel or sand bar in a river on which to locate the fire. By choice, I always search for mineral soil, such as mud or sand. Choose level ground close to the resources you will be needing: dead fallen wood and, if possible, water.

Before doing anything, take a long hard look at the area: what you see is what you will aim to leave when you depart. Next, clear away the surface humus layer; this can ignite and will be needed when restoring the ground when the fire is extinguished. Create a circular space three times the diameter of the fire you will be employing. Site the fire in the centre of this circle. Do not surround the fire with rocks; this will only lead to permanently scorched rocks and will reduce the efficiency of the fire's ventilation.

Burn only dead fallen wood, keeping the fire small. Large logs will not be consumed and will remain afterwards as an unsightly sign of your passing. Instead, we shall burn firewood of a dimension that will be consumed totally to ash during the life of our campfire: finger thick for a quick trail fire; no thicker than wrist diameter for an overnight fire. A small fire is all that is normally needed; we only make the fire larger when the weather is cold, excessively wet or if it is needed to repel predatory animals.

A fire is most easily removed when it has burned completely to ash. To aid this, anticipate the end of your fire so that the stub ends of firewood, known as 'fire dogs', can be turned into the fire and reduced to ash. Ideally, do this last thing at night, and use your stove for breakfast.

When it comes to extinguishing a fire, begin by spreading the embers out into a thin layer to cool and separate any remaining firewood. Left in this way, a fire is starved of fuel and warmth and will usually go out naturally of its own accord. In arid regions, this may be the best option for extinguishing a fire. It should not be left unattended until the embers and ashes are cold to the touch and can be removed with a bare hand. Where water is in good supply, having given the fire time to reduce by cooling, use water to ensure that the fire is truly extinguished. Use a sharpened stick to pierce the ground in many places to a depth of ten centimetres to allow the water to penetrate the ground and ensure that nothing is smouldering underground. Drench the fire with water and mix it through the embers and ashes with a stick. Once all is cool, the embers can be raked together by hand and placed in a billycan and then walked away fifty metres or more into the surrounding area and widely scattered by hand. This will certainly take several trips. Once this is done, sweep back the humus removed initially, and brush away any depressions where you have been standing, sitting or where packs have been resting. Your aim is to restore the scene to the one you carefully observed before the fire was ignited.

Finally, wash your hands, pack the billycan and head out on the trail. It may seem a hassle, but this simple method will ensure the fire is safely extinguished, and that you leave little sign of your passing and no encouragement for less-skilled hikers to light a more damaging fire. When you look back over the scene, you should feel pride in a job well done and the certain knowledge that you have shown respect to the land.

DANGER

To be afraid was natural and not cowardice: it kept one alive in the bush and on the lakes. The [Zulu game] guards seldom, if ever, gambled with their lives. They had too much respect for themselves and the environment they lived in. All life was precious, and you had to hlonipa *(respect) it. To challenge wild animals out of bravado was neither heroic nor wise, only insulting.*

Ian Player, *Zululand Wilderness: Shadow and Soul*

Growing up in the UK, the outdoors was a wonderful place to explore. In fact, a more benign environment to enjoy would be hard to find. Long ago, our native bears and wolves were hunted to extinction; even malaria was eradicated in the 1950s. Apart from wasps, hornets, bees, ticks and the adder – our only venomous snake, which is shy and retiring by nature – there are few threats to be concerned with.

The greatest threat to life in the UK is without doubt our fickle maritime weather and the resulting risk of exposure to the cold, wet and windchill, which can lead to hypothermia. This is a problem for those lost in our mountains and moorlands, who after running out of food become exhausted and dehydrated, both significant contributors to hypothermia. Although small by comparison to many other countries, Britain's wild lands should never be underestimated; map and compass skills are a prerequisite for outdoors safety. As is always the case, preparation is the key. Even on a day hike, it is wise to carry extra food, warm clothing, a first-aid kit, a whistle and a torch. Ideally, you should also have a way to heat water, a shelter and a reliable means of communication or an emergency battery for a mobile phone. With these few items, your chances of survival if caught out by rapidly changing weather or injury are greatly improved. What might otherwise be a life-threatening circumstance can instead be a harmless adventure.

As experience grows, so too does confidence, and a day may come when you want to look farther afield for more remote wilderness expeditions, at which point you might find yourself walking in country where there are more tangible threats to life than the weather. With the right attitude and knowledge, these dangers can be effectively managed and safety maintained. I have been doing just that for nearly forty years, during which time I have traversed wilderness regions containing every conceivable threatening creature, from cape buffalo to polar bears. I do not say that in a macho way, just as a statement of fact. Dealing with dangerous wildlife is no place for Hollywood-inspired heroism. Rather, it requires calmness, presence of mind and an in-depth knowledge of wildlife to read the mood of a situation and to instantly take the appropriate action.

It is impossible in the space here to give detailed advice for every conceivable threat. Indeed, when it comes to big game, volumes would have to be written for each animal. What I want to do, though, is introduce the thought that it might be possible to walk safely in such places, and that walking in country where you are no longer top of the food chain can intensify the experience of being alive. But please do not rush out and hike into dangerous wilderness alone. It is far wiser to travel in such places with an experienced local guide, at least until you have learned to handle yourself in such circumstances.

It is strange how voices and advice from the past can echo in one's mind decades later. Perhaps the sagest advice I have ever heard was that from an Aboriginal elder responding to a colleague who was keen to see a saltwater crocodile. He explained in the Yolngu language, although it later transpired that he spoke perfect English, that his people had a way of avoiding dangerous interactions with crocodiles in the bush. I noticed a twinkle of mischief in his eye as he waited for his words to be translated by a younger man. My colleague leaned forward with excitement and anticipation of becoming the recipient of this ancient Aboriginal secret. It looked to me as though he was trying to strain the unintelligible words from the air as they passed to the translator. Once delivered, he turned eagerly to the interpreter, who said, 'The old man says that we leave them crocodile alone and they leave us mob alone.' My colleague turned back disappointed, realising that he was the butt of a masterfully delivered joke. The old man had already walked away chuckling. It was funny, but I doubt that any wiser advice could ever be offered on the matter of dangerous animals. Leave them alone, and they will leave you alone.

Later, talking quietly with the old man, I was able to learn more. He told me in all seriousness that he believed that if you think about an animal, you will attract it. ESP (extrasensory perception) was a real and important concept in Aboriginal life. A thousand miles south into the Australian desert, a Pitjantjatjara man explained that he had a scar that he'd sustained when play fighting with his brother when they were children. If this itched, he knew his brother was thinking about him. Then he laughed, and, pointing to the somewhat incongruous solar-powered phone booth in the centre of the outstation, he told me, 'Telephony has replaced telepathy these days.' Again, a true and sagely observation.

As I have already explained, one of the great joys of walking silently in the wild is that we reconnect with our latent intuitive senses. At no time is this more comprehensively experienced than when we are walking amongst dangerous game, for now our very survival depends upon our situational awareness. This can manifest itself in many surprising ways; for example, becoming alert to the presence of an animal before there is any obvious indication of its proximity, pre-empting a wildlife encounter shortly before it occurs or instantly understanding the mood and intentions of a threatening animal we encounter in the bush. We should never disregard these intuitive alerts, but instead strive to pay attention to such feelings, incorporating them in our general alertness. In time, with consider-able effort, many years of field experience and the appropriate frame of mind, it is possible to learn to trust and rely upon them.

One of the problems here is that as a species we are very willing to accept the concept of ESP, imagining we can sense more than is the case. Before we leap to thoughts of reading 'The Force', remote sensing like a Jedi, I must qualify my assertions. As a tracker, I cannot simply rely on intuitive feelings; whilst I am open to accepting them, I must always search for empirical evidence to back them up. When I cannot find such evidence, I assume that I am failing to detect it, but without ignoring the feeling I remain on higher alert. This has proven to work extremely well for me.

It has been my observation that this intuitive ability improves the more we devote time to using our regular, conscious sensory awareness, particularly when we have been using our senses fully for prolonged periods of time, as we do when silently trail walking. It has also been my observation that this intuition is most accurately felt by those with the most detailed knowledge of the local wildlife and environment. These observations lead me to believe that our intuitive abilities are mostly the result of our subconscious mind detecting the subtlest indications and changes of atmosphere in the environment; for example, the discreet flight of a bird fleeing in the distance. These indications may already have passed by the time our rather myopic conscious mind catches up, or they might even be too cryptic for it to interpret. But the subconscious seems to be able to interpret these observations swiftly, without bias or prejudice, and is hyperalert to their significance or meaning, instantly comparing them with both conscious and subconscious memories from previous encounters.

That we have this ability suggests that it was once vital to our survival, and exercising it is rewarding and can transform our experience of living on the trail. I long ago ceased trying to explain it, instead dedicating myself to being better able to read it reliably. But this is perhaps the most difficult task of all, for the moment our conscious mind probes our intuitions it is apt to pollute them with its own priorities and preconceptions. In fact, the more we focus our mind upon these intuitive feelings, the more invisible they become.

Intuitive alerts seem to break through to our conscious mind best when we are distracted by another activity, on first impressions or when our mind is empty and fully receptive to stimuli. Our subconscious mind is particularly obscure, but with practice it is possible to turn up its volume and to allow it to play a larger role in our decision-making process.

Personally, when I read the landscape, I do so with my conscious mind in a wide-angle, passive state, allowing information to reveal itself to me, while simultaneously, in the background of my consciousness, providing my intuitive mind with the opportunity to feed into the assessment like a Geiger counter constantly supplying feedback on the strength of my observations. It is a poor description, I know, but the best I can muster for such a nebulous ability. Perhaps most important of all, though, is the necessity for analysing those occasions when it has proven useful, playing back in the mind the events and observations which occurred, even walking back over the ground to better differentiate between what was observed and what was intuited. There is no place here for dreamy self-delusion. This is not a game, nor is it all-in-my-mind extrasensory perception; this is hypersensory perception – the combination of heightened sensory awareness with detailed knowledge of nature.

There have been many occasions when walking back over the ground of a sighting, reading the tracks of the event, I have come to better understand the full dynamics of the moment. For example, I was once cutting wood in the Arctic forest of northern Sweden when I had an overwhelming feeling that I was being watched. At the time, I did not have a binocular with me, and, search as I did, I could not see anything observing me. Later the same day, I returned to that place only to discover the clear tracks of a wolverine leading straight to where I had been cutting the wood. It had sniffed around where I had been standing and then carried on. I was massively disappointed not to have seen this wonderful animal but happy that my instinct had proven to be reliable.

For the most part, these intuitive alerts serve mostly as stabilisers to our conscious reasoning. But just occasionally they play a more prominent role. On a tracking safari that I was leading in Namibia, we were trying to locate two wild elephants that were heading towards the reserve we were working out of. They had been seen in the thick thorn scrub around the guides' accommodation. Travelling in two game-viewing vehicles, we cut for the elephant spoor, which despite their great size can be difficult to find, particularly on sun-baked ground.

Eventually, we came across a fence the elephants had demolished and followed their spoor downhill to a dry watercourse. The vehicle ahead radioed, having found clear tracks in the sandy riverbed just as I spotted them from my vehicle. As we crossed, I gazed at the tracks, and I received a subconscious jolt: I felt that these were the tracks from three elephants not two. Calling a halt, we stopped, and I examined the spoor, but from the way that they had meandered while grazing it was impossible to say for certain that there were more than two. However, try as I might to reason with it, that intuitive feeling would not budge.

This was important. If later we were to approach these animals in the thorn scrub, we would need to know for certain whether there were two or more. If we approached them on the assumption that there were only two when in fact there were three, we could quite easily walk into a situation where we failed to perceive the threat posed by the third elephant, with potentially fatal consequences. We agreed to assume a minimum of three elephants for safety.

When an elephant walks, we must take three steps to its one to keep up, so rather than attempt to follow the already twelve-hour-old trail on foot through the dense thickets, we searched ahead to the far side of the thorn scrub. With the lead vehicle cutting for spoor, I stopped my vehicle on all prominent rises where we could glass the terrain with our binoculars. On one of these stops, when it was approaching midday, one of my guests, demonstrating great observational skill, spotted the dark silhouette of an elephant standing motionless in the shade of an acacia several miles away. With our binoculars stabilised against the roll bars of the game-viewing Land Rover, we carefully scanned the distant hillside, eventually finding two more elephants standing perfectly motionless, well concealed in the shadows of the shady scrub, vindication of my intuition and the importance of paying it regard.

As a species, we humans seek always to tame nature, using our gadgets and technology in order to reduce and, where possible, to remove all risks to our lives. It is common sense – it is part of what makes us special – but the problem is that in the process we risk taming ourselves to the point where we lose sight of our place in nature, are no longer respectful of other species and cease to value the gift of life itself.

When we enter a wilderness on foot, we sign an invisible contract. It states that we agree to survive by our senses, our wits and our intelligence. With the very first step we take, we cease to be mere observers of the wild and become full participants, living by the rules imposed by untamed nature. But if we have made our preparations, pay respect to the wildlife we encounter and keep a calm head, we have little to fear and much to gain.

It is perfectly rational to experience fear and trepidation when first exposed to potentially dangerous wild animals. Certainly, we cannot ignore the dangers – to do so would be foolhardy – but the greatest danger we face is not from the wildlife but from our own actions and decisions.

Every year, the news records horrific human deaths and injuries caused by large animals in the wild. It is rarely made clear that the fault, in nearly all cases, lies solely with the victim. 'Man Bitten on Head by Crocodile' was one such front-page headline. The full story was that this individual had chosen to swim in a watercourse known to be full of large crocodiles, with warning signs to that effect posted throughout the area. He reasoned that he would be safe – he wasn't. But he was lucky that it was only a relatively small croc which tried to eat him. Realising that it had bitten more than it could chew, it spat him out, and he survived at the cost of a few unsightly scars.

Fortunately, these situations are extremely rare and are avoidable. They usually result from a toxic cocktail, mixed from the following ingredients:

- ~ ignorance of the animals concerned and their natural history.
- ~ failure to notice or ignoring behavioural signs that warn of danger.
- ~ misplaced bravado and daring.
- ~ overestimating our speed and strength in comparison to that of the wildlife.
- ~ plain stupidity, such as approaching dangerous animals, in search of an adrenalin rush.

Obviously, these are all factors which can and should be avoided. In any physical conflict with large game, humans are frail by comparison. Even if the animal concerned is only providing a warning bite or scratch, we are likely to sustain serious injury.

But before our fears go into overdrive, there is good news. With only a few exceptions, the default position for most wildlife, large predators included, is to avoid contact with humans. Nature hardwires all animals to avoid injury through avoidable conflicts. Even during mating contests, fights between rival males are mostly decided by posturing and display, with physical fights limited to only the most dominant, closely matched individuals.

We are the most dangerous predator on the planet, a dubious reputation some might say, but one that is not lost on wildlife, and which largely affords us a degree of protection. Many aggressive animals can be persuaded to back off from physical conflict by making a suitably impressive vocal display and demonstration of fearlessness. However, there are a few animals that are brave enough to attack us without apparent care of the risk to themselves, such as the leopard or the cape buffalo to name but two. Learning the personality traits of the species you might encounter before hitting the trail is essential homework.

There are also a variety of circumstances under which even the timidest wild animals become more willing to risk injury in physical confrontation. Understanding these is critical to our safety.

When We Are Food

Perhaps the most commonly held fear is that large predators want to eat us. This is usually not so – even predators are more often than not wary of humans. However, the largest predators, such as polar bears, tigers and lions, are certainly capable of regarding us as prey on occasion.

While the internet is filled with footage of tigers chasing safari jeeps full of tourists, it should be remembered that these tigers are reacting instinctively in the way that evolution has trained them to – that is, to chase a creature that is running away. If you unexpectedly encounter a strange person outside your house and they dash away as though surprised, it is highly likely that you will respond to the same instinctive urge and give chase. In the case of those jeep encounters, these tiger chases are being encouraged by the safari drivers in the hope of earning a healthy tip from their guests at the end of a thrilling game drive.

Never underestimate instinctive responses. They are very powerful motivators, particularly in the big cats. Great opportunists, they will respond swiftly to chance encounters where they sense that they have the advantage. For this reason, we must always project confidence and latent strength in our posture and demeanour. Turning our back on a big cat is particularly dangerous, exposing the blind spot in our vision. This can be all it takes to precipitate a predatory response. Worse of all is to do so when squatting down. Squatting, we lose our vertical silhouette and more closely resemble the predator's normal prey species. Equally, staring into the eyes of an animal is interpreted as a sign of aggression and can precipitate a defence attack. Leopards are particularly sensitive to being stared at. Should you encounter one close up, avoid peering or gazing in amazement and walk on to a safe distance, keeping it in sight from the corner of your eye.

Generally, big cats are encountered in country rich in their natural prey species, for which reason they have little reason to risk a human encounter. The exceptions to this are injured animals, starving animals, those that have lost their fear of mankind or those that have developed a taste for human flesh.

In India, the tiger has a fierce reputation for human predation in regions such as the mangrove swamps of the Sundarbans, where it coexists with humans who are unable or culturally unwilling to defend themselves. The tiger is the largest and most powerful big cat. The large rear pad in its track reveals it as a specialist in silent, stealthy stalking. Post-mortem examinations of tiger victims show that the animal nearly always pounces on unwary victims from behind. Foot travel in big-cat country, when permitted, should be in the company of a professional guide, who may be armed, depending upon the local laws. If so, it must be remembered that the rifle is the absolute last resort and even then no guarantee of safety. The most important tool for self-protection is our sensory awareness.

Despite the big cat's terrible reputation, it is the polar bear that tops my list of dangerous animals. Although they may appear lumbering in size, polar bears are fast, agile, stealthy and intelligent hunters. Living as they do in the barren lands of the high Arctic, there is generally less cover for concealment and prey can be hard to find. If you encounter a polar bear in the wild, keep them in sight at a safe distance, for if they seem to take an interest in you and slip into cover, there is a high probability that they are using dead ground to close the gap between you, just like the one that stalked me by sliding on its belly for hundreds of metres. If travelling by snowmobile or quad bike, turn the engine on so that you are ready to depart without delay or risk of stalling; the stress of a close encounter may lead to an engine being flooded by anxiety-induced error. Plan the route you will retreat by and maintain a safe distance of at least 300 metres from the bear.

It is normal to carry a rifle for self-defence in polar-bear country, but you should only consider doing so if you have the appropriate training. Shooting at a paper target at 100 metres does not teach the skills necessary to neutralise a charging bear. For those readers who do have the appropriate experience or training, it is in some locations recommended that a .30 calibre rifle is suitable for the task. While this has proven to be the case, I would argue in favour of a heavier calibre to provide more reliable stopping power: a .375 or, better still, a .416.

Despite their potential threat, negative encounters with polar bears are extremely rare, with both bears and polar travellers sensibly giving each other a wide berth. Most negative encounters occur when bears try to access human food, break into cabins or hang around communities. In the wilderness, it is mostly cases of misidentification that are the problem. Inuit hunters who have survived being attacked when camping in a tent, frequently exhibit injuries consistent with the pounce a bear makes when breaking into a seal hole.

Healthy polar bears usually show some interest in human travellers, glancing towards them and sniffing their scent, but walk away with a confident air of disdain that implies their strength and ability. The most dangerous bears are those that are injured or underweight, particularly at the end of the summer. Hunger can force any predator to take extraordinary risks out of desperation, including actively hunting humans. A starving or injured bear may appear sallow, unkempt and underweight, and it will usually behave differently, taking a more certain, focused, staring interest. Very often they are encountered more than once in a short period of time and possibly at uncomfortably close quarter. Coming across the same bear more than once in this way is a sign that must never be ignored. An encounter with such a bear should be taken very seriously. If possible, it is best to depart from the area at the first opportunity. Certainly, ensure that everyone in the party is on full alert and that all bear safety measures that you are employing are fully functional. These may range from a bear sentry watch, bear bangers (fireworks designed to deter a bear), a portable electric fence and bear pepper spray. All good, but, quite honestly, when facing a desperate, predatory polar bear, a rifle is absolutely essential.

Beyond those animals that might be tempted to invite us as unwilling dinner guests, there are a range of other circumstances that can precipitate a dangerous wildlife encounter. It is these situations that we are most likely to encounter and that we must strive to understand and to avoid.

Fear

Regardless of whether they are a predator or prey, when any animal senses it is in mortal danger, it will act to preserve its life. It is the most powerful motivation any animal can experience, one which can trigger a response with lightning reflexes, either fleeing or attacking. In either case, we can find ourselves in harm's way, being mown down by a hippopotamus fleeing to the safety of water, or sliced by the claws of a leopard that feels hemmed in. Here is the point to remember: it is not the emotion of fear itself that is the danger but the circumstance which generates it. In the case of the hippo, it is the vulnerability of being out of water; for the leopard, it can be the lack of an escape route.

Surprise

Perhaps the most common cause of fear occurs when an animal is surprised. If we suddenly appear at close quarter, either visually or by scent or sound, there is no space and time to evaluate the situation and for both parties to negotiate a mutually satisfactory avoidance strategy. Instead, the dice of instinct is rolled: the animal may flee or choose to defend itself by attacking the intruder. This is a particular risk in cape-buffalo country, where it is all too easy to mistake the form of a recumbent buffalo that has been rolling in dust for that of a large boulder, only to watch it stand up and turn towards the scent of the intruding threat, us, with total hatred in its eyes.

Injury

Injured animals, particularly dangerous predators, feel exception- ally vulnerable, which raises their willingness to defend themselves and increases their unpredictability. Novices often fail to recognise that an animal is exhibiting unusual behaviour traits and mistakenly approach them oblivious to the mounting danger. Always ask the question: 'Why is that animal not leaving?' While obvious signs of injury might not be immediately obvious, the animal's abnormal, awkward posture and demeanour should alert you. A seriously injured animal may choose to remain where they are rather than fleeing, lying down flat to the ground with their ears back, staring wide-eyed. In such a circumstance, you should back off immediately and give the animal space. A bared-tooth snarl is a final warning that should not be ignored.

Memory of Prior Experience

Animals have varying degrees of memory. The more intelligent animals, such as elephants, have good memory capacity. If they are abused by humans, they may harbour a deep fear for humans that can manifest itself as seemingly malice-filled aggression. Just last year, a friend of mine actively engaged in teaching safari guides to conduct walking trails was pursued for many miles by a bull elephant in musth, a period in a bull elephant's year when he becomes engorged with testosterone, causing a dramatic, dangerous change in personality (see below). To all intents, it seemed to be crazy, actively hunting his party down. Fortunately for all concerned, a day-long series of swift sprints downwind averted a disaster for both parties. What no one had told my friend is that the year before, that same elephant had been pelted with rocks by another guide attempting to prevent it pushing down an electric fence. When we encounter animals in the wild, we have no way of knowing what prior experiences they have had with our species.

Defending Offspring

One of the most powerful biological motivators is defence of the species. Adult animals will demonstrate seemingly irrational bravery and ferocity to defend their, or the herd's, offspring. Encountering the naive young of any potentially dangerous species should trigger the question: 'Where are the adults?' An immediate and discreet retreat from the scene is essential. Animals protecting young are notorious for not offering an opportunity for negotiation, instead mounting an intense attack.

Defence and Theft of Food

If you have by now undertaken some survival training, you will be aware that wild food to sustain life is difficult to obtain. Wild animals will seek out any easy opportunity for a meal, particularly bears that must accumulate significant reserves of fat to see them through their winter hibernation. Walking on the trail with a pack full of rations is akin to carrying gold bullion in front of a bank robber. The food and any strongly scented items that may be mistaken for food, such as toothpaste, must be kept in scent-proof packaging and stored away from where we are sleeping at night, ideally in a container that is bear proof. Food scraps must be burned or buried away from the campsite and dishes cleaned of all food scent, again away from the camp. Where suitable trees are to be found, our food pack can be suspended four metres above the ground, out of bear reach from the trunk (two metres) or from overhanging or nearby branches. If a bear locates your food, it will

234

mercilessly dispossess you of your treasure. Trying to retrieve it is an act of the greatest folly and danger to life.

I remember watching a black bear with fascination in British Columbia. I was cooking a wild salmon over a fire. Downwind, the bear had attached his nose to the scent trail like a karabiner to a lifeline and was working his way up towards it. The question was whether the fish would be cooked before he arrived, as I was convinced he was timing his arrival with perfection. Eventually, he passed the fire on the opposing bank of the inlet some 200 metres away. Feigning disinterest, he then disappeared around a bend in the inlet. The fish being ready, my party and I tucked into the seasonal culinary wonder. As we ate, I kept my attention towards where the bear had been. Doing so, I noticed movement and with my binocular saw his rather wobbly backside slip into the water. He was attempting to swim the inlet, crossing to our side while concealed from our view. With some urgency, we burned the remains of the fish on the fire, put it out, removed all trace of our presence, packed up and headed back to our canoes. As we paddled away, that rascally bear emerged from the thickets of devil's club and salmon berry just ten metres from our campfire and with the fanatical determination of a metal detectorist started to sniff the ground for traces of the salmon. I wished him better luck next time.

When Mating

Animals engaged in mating are little impressed by our sudden appearance at their side and may react aggressively in response. This is particularly the case with lions, who only mate in the wild once every two years. At these times, the female is receptive for three to four days, during which time the pair will mate every twenty to thirty minutes, or more than fifty times a day.

Misidentification

It is not only humans who make mistakes in wildlife encounters; animals can too. And the greatest danger to us is when we are misidentified by wildlife. This is the situation surfers face when attacked by sharks mistaking their profile in the surf for that of a seal. On land, some of the animals we might encounter can have eyesight that is poor in comparison to their other senses. Sometimes we might need to identify ourselves vocally with a confident call to help realign their threat assessment. Bear in mind that fear can transform a bass voice into a sopranino, so concentrate on making a deep, confident call rather than a fear-filled squeak.

The Unexpected

However well we think we understand animals and can read their behaviour, there are times when we might encounter something completely out of the blue: perhaps an animal that is still engorged with adrenalin from a fight-or-flight encounter; perhaps an animal suffering with toothache; even an animal that was orphaned and did not have elders to teach it how to behave appropriately. The point is, we can never really know another species, no matter how well we think we do. It is a natural law that some degree of physical separation is necessary for maintenance of the wild status quo.

Children

Young or small children should never be taken on foot amongst large predators. Evolution has taught predators to seek out young animals as easily caught low-risk meals. Equally, young children should not be allowed near gorillas, chimpanzee or baboons. While some safari operators will allow twelve year olds on walking safaris, my advice would be to consider sixteen as the minimum age requirement. Wisdom is far better than lifelong regret.

Rabies

Animals infected with rabies can exhibit very abnormal behaviour, ranging from fearfulness to unconstrained aggression. They may appear to drool excessively, and some are unusually calm until closely approached, at which time they react viciously. They should be given a wide berth.

Zones of Awareness

If you have ever been on an underground train and had a stranger stand very close to you, you will know that it is normal to feel uneasy. This feeling is intensified if the train is not crowded. In these situations, we say that our personal space has been invaded, and we are suspicious of the intruder's motive. Animals feel the same way, depending for their survival on an acute awareness of their personal space.

Under ideal circumstances, we walk in the wild with the intention of approaching wildlife closely enough for observation. To do this, we

Is Running Away an Option?

I suspect that you already know the answer to this question. It may be that a quick dash into cover or to the safety of a climbable tree might protect us from a cape buffalo or rhinoceros, or that running downwind and out of sight can take us to a safe distance from an elephant. But for the most part we do not attempt to run away from wildlife.

As I have already explained, flight will trigger a pursuit response in many animals, so do not think for one moment that you can outrun dangerous wildlife. If you look at the following table, the answer is clear: the only creature that we can confidently outdistance is the black mamba (the fastest snake), assuming that we are well clear of its striking range and respond instantly. Mostly, though, people stare in horror at snakes, frozen to the spot with fear.

This table should only be seen as a general guide. It does not take account of the fact that elephants can run through thorn scrub with impunity, whereas we would find our clothes and skin stripped from our bodies. Or that a rhinoceros can run across a field of boulders in which we could barely stand upright. Nor does it reflect the animals' reaction speeds. Wildlife lives by the rules of the wild. Every day, animals face the challenges of survival posed by claws, talons, teeth, horns and venom. Their reflexes are honed to the highest pitch – they know far better than most humans that hesitation can cost them their life.

As we shall explore, distance is the critical factor in a wildlife encounter. The closer we are when detected by an animal, the greater the threat they perceive, the shorter the available processing time and the more reflexively instinctive their response will be. We need to understand how to approach or retire from an encounter, how to read the body language of the animal and how to send out the appropriate body language ourselves. The golden rule is to never underestimate the possible speed and ferocity of a negative wildlife encounter.

Animal	Speed (metres per second)	Time to cover 30 metres (seconds)
Lion	22	1.3
Jaguar	22	1.3
Tiger	21	1.4
Human (Usain Bolt)	19.9	1.5
Cougar/Mountain Lion	18	1.7
Leopard	16	1.9
Cape Buffalo	16	1.9
Moose	16	1.9
Hyena	14	2.1
Grizzly/Brown Bear	14	2.1
Black Bear	14	2.1
Baboon	13.4	2.2
Rhinoceros	11–13.5	2.2–2.7
Human (Average)	12.5	2.4
Polar Bear	11	2.7
Elephant	11	2.7
Gorilla	11	2.7
Hippopotamus	10	3
Black Mamba	5.6	5.4

move silently, travelling into the wind, or with the wind quartering towards us (a technical term for wind blowing towards you from a quarter to the left or right), so that we minimise the chance of our detection and maximise our opportunity of encountering wildlife. In dangerous country after sunset, if we must walk, we do so with the wind behind us to provide ample warning of our presence, giving wildlife the opportunity to yield and to avoid surprise encounters.

What we want to achieve is an approach that provides good visibility, such that we and the animals we meet both have the time to assess the threat level and the space necessary for de-escalation or flight. This will inevitably have a bearing on our route planning and the type of vegetation we will negotiate. As visibility reduces so too must our alertness be raised. This is the same for the wildlife we encounter.

Biologists frequently explain that wildlife exists within invisible threat zones, sometimes referred to as the sight, flight and fight zones. This is a useful concept for explaining that the nearer we encroach within an animal's personal space, the more threatening we appear and the more energetic will be the animal's response.

The first zone we enter is the sight zone. I prefer to refer to this as the SUFFERANCE ZONE, as many animals rely far more on their sense of smell or hearing than just their eyesight. This zone represents the extreme limits of the animal's personal space, as defined by its sensory reach, in which it is prepared to tolerate our presence, although our movement will be monitored carefully. As we proceed closer, so our presence is more noticeable and the degree to which we are watched will increase. The extent of this and any of the zones will vary with the terrain, the weather, the time of day, the mood of the animal and the presence or absence of other predatory threats. If we are seen to be observing the animal carefully or making a beeline for it, we will appear more threatening and the extent of the zone will diminish. For this reason, we usually approach at an oblique angle from downwind. And always bear in mind that the wind can change at a moment's notice, totally altering the dynamics of the threat zone.

Eventually, we will pass into the flight zone, which I prefer to call the WITHDRAWAL ZONE. In this zone, the animal feels sufficiently ill at ease as to withdraw to a safer distance. Usually, this is simply a swift exit from the area without an alarm call. If we are not detected until we have entered this zone, it will surprise the animal, causing it to withdraw immediately, often vocalising an alarm call and fleeing in a manner designed to deflect pursuit. Deep in the withdrawal zone, we can anticipate obvious signs of increased alertness and stress bordering on aggression.

Moving closer, we enter the fight zone, which I prefer to call the EMERGENCY ZONE. Here our presence will elicit an emergency response, immediate flight or a definite indication of aggression, including the possibility of a mock charge. We should be asking the question: 'Do we need to be this close?' Here a mistake by either us or the animal could have unforeseen consequences; for example, an antelope attempting to flee and discovering its exit blocked may panic and decide instead to turn and fight.

If we push closer, we enter a zone I refer to as the SURVIVAL ZONE. In the survival zone, the animal feels imminent mortal threat and will act accordingly, decisively and without negotiation, fleeing at breakneck speed or acting to neutralise the threat, attacking with sustained fury. Even an antelope that would normally choose to flee may lower its head and attack with its horns.

• • •

It should now be apparent that the wilderness is not a theme park. Unlike most outdoor pursuits, which develop individual growth in the safe gap between managed risk and perceived risk, the risks are all real when we walk in the wilderness. This is not a game and certainly should never be viewed as a source of an adrenalin rush.

When guided by an expert carrying a rifle, there is still no absolute guarantee of safety. Stopping a charging animal is difficult, there can be mechanical failures, errors in weapon handling and even the best guides can be taken by surprise. Your best defence is your situational awareness. As part of a walking party, you have a responsibility to contribute to the overall safety of the group. Nothing is more disheartening for a professional than seeing a guide leading a party of tourists with their heads down oblivious to what is around them. When it comes to walking, there are no 'guests'. Everyone walking is a 'participant' and must be willing to act accordingly.

Signs of Aggression in Animals

Reading and interpreting patterns in animal behaviour, and making an accurate deduction in dangerous country, is a lifesaving skill, one which is never fully learned and always being improved. By this skill alone it is possible to avoid a dangerous wildlife encounter, relying on the sharp eyes of other wildlife as sentinels warning of the proximity of a dangerous animal and if encountered, reading the mood of the animal and predicting its intentions.

While this skill may seem unattainable, it is actually very easy to acquire. All that it takes is dedication, and many hours spent watching and listening with a mind openly curious and alert to subtle changes in animal behaviour. Most of the information we need will be found in the vocalisations, posture and behaviour patterns of the wildlife around us. These details are always there; we just need to make a point of noticing them and connecting the dots between the causes and effects. I have never found this study to be a hardship, quite the opposite, as it encourages more detailed, inciteful observations of nature and quickly finds employment, improving our ability to read a landscape and locate wildlife. This practice more than any other enables us to hear with our eyes and to see with our ears.

Walking in the wild, our needs, in terms of understanding animal behaviour, are almost solely concerned with maintaining our safety and so are predicated on recognising signs of stress, irritation and aggression. But a wider study of animal behaviour can reveal astonishing information about wildlife, including how other lifeforms are responding to the changes we are making to the world: habitat loss, the impact of insecticides and extinctions, to name but a few. If I had my youth over, I think the study of animal behaviour, ethology, would be one that I might take up academically.

When I am walking in the bush, rather than trying to visualise the zones of awareness, I prefer instead to rely on my actual or sensed proximity, the visibility of the terrain, the direction of the wind and the presence of possible escape routes. As I move closer, so I can expect the animal to exhibit increasing signs of unease and irritation prior to a warning that I am too close. Stopping and standing silent and motionless often puts an animal more at ease, allowing it to regain its composure. I prefer not to approach so closely that I cause an animal visible stress. I never try to impress my fellow participants or to show off, always putting the animal's welfare first, treating it as I would wish to be treated in its place. It is always worth remembering that as we move closer, the options available to us are decreasing. When we detect a sign of aggression, it is a certain indication that we should consider backing off or acting to defuse the situation.

For the most part, I have found animals to be good at signalling their unease and rising stress levels. The problem is that humans are notoriously poor at noticing these indications, which can appear very subtle to untrained eyes. These signs vary from species to species and can range from tail flicking and ear flattening in cats to yawning with erect ears in grizzly bears. But any generalisation is fraught with danger, and attempting to list all these characteristics, species by species, is beyond the scope of this book. However, you must study the signs of unease in the animals you anticipate that you might come across. As an example, we can consider encountering a lone elephant bull. It is vital that we determine swiftly whether it is in musth, when elephants are notoriously unpredictable and aggressive.

Musth is a mysterious period of hormonal excess that adult male elephants experience for a month or longer each year. During the musth, they experience a Jekyll-and-Hyde-like transformation in their personality. This results from a massive increase in their level of testosterone, which rises to more than sixty times its normal level. This causes the elephant's temporal glands to swell, doubling in size and pressing on the eye socket. It has been suggested that this pressure causes a pain akin to severe toothache and that this may account for the dramatic changes in an elephant's demeanour during this time. What is certain is that elephants in musth are unpredictable and can be violently aggressive to any creature they meet. As such, they are highly dangerous and should be avoided at all costs when on foot. Although the term musth is derived from the Persian for drunk and refers to the elephant's behaviour, I prefer to think of it meaning 'must', as in must be avoided.

Frequently, the first indication of a nearby elephant in musth is an overpoweringly sickly-sweet odour permeating the air over a wide area. In the right conditions, it can be smelt by humans more than a kilometre away. Walking into this scent is like walking into a cloud of danger; it seems to linger like a fog over the landscape, making it difficult to determine the direction from which it emanates. The only certainty is that a cranky, potentially lethal bull elephant is close by. Encountering this scent, we must remain on high alert, for despite their massive size, elephants can walk incredibly quietly and are masters at vanishing from sight in woodland.

The scent is produced by a cocktail of chemicals being excreted by the elephant. When in musth, elephant bulls discharge a sticky, tar-like secretion called temporin from the swollen temporal ducts on the sides of their heads. This is visible as a dark, streaming stain that runs down behind the elephant's eyes. They also leave a scent trail of hormone-rich green urine, which dribbles continuously from their penis – up to 300 litres per day. This stains the penis sheath with a green or sometimes a white tinge and leaves smelly dark stains down the inside of the hind legs. It is this urine that is mostly responsible for their perfuse odour.

While these discharges are usually obvious to view from a distance with a binocular, there can be times when they might not be easily seen at all. For this reason, we must also be able to spot behavioural indications. Musth bulls exhibit a distinctive posture and pattern of behaviour. With their ears held somewhat stiffly, they stand tall, holding their head high, emanating a strong sense of confidence. As they walk, they place each foot with deliberation, affecting a distinctive, showy swagger. Part of their musth display includes characteristic ear wafting and the 'musth rumble', a deep, powerful, resonant vocalisation that reminds me of an old engine spluttering into life. Musth bulls may also pierce the ground with their tusks, kneeling on their front knees for extra power and emphasis.

Described in this way, it would appear easy to recognise an elephant bull in musth. However, nature's signs can be subtle to read, and we are far from infallible. The school of hard knocks teaches us that sometimes even the most obvious indications can pass unnoticed, even by experienced guides. Accepting that we are all fallible is an important frame of mind, one which should serve to remind us to look carefully and to always seek confirmation. Follow the carpenter's maxim: 'Measure twice, cut once'.

Proximity to an elephant in musth is best avoided due to their unpredictable nature; however, none of the above patterns of behaviour and signs are in themselves indications of aggression. When an elephant does choose to exhibit aggression, it is a very dramatic display.

Elephants are highly intelligent animals, with calculating minds, emotional temperaments and, as I've said, good memories. A large bull may weigh in at 6,000 to 7,000 kilograms and a cow at 4,000 kilograms. For this reason, seeing them at a distance in the comfort of a safari vehicle is quite different to staring up at one from ground level. A full-sized bull stands towering over us, three to four metres at the shoulder.

Apart from the unusual behaviour exhibited by bulls in musth, elephants do not seek out conflict with other animals, certainly not with humans. However, their size and strength, provides them with the confidence and ability to defend themselves if push comes to shove.

If we encounter an elephant while on foot, our aim should be to increase our distance from it, staying downwind so that we cannot be smelled, out of sight and moving quietly. Elephant eyesight is not their strongest sense but is equally not to be ignored; they are particularly sensitive to silhouettes on the skyline. If possible, we should attempt to keep a geographical obstacle such as a ravine, donga or dry riverbed between us and the elephants.

In many cases, this will serve as a psychological no-man's-land for both parties. However, it is not fail-safe; an aggressive elephant will not hesitate to cross such a boundary, and they can negotiate the steepest rocky ground with ease. We must always remain alert to this possibility, and be prepared to respond quickly, with an escape route already picked out, one that will allow us to stay out of sight and downwind. You cannot outrun an elephant, and climbing into a tree is also not an option. An elephant can easily rip a person from the branches of a tree, push over healthy trees fifty centimetres in diameter and overturn a vehicle. Also bear in mind that elephants are herd animals; there may be individuals nearby that have not yet been detected.

Early indications of their unease to watch for are an elephant with its trunk held up, sampling the scents in the air, and a tensing of the posture, holding the body tall and upright. Intently staring in your direction is also a sign of an escalation in interest. When coupled with ears fully spread out, the message is clear: the elephant is feeling threatened and making itself appear as large as possible, as well as demonstrating that it knows where you are. A subtle indication often missed is the elephant folding back the lower part of its ear to create a horizontal crease; this reminds me of a pharaoh's hat. It might now approach you with menace. If you are not intimidated by this, you certainly should be. As the elephant's response to a threat increases, so the possibility of a harmless encounter diminishes.

Beyond actively maintaining a safe distance, there is never certainty in any encounter with a potentially dangerous wild animal. If the elephant decides to provide more warning, it will most often do so in a most impressive display of strength and agility: shaking its head violently, causing its ears to make a flapping sound, swinging its trunk forwards, making a whooshing trumpeting noise. It might kick up dust and pick up sticks or other items of debris with its trunk and fling them towards you, sometimes with astonishingly good aim. It might make a mock charge, rushing up, ears displayed, demonstrating its prowess. In many cases, it might not have identified you, so calling out to it may assist here. If you remain still and very calm, there is a possibility that it will halt and gradually retire; you would be well advised to do the same. From experience, I would say that in most close encounters with dangerous game, simply standing still very often suffices to de-escalate the situation. But here is the rub: an elephant can launch a full-on, committed charge at any time without warning. The signs of an imminent charge are the ears flattening back against the head and the trunk tucking under its body, running silently. If all else fails, it might just be possible to dodge out of the way, but you need to remain calm and get out of sight downwind.

Managing Our Fear

If we encounter a potentially dangerous animal while walking in the wild, it is only natural to experience anxiety and fear. These are ancient emotional responses that serve to heighten our senses and prepare us to respond swiftly to meet the possible emergency. In a crisis, they trigger strong psychological and physiological responses that should improve our performance under stress. However, if we fail to manage our fear, the result can be a panic that reduces our chances of survival and often leads to lethally inappropriate and clumsy responses to a situation.

Part of our evolutionary history, these responses are hard-wired into us, but the knowledge we need to manage our anxiety has to be learned. Our distant ancestors had an advantage: they were extremely familiar with the wildlife around them, they were alert to their behaviour traits and able to read their mood, and from childhood they learned how to respond when confronted by dangerous animals. Prior experiences coupled with this detailed knowledge gave them confidence, providing a framework for analytical thinking and positive problem solving. This was their key to managing stress during such encounters. Few people today routinely spend time near dangerous wildlife and consequently we are mostly blind to the most subtle behavioural signs and indications that telegraph an animal's intent, small details which can afford us a lifesaving, split-second advantage.

Managing an encounter with a dangerous animal is a sober business that requires us to think maturely about the consequences and realities. In fact, our general attitude towards an animal is as important as our response to it in the field. If our minds are filled with scary stories about the power and danger of an animal, we may be predisposing ourselves to a higher level of fear and the stress it induces. It does not matter whether these thoughts are real or imagined. The most important thing is to accumulate accurate knowledge focused not on the devastating power of an animal but instead on those telltale indications that reveal that it is feeling stress or beginning to behave with aggression. In other words, focus on the information that is truly useful in a crisis.

One of the fascinating things I have observed when living with San bushmen is that their folk stories relate how their ancestors were able to outwit dangerous animals. Considering that these are told by firelight, where the threat from predators in the shadows is a real danger, they clearly serve to bolster confidence. They are a coping strategy to reduce the stress of close encounters.

In an ideal world, you will only head into the wild in the company of an experienced guide to begin with. While they may be carrying a rifle, their most important contribution to your safety is their wisdom. They will provide an accurate context for your anxiety, and his or her briefing will help to prepare you with an immediate action drill in case of an encounter. However, even a novice without a guide can walk away from the most dangerous encounter if they manage to keep a calm head and control their fear.

For those of us who are used to walking in country where there are dangerous animals, we walk alertly but in a relaxed state. Experience enables us to read the atmosphere and to anticipate places of danger. We utilise all the awareness skills and methods we have already explored to maximise our opportunity to spot a danger before it spots us. We are in good company, for this is the same for San women who routinely gather edible roots and berries armed only with their digging sticks.

Adrenalin Rush: Friend or Foe

I have already explained the need to always prepare for the worst, so it is vital that we understand the physical cause of our fear and its management. If we encounter a dangerous animal uncomfortably close within our personal space, the tables are turned; now we are the animal feeling anxiety and mortal fear.

In these situations, our body responds physiologically to increase our chances of survival. The response is incredibly quick and testifies to our long history of coping with such dangers. Our amygdala, the part of our brain that is responsible for emotions, triggers our hypothalamus, which regulates our hormones. This in turn sends a signal via our sympathetic nervous system to the adrenal glands located on top of our kidneys to secrete adrenalin into our blood stream. Adrenalin is the fight-or-flight hormone. It raises our heart rate, increases our blood pressure, sharpens our sensory awareness, reduces our sensation of pain, and improves our physical strength and performance. We can recognise this as a pounding of our heart in our chest. We also breathe more rapidly, our sweating increases, we feel on edge and our pupils dilate.

This is the beginning of a rush of adrenalin that will take roughly two to three minutes to develop fully. At this early stage in the adrenalin rush, we have the opportunity, to harness these changes as the physiological advantage they are meant to be, giving us temporary superpowers.

To do this we need to control our breathing, remaining calm and alert. Our focus should be on positive actions and, most importantly of all, maintaining a wide situational awareness. Now is the moment to employ our training and knowledge. But as soldiers often say, 'The plan is the first casualty of war.' So it is in wildlife encounters. While we may have visualised such a situation in training and repeatedly rehearsed our responses, in reality there can be a thousand unforeseen circumstances, to which end we must follow Major Robert Rogers' maxim and 'act to preserve firmness and presence of mind on every occasion'.

Look for other animals yet unseen, feel for the wind direction on your skin, look for possible escape routes and pay attention to what the animal is trying to express. You have not yet been charged – this is a good indication. As soon as you start to think positively, you will take a grip of your emotions and master the fear.

If we fail to overcome our fear, we risk losing control to our adrenalin-fuelled emotions and a resulting downward spiral of negativity. Nature has invested us with a bias towards self-preservation; our automatic response is to focus our attention on the perceived danger. With adrenalin stimulating our sensory alertness, we become hypersensitive to the threat, experiencing tunnel vision in which we are only able to see the thing we are most concerned with – perhaps the teeth of a predator, whose snarl is only a late-stage warning. We also become less able to respond to more than one stimulus at a time. This narrowed perception contributes to a feeling of sensory overload in which we are easily distracted by irrelevant stimuli and can become dangerously fixated on one threat or action, oblivious to everything else around us.

This loss of control causes us to focus repeatedly on the threat, reinforcing the negative stimulus, making it increasingly difficult to see a solution or any positives. As the unharnessed adrenalin rush intensifies, it accelerates our sense of fear, and the production of adrenalin becomes self-sustaining. As this occurs, the adrenalin causes the release of cortisol, which in turn provides a higher blood-glucose level, providing energy for fight or flight. Moving rapidly towards panic, we make increasingly irrational, emotional decisions and our motor skills become impaired. Simple manual tasks become impossible, as though we are wearing boxing gloves, and we might become fixated, executing the same action repeatedly, over and over again, despite it obviously failing.

While a very strong mind may force its way through this adrenalin-fuelled fog, in most cases rationality is lost and a blind panic follows, which massively reduces our chances of survival. Remember, focus on your training, look outwards to the wider picture, look for options. Every positive thought or action contributes to success and to survival.

Managing Stress

It is vital that we learn to actively manage our stress levels. Doing so sets in motion a positive frame of mind that makes it much easier to cope with the most dangerous encounter. Stress is cumulative, and we each have a different capacity to absorb it. You can think of it as a liquid filling a vessel: for some the vessel is a forty-five gallon oil drum; for others it is a bucket. The problem comes when the vessel is full and overflows; in such a circumstance, an individual may be overwhelmed by fear and suffer lasting psychological trauma.

Our stress vessel may already be partially filled from psychological stress at work, previous unprocessed stressful encounters, emotional upheaval at home or irrational fears. Guides must bear in mind that novices might already be carrying a considerable volume of stress simply from unfamiliarity with the situation, anticipation of dangers, the environment and the sense of a lack of control. Stress can also be induced physically from feeling cold or excessively hot, being ill or thirsty, fatigue, sleep deprivation, or if under the influence of drugs or alcohol. For the most part, these physical stresses are easy to fix. As with most things concerning the mind, it is the psychological stress burden that is more difficult to deal with.

As I have already explained, acquiring accurate knowledge is a good first step, but there are also other things we can do to alleviate stress – so-called coping mechanisms. These do not prevent stress, but they do punch a hole in the side of our stress vessel, relieving the pressure and allowing some of it to empty out, effectively slowing the rate at which it fills. There are several coping mechanisms that we can employ. The first of these is staying alert, contributing positively to the safety of the group. The participant that merely follows along with their head down is more likely to dwell on their fears, more likely to experience the shock of encounter and denies themself the positive uplifting stimulus of nature encountered on the walk. If we maintain a lively banter and good humour (although not at the expense of the silence needed when walking), well-motivated and happy participants are better able to cope with stress and more likely to help each other out.

Support within a group, where each member shows consideration for those around them, reduces a sense of personal isolation and contributes to team spirit. Being part of a team provides powerful psychological strength. Remember, 'One stick is easily broken, but many sticks together cannot be broken.'

Staying alert to events during the walk promotes a sense of control and reinforces the belief in a positive outcome of a more threatening encounter. Perhaps the most important thing of all is following the instructions of the guide. In a wildlife encounter, the guide will be focusing on the animal's behaviour, maintaining a wide overall view of the situation and negotiating a positive outcome with the animal or animals through their posture, body language, voice and actions. A participant that fails to follow the guide's instructions increases the stress the guide is experiencing, may precipitate an attack and if not making a target of themselves, may endanger the rest of the group.

• • •

It should be obvious by now that walking amongst dangerous animals is not your average stroll. But in recent years, the safari industry has received increasing demands from guests to walk within game reserves. The normal procedure is very sensibly a total prohibition on guests leaving a vehicle whilst in a game reserve. And it is my belief that trail walking should remain within the scope of specialist operators only. If walking amongst dangerous game becomes just another safari tourist activity, easily purchased at the lodge reception with a credit card, then either a guest or an animal will inevitably become a casualty.

While excellent training for walking guides is now available in South Africa, the fact remains that not all those who put their hand up and say 'I want to guide on foot' are cut out for that responsibility.

Training, no matter how good, can only provide the skill and knowledge; it cannot impart the attitude and personality traits required for such responsibility. Unless the individual guide has a passion for it, this is a skill set that will fade and require considerable support from the lodge to maintain. Also, to make the most of a trail walk requires a guide of exceptional ability. Such individuals can offer a life-changing experience, but they are, always have been and always shall be, few and far between.

Sadly, I have also encountered guides qualified to lead walking tours who profess an ideological unwillingness to ever use their rifle. Of course, no one wants to shoot an animal we are simply intending to observe; the guide is there to prevent such a circumstance. But nature is unpredictable. The guide's ultimate duty is the safe welfare of their guests. Not being willing to act is a very dangerous attitude. It would be far better that they avoid guiding trail walks. In the heat of an unforeseen close encounter, when communication between man and animal is reduced to body language, read at lightning speed, the body language accompanying a guide's willingness to act may be the final deciding factor that dissuades a charge.

The Real Dangers

It was my first expedition to the equatorial tropics. I was sitting on a handmade stool beside the campfire cooking. The sun had dropped like a stone, plunging my improvised kitchen into darkness. I was tired and trying to get things done quickly. What I didn't realise was that as I was sitting there preparing a meal, a multitude of mosquitoes were feasting upon me. I had foolishly accepted the advice in a London outdoor shop and purchased a very lightweight pair of trousers for the trip. Certainly, they were comfortable to walk in and they dried quickly when washed. But they offered zero protection from the needle-sharp probosces of mosquitoes. In fact, with the luxury of hindsight, I would say they provided the perfect landing site for those loathsome insects to arrive for their blood meal.

The next morning, I discovered that I had more than a hundred bites to the backs of my legs, just where the fabric had stretched most tightly. A month later, I would pay the price. Despite taking the recommended dose of prophylactic medication, malaria would catch me unaware, a stark reminder that the greatest and most constant threats to our safety come from the smallest creatures. While an estimated 250 people are killed by lions each year, approximately 500,000 people die from malaria and 3.4 million deaths result from waterborne infections.

In tropical and subtropical regions, where there is poor access to potable water and inadequate provision for sanitation, there is a significant risk from waterborne parasitic blood flukes and soil-transmitted parasitic worms.

Waterborne blood flukes cause schistosomiasis (bilharzia). It is estimated that 200 million people are affected by bilharzia and that in Sub-Saharan Africa it is responsible for 200,000 deaths each year. The life cycle of these flukes begins when an infected person's urine or faeces enter a freshwater source such as a river or spring. Here they hatch and enter the bodies of freshwater snails, where they multiply, later emerging as cercaria, which swim and can penetrate the skin on contact, thus infecting a new host. To avoid contracting bilharzia, avoid swimming or wading in water sources in areas known to be infected and minimise contact with water from these sources.

Soil-transmitted-parasitic-worm infections happen where the soil is contaminated with worm eggs. This usually occurs where people defecate outdoors, where there is poor provision of hygiene and sanitation or where human faeces are used as fertiliser. There are many types of such worms, the most common being roundworms, whipworms and hookworms. These infections are very common; it is estimated that 1.5 billion people worldwide are infected at any one time. Infection occurs when the eggs are ingested as a result of poor hand hygiene, where food is consumed unwashed or uncooked, or where water hygiene is inadequate. In the case of hookworm, people can also become infected by walking barefoot on contaminated soil. To prevent infection, maintain a high standard of hygiene, washing your hands and food well. Use water you absolutely know to be from a safe source or that you have disinfected yourself by filtration, chemical disinfection or by boiling, and avoid walking barefoot, particularly around communities and livestock.

When we travel in remote country, we need to ensure that we are alert to the wider health threats, understanding how they are spread, how they can be avoided and what their symptoms are. Always carry a suitable medical kit for your adventure, along with insect repellent, insect-proof clothing and water-purification equipment. Such items need not occupy much space in your baggage, and they will provide significant protection and peace of mind.

There are many other odious parasites that can cause discomfort, such as jiggers, chiggers, putse fly and bot fly to name a few. I have encountered rather more than my fair share of these, but none have thus far spoiled a trip or even linger in the memory of my past adventures.

Waterborne Diseases

Virus	Hepatitis A
Bacterium	Typhoid
	Cholera
	Dysentery
	E. Coli
	Salmonella
Parasite	Giardia
	Cryptosporidium
	Bilharzia

Diseases from Insect Bites

Vector	Disease
Mosquitoes	Malaria
	Dengue Fever
	West Nile Virus
	Chikungunya
	Yellow Fever
	Lymphatic Filariasis
	Japanese Encephalitis
	Saint Louis Encephalitis
	Western Equine Encephalitis
	Eastern Equine Encephalitis
	Venezuelan Equine Encephalitis
	La Crosse Encephalitis
	Ross River Fever
	Barmah Forest Fever
	Zika Virus
	Rift Valley Fever
	Keystone Virus

Diseases from Insect Bites (cont.)

Ticks	Lyme Disease
	Rocky Mountain Spotted fever
	Q Fever
	Tularemia
	Relapsing Fever
	Ehrlichiosis
	Colorado Tick Fever
	Crimean Haemorrhagic Fever
	Babesiosis
Mites	Q Fever
	Rickettsiosis
Deer Flies	Tularemia
Tsetse Flies	Sleeping Sickness
Black Flies	Onchocerciasis
Muscoid Flies	Yaws
Sand Flies	Leishmaniasis
	Sandfly Fever
	Vesicular Stomatitis
Lice	Epidemic Typhus
	Trench Fever
Fleas	Endemic Typhus
	Bubonic Plague
Reduviidae	Chagas Disease

Venomous Snakes

A large portion of humanity living in tropical and subtropical regions make their livings by simple manual-farming methods. This brings them into regular close contact with venomous snakes. Footwear capable of affording protection from snakebites is also rarely worn in these regions. These factors combined with poor access to emergency medical care result in a high number of snakebite deaths each year.

It is estimated that there are more than five million people bitten by snakes annually. Of these, around 2.7 million cause envenomation, with between 100,000 and 150,000 deaths, and perhaps three times as many serious bites that result in disability or amputation. When walking in snake country, we never step over logs or large boulders in case a venomous snake is coiled in the shade beneath it. Far better to step on the log or boulder, providing the snake with an opportunity to depart. It is worth remembering that many snakes are so well camouflaged as to be effectively invisible. They do not hear but instead rely upon detecting vibrations. Unfortunately, not all snakes will depart if disturbed; some instead prefer to rely on their camouflage and remaining motionless.

It is best to avoid thick brush where visibility is compromised, and never ignore local warnings of places where dangerous snakes are frequently encountered or known to be resident. Depending on the species, a snake may signal a warning by rearing up, shaking its tail (with or without rattle) or coiling back in an S shape, poised to strike. Stillness is my first reaction in such moments, carefully looking for an exit route. Usually after a standoff, the snake moves away cautiously. If not, I will carefully back away, ready to spring away quickly if necessary. When I traverse terrain with a high risk of a snake encounter, I always carry a walking staff. Not so much as a weapon but instead to provide an alternative target for the snake to strike at and a means of fending it off as a last resort. It is highly unwise to throw objects at venomous snakes or to attempt to kill them; doing so is to incite a more deadly response. Never underestimate the speed or reach of a snake.

Most snakebites occur to feet and lower legs, followed by hands and forearms and then faces. The message is clear: avoid walking in thick vegetation, and wear sensible footwear and long trousers where practical. Never reach into recesses or places where you cannot see clearly, and never peer into places that may harbour a snake. If we must lift rocks or logs, we do so by levering it towards us so that the rock or log is between us and whatever may be lying beneath it.

Before heading into snake country, familiarise yourself with the species of snakes you may encounter locally, and pay special regard to the venomous species, their habits and nature. Make a note of the type of venom they are equipped with, the symptoms of envenomation and ask local experts for the recommended first-aid procedures (these can vary from country to country depending on the species of snakes which occur there), the location of the nearest hospital capable of treating snakebite casualties and the availability of anti-venom.

A HANDFUL OF SAND

The greatest danger to our future is apathy.

Jane Goodall

This book has been written in what I can only describe as the most extraordinary period in my life, during the coronavirus lockdown of 2020. Writing at this time has been strange. In the first instance, it has given me purpose and a focus – I am in many ways a workaholic. At the same time, sharing these thoughts has given me the opportunity to revisit memories of past experiences, places and journeys.

Despite the terrible impact of this virus and the tragedy it is currently visiting upon many families around our planet, it has highlighted how interconnected our communities are, raising awareness of things that in the normal course of life we take for granted; for example, how we cherish human company and how important nature is to us. I wonder if we have ever valued our green spaces more than now.

With hardly any cars on the road for a while and few planes taking flight, our skies have been purged of pollution and are visibly clearer. Here at home in the UK, the moon seems to fill the sky, as clearly defined as I would view it from my favourite remote wilderness regions. Seeing it like this reminds me of many happy nights on the trail. One of the greatest joys of being out on expedition is to lie beside the fire and to gaze into space, marvelling at the vastness of the universe, daring to consider our own place in the larger scheme of nature.

When I first began teaching bushcraft way back in the early 1980s, I would encourage my students to lie back and search for a satellite. This was a task that took some time. Today, with more than 2,000 satellites in orbit, it takes only a few seconds to spot one. It is amazing how in just a few decades satellites have come to dominate our lives, so much so that the world's great powers are now vying for military dominance over the space that surrounds our planet.

In 2020, China tested a new missile, destroying one of its own satellites to prove its ability to destroy an enemy's satellite. What might have seemed like a demonstration of military prowess to a foolish general simply eroded the trust of other nations, fuelling the proliferation of yet another arms race. It also contributed to the ever growing cloud of orbiting space junk.

I have lived through the Cold War and the first great era of space exploration. When I think back on what we have learned from those space missions, there are several truly awesome things that have stood out. To begin with, that first marvellous image of our planet seen from space, *The Blue Marble* photograph that was taken on 7 December 1972 by the crew of Apollo XVII. This is perhaps the single-most inspirational image I have ever seen. The beautiful blue Earth, the planet of water, planet of life, our home; it is an image that makes my heart sing.

Then between 18 and 28 December 1995, Bob Williams, director of the Hubble Space Telescope, did the unthinkable. He pointed the Earth's most expensive telescope at a patch of the heavens close to the handle of the Big Dipper, where there was nothing to see. It was an act so seemingly disrespectful to the value of the telescope that it verged on the sacrilegious and could easily have cost him his job. He went on to record 100 hours of nothing, taking 342 pictures with exposures of between twenty-five and forty-five minutes in the red, white, blue and yellow wavelengths of light.

What a genius he turned out to be. By his act of courage, our understanding of the universe and our place within it was for ever changed. There, for all to wonder at, was evidence that in the dark spaces in the night sky there are millions of distant galaxies too dim for us to see from Earth.

That Christmas, the Hubble Deep Field image increased the number of galaxies in our universe fivefold to fifty billion. Since then, the Hubble Space Telescope has been tasked to peer deeper still into dark corners of the night sky, producing further astonishing images: Hubble Deep Field South (1998), Hubble Ultra-Deep Field (2004) and Hubble eXtreme Deep Field (2012). Despite the rather unimaginative naming of these missions, each time we have scrutinised the dark spaces in the night sky we have been forced to increase our estimate of the magnitude of our universe. It is currently believed to contain hundreds of billions of galaxies.

The scale of the universe is too expansive for any human mind to truly envisage. But what we can grasp is that each time we increase the size of our universe, so our presence within it diminishes exponentially. Humanity seems atomically insignificant and shrinking, not an easy thing for an organism that likes to feel it is special, superior, the lord of all that it surveys. When I gaze into the night sky and contemplate the magnitude of our universe, it makes me realise that the greatest gift we possess is life itself; to be a part of such an immensity for however short a span of time is a sacred gift and surely must be significant.

As certain as the twinkle of light from a distant star in the heavens, each of us is a sparkle of life contributing to the multiverse.

As such, we are each bound spiritually to every other lifeform past, present and future. This thought inspires me to strive to use that gift, to try in some way to make a meaningful contribution with my life.

• • •

In the early 1990s, I was engaged to provide bushcraft training to a Greek trekking company, in the pine-covered mountains of Attica, north of Athens – retsina wine country. I remember the days were beautifully warm and the nights chillingly cold. The dry, rocky limestone hills were clad in pine forests, perfuse with the rich scent of the valuable pine resin being tapped from the trees.

One morning, I set out with a survey map and compass to find a suitable water source to present a lesson on water safety. The map provided many options, with lots of blue marks indicating a variety of local sources. But having spent the better part of the morning without success, I sat in the shade of a spreading pine branch to consider my dilemma. I had visited many of the water sources only to be astonished to find that the marks were totally spurious; in one case, they had led me to a large monolithic limestone boulder. I came to the inevitable conclusion that either there was a cartographic printing error or the surveyors had been drinking too much retsina.

Not to be deterred, I studied the map for some other feature. There was one that attracted my interest: a S-shaped thin blue line. What interested me was that it followed a crease in the contours of the landscape, precisely the sort of place I would expect to find water. As I approached the location, I could hear the occasional report of a shotgun. Perhaps I would have the opportunity to meet a local hunter.

The place I was searching for ran north at ninety degrees to a track and proved easy to find. Even as I made my way into the gully, it felt promising, with thicker, greener vegetation, mostly spikey juniper trees lining a narrow game trail. Here the soil was darker, and whilst not wet, it was certainly damp and clearly held a fresh set of human footprints. A freshly spent twelve-bore shotgun cartridge case suggested that it was the trail of a hunter, perhaps the one I had heard earlier. The tracks led exactly in the direction I was heading, and as I proceeded I heard the report of a few more shots.

Eventually, I found a thin strip of very moist ground, exactly as represented on the map. It was a poor source of water for a hiker, but one which, with the right knowledge, could sustain life in an emergency. Hearing another shot and having satisfied myself with the water source, I thought I would continue past and follow the tracks to say hello to the hunter.

One of the joys of tracking in places as quiet and remote as this is that there are no other fresh human tracks to provide any confusion. As I followed the spoor, I could clearly make out where the shotgun had been fired by the discarded cartridges and in which direction the hunter had been facing. What puzzled me was that the hunter never left the track. In the normal course of rough shooting, a hunter will have to walk out and retrieve his bag, the hunting term for what has been shot. I checked carefully; there were also no signs of a dog to do the retrieving. Then I had one of those intuitive alerts and started to wonder what the hunter was shooting.

Returning to the last place I had found evidence of a shot having been made, I scanned the vegetation carefully. I couldn't see anything. Reading the tracks more carefully, they suggested that the hunter had been shooting low. This would place his point of aim above the nearest vegetation: low junipers towards the middle of the pine trees behind them. Given the steepness and narrowness of the gully and the clear imprint of his feet, he could not have been shooting into the air above the vegetation. This seemed odd.

Picking up a stick to represent a shotgun, I placed my feet in the same manner just to the left of the tracks and mimicked the shooter's stance to try to estimate his point of aim. This exercise suggested that he was shooting slightly lower than I had estimated. When tracking, if something seems odd with the trail, it must be paid greater attention, as it usually proves to be significant.

Pushing through the wiry vegetation on the line of the shot, I searched for any sign of success, perhaps some pigeon or quail feathers. What I found was one of the saddest sights that I have ever seen. Lying on its back deep in the thickets was a small songbird, its feathers distressed by the lead shot, but not as badly mangled as I would have thought a small bird would have been by a twelve-bore load. At the time, I could not recognise the bird; later, when I found a field guide, I learned it was a very aptly named sombre tit (*Poecile lugubrisi*). I picked it up, cradling it in my hand, its head flopping loosely over the edge of my right finger. I could clearly see it had been shot; beneath its plumage it was utterly broken but still in possession of some of its life warmth. I was shocked. Why would any adult seek to end the life of such a beautiful and harmless creature, let alone with such an excess of violence? It seemed more like the crime of a small boy with an air rifle.

As I contemplated what I had found, I heard another shot ring out from further down the gully. Laying the little bird's body respectfully on a shaded rock, I picked up the trail again. Fifty metres further on was another cartridge, again shot towards the right of the track, where I found another songbird. On again and another cartridge, but I could not find a bird this time. Either the shot was a miss or the body was concealed in the thickets. In all, I found nine cartridges and seven songbirds, all tits excepting one sparrow, and all left where they had fallen.

I never caught up with the hunter. When eventually the little gully levelled out and emerged again onto a rise, I found the trail led me to the tracks left by a car that had been parked in the shade of a pine tree. This is where the hunter's trail exited the scene. I am loathe to call him a hunter, for any true hunter would demonstrate more respect for his prey. Neither was he a poacher, for he had no interest in the things he killed. A far better term would be murderer.

I studied the tracks with a forensic interest. He had walked to the rear of the car, perhaps to stow his shot gun and cartridge belt, and then climbed in and driven away. What was interesting was that the rear wheels of his car had totally different tyre treads: the left a chunky off-road tyre, the right a fine-filigree road tyre. From a quick cast around, I deduced that he had walked a loop around the hill that formed the western side of the gully. I was angry, deeply saddened and frustrated. In hindsight, it was perhaps best that I never met him, otherwise I might have spent the intervening years languishing in a Greek prison.

A few days later, as we were driving away from those beautiful hills, I suddenly realised that on the road in front of us were the tracks of a vehicle with odd tyres, the left rear with a heavy zigzag, the right with a fine road pattern. As we climbed the dirt road, we came up behind an old rusty, filthy, cream-coloured car, burning oil, trailing a black exhaust cloud, struggling to climb the grade – this was the car.

Just below the crest of the hill, in a dangerous move, my host dropped a gear and overtook it. As we passed, I could see that the car was being driven by an unshaven local in a dusty white shirt in his late forties. As I stared at him, he misread my interest, and smiling he waved to me cheerily. Then as we crested the hill my driver decided to demonstrate his best rally-driving prowess, and my mind moved to more pressing thoughts, those of my own survival.

Apart from that encounter, I enjoyed those few days. Greece is a stunning country, and the trekking team I was working with were wonderful company, all devotees of nature, committed to conservation and wildlife education. The man with the shotgun was a frustration. Whilst I could place the car at the scene of the crime, it would have been another thing to prove with certainty who the shooter was.

Noticing crimes against nature is perhaps the inevitable price we pay for raising our levels of awareness. Since that afternoon, I have encountered many far worse events. I realise now that as wildlife crimes go, the deaths of those birds in Attica were but a speck of dust in the sands of the Sahara. But I have a long memory, and I have always carried the sights of that day with me – the man killing birds with a shotgun needlessly symbolises for me humanity's often corrupt relationship with wildlife. It is not a new thought. In 1869, Alfred Russell Wallace, the co-originator of the theory of evolution, wrote in *The Malay Archipelago*:

> Should civilised man ever reach these distant lands, and bring moral, intellectual, and physical light into the recess of these virgin forests, we may be sure that he will so disturb the nicely-balanced relations of organic and inorganic nature as to cause the disappearance, and finally the extinction, of these very beings whose wonderful structure and beauty he alone is fitted to appreciate and enjoy. This consideration must surely tell us that all living things were *not* made for man.

It was 100 years later, in the summer of 1969, when I was five years old, that my interest in wildlife began. On the way to visit relatives in the West Country, we stopped off at Longleat Wildlife Safari Park. These parks were a novelty in the 1960s and '70s, providing a unique way to observe exotic wildlife at close quarter. In those days, visitors could even picnic amongst the giraffes. I remember my father being concerned that the monkeys would break the windscreen wipers off his cherished Humber. I also remember feeling rather tired of being trapped in the car for so long. It was a sultry day.

Eventually, we parked and walked around, and I found myself gazing in wonder at a rhinoceros. I clearly remember leaning on a fence in the shade of a spreading oak tree, staring in awe. I knew it was a powerful animal, but it seemed much gentler and more innocent than I had been taught. I do not for the life of me know why, but something clicked for me that day, and ever since I have been a devoted fan of this extraordinary animal. What I could not have guessed is that since that day in 1969 the remaining population of wild rhinoceros in Africa would be more than halved, a result of a demand for coveted rhinoceros horns to make high-status dagger handles in the Arabian peninsula and for its wrongly supposed medicinal properties in Asia.

Through the intervening decades, Africa was a troubled continent, beset by severe environmental problems, ecological degradation, endemic diseases, desertification, deforestation, loss of biodiversity, droughts and famines. As with global warming, the factors leading to these interconnected environmental troubles were very complex, but there can be no doubt that they were exacerbated by human influences, such as the exponential population growth that followed the introduction of Western medicine and public-health regimes, as well as the social and cultural disruption of colonisation. Add to this economic and political instability, and the wars and insurgencies that arose from the Cold War struggle between the conflicting ideologies of Marxism and Western liberalism, and the picture was bleak, especially at the grassroots level – an ever increasing competition between human communities with each other, and with wildlife, for land, food and water.

Throughout the 1970s and '80s, central, eastern and southern Africa became the bloody battlefield on which the Cold War was fought. Quiet rural homesteads became the scene of political indoctrination and intimidation. Once-peaceful peasant and pastoralist communities were flooded with Kalashnikov rifles, landmines and rocket-propelled grenades. Regardless of race, tribe or religion, the resulting border wars, guerrilla insurgencies, brutalisation of child soldiers and ethnically motivated genocide brought misery to the peoples of Sub-Saharan Africa, in many cases only serving to deepen crippling poverty and social inequality. Cruel dictatorships and endemic corruption have been the almost inevitable consequence for postcolonial Africa. While it is testimony to the enduring spirit of the peoples of Africa that they weathered such a fire storm, when human survival is such a ruthless struggle it is hardly surprising that it was the wildlife that suffered most.

When war-weary rural communities, with easy access to modern automatic rifles, come into conflict with wild animals for grazing, water and land, they are unlikely to value the life of an elephant or a rhino; unless that is, they are given compelling reasons to preserve them. Such reasons do exist, as the selfless efforts of generations of African conservationists and game rangers testify, but they are complex, altruistic and difficult to convey to a struggling peasant farmer who sees his entire corn crop destroyed in a single night by a herd of elephants. The poverty and necessarily short-term view of rural communities, living a hand-to-mouth existence, have been exploited by grasping and unscrupulous businessmen throughout Africa, seeking to make a quick profit from the equally greedy Middle Eastern and Far Eastern demand for rhino horns.

Today, a foreboding sadness, a darkening cloud of shame, hangs over Africa's forests and savannah. Pangolin cannot sleep for his fear; elephant longs for a place to hide; while hyena grows fat and vulture has difficulty flying, so filled is his belly from the endless glut of rhino's flesh left in the wake of mankind's insane greed for the body parts of other animals. Daily, inexorably, the very lifeforce of these and many other species are haemorrhaging onto the blood-red soil of the Dark Continent.

If you have ever walked in the bush and encountered a rhinoceros in the wild close to, you will understand the meaning of the word megafauna. For seen from ground level they seem impossibly large for the landscape. Rhinoceros are amongst the largest land mammals. Weighing up to 2,300 kilograms and standing two metres tall at the shoulder, it is the white rhinoceros (*Ceratotherium simum*) that is the largest of the species. Grazers of grasses, they have a wide, almost square, lip adapted to the task. Their distinctive head and neck shapes have evolved to facilitate a lowered head position suited to grazing; they sometimes even drag their lower lip along the ground. Like all rhinoceros, white rhinos create dung middens to demark their territory. Their dung is similar to elephant dung, although somewhat darker and smoother in texture. White rhinos are the more docile of the African species, mostly preferring to withdraw to the bush in response to surprise encounters.

DNA analysis has revealed that there are two subspecies of white rhino: the southern white rhino (*Ceratotherium simum simum*) and the northern white rhino (*Ceratotherium simum cottoni*). After decades of poaching, the northern white rhino is teetering on the brink of extinction. With no males left alive to sire young, and just two elderly cows that are no longer capable of reproducing, only frozen sperm, eggs and surrogacy present a possible solution. But rhinoceros reproduction is a notoriously difficult process. The task of saving this species is Herculean and time is running out.

Despite their size, armour-like skin and intimidating horns, rhinoceros are paradoxically tender and vulnerable creatures. Their skin is five centimetres thick but if cut, cannot heal. When I was a boy, Hollywood movies set in Africa depicted them rather differently. Virtually every such movie had to contain a dramatic scene with a rhinoceros charging a vehicle. These chase sequences typically ended in a hair's-breadth escape, an injured gun bearer and a truck crash; for example, *Hatari*, starring John Wayne, or *The Last Safari*, starring Stewart Granger. While I hate to think how many takes were filmed to capture the action sequences in these movies and the stress the animals may have experienced being goaded into charging, they do serve to demonstrate the astonishing speed and power of these magnificent creatures that are built like bulldozers with a spike on the front, possessed of racing-car speed and the manoeuvrability of a trail bike.

Survivors from a more ancient time, they have been walking the earth for fifty million years. The collective noun for a group of rhinos is 'a crash', a good reflection of their Hollywood persona, but perhaps more faithfully describing their fate at the hands of humanity.

It is often stated that rhinos have no other threats than humans. This is not strictly so. Young rhinos and the infirm can and do fall prey to large carnivores. A pride of lions will also sometimes play the ultimate 'cat and mouse' game with a rhino, making many daring and risky attempts upon one, hoping to subdue it once it becomes exhausted.

I long ago lost count of the times I have tracked rhino on foot. But I clearly remember the very first opportunity to do so, in the company of expert conservation rangers who daily tracked and monitored the wellbeing of a black rhinoceros population. The black rhinoceros (*Diceros bicornis*) is the smaller of the African species, the adults weighing in between 900 and 1,400 kilograms. They are browsers, with a narrow, hooked lip that enables them to grasp leaves, fruits and branches. Their head and neck shapes result from their need to reach upwards for vegetation, which also affects their posture. Their dung is characteristically more coarsely textured than that of the white rhino and contains small twigs that show a clean forty-five-degree angular cut where they have been bitten through.

The black rhino, like the white rhino, has two horns, but it is the black rhino that has the reputation for being the most aggressive of the African species. They are certainly very willing to charge at perceived threats, and mothers with calves should be avoided as they may charge unexpectedly. Injuries due to combat between rival males courting a female in heat are relatively common, sometimes even resulting in deaths. Perhaps the most astonishing aspect of their natural history is their ability to survive in the most arid terrain, which was precisely the conditions where I first tracked them. Because the vegetation was so sparse, they were browsing on naboom (*Euphorbia ingens*), a cactus-like tree that contains a milky latex that is toxic to most other animals, can burn human skin, and cause blindness or even death if ingested.

The trackers' process was simple in concept but required great skill to execute. At first light, we drove the vehicle trails looking for crossing places where fresh spoor could be found. Finding such a trail, we searched for a dung midden to confirm the age of the trail. This was our starting point. You can be forgiven for imagining that a rhino track is deep and easy to follow. Their broad feet combine with ground that is sun-baked to an iron-like hardness to leave a trail that is often subtle and surprisingly indistinct. This is particularly so for the black rhinoceros, which inhabits many of the most inhospitable, rocky desert regions.

As we progressed, close attention was increasingly paid to the tiny succulent plants that emerged from between the rocks. Bruising to these hardy herbs is not easily seen but is nonetheless the most accurate means of ageing the trail in such an arid landscape. The age of the trail is critical in this type of tracking. As the sun approached its zenith, the rhinoceros was traveling downwind, searching for a shady place to lie down. The trackers knew that when it did, it would lie so that it was turned to face into the wind. If we had blindly continued along the trail, our scent would have been detected by the rhino long before we had located it, in which case we would have walked directly into a head-down defensive charge.

The skill in the tracking was choosing the perfect moment to turn off from the trail and then, staying downwind, to circle round via the high ground, glassing the landscape to find the rhino. It was wonderful to observe the trackers' practised skills. Once they were on the trail, the outcome was assured, and they unerringly located the rhino. Now the challenge was to approach the animal close enough to observe its health and to identify it by the shape of its horn and ears. These details would be recorded by sketching in a field report form and by photograph. The trackers headed off to make their observations, using some bushes on the right for cover, while I stayed in position to film.

The scene was like something from a surreal newspaper cartoon. The landscape resembled the surface of Mars. There in the distance was the lonely rhinoceros in the tiniest patch of shade from the only tree for miles around. To say that I was poorly concealed by a thin and decidedly too short trumpet thorn bush would be an abuse of the word concealed. Then, as is the way of the wild, the sun won its daily wrestling match with the cool morning breeze for control of the wind. Ever so gently, I felt the passage of warm air across the back of my neck. As it passed, it picked up scent molecules from my skin and carried them with mischief straight to the waiting nostrils of the rhino. I tried to estimate the speed of the breeze and how long it would be before my scent would reach the attention of the sleeping giant – but it was already too late.

The rhino's head moved first and like lightning he was on his feet, raising a small cloud of dust. Clearly led by his nose, his head lifted slightly and his posture tightened. He demonstrated that he could pirouette with the ease, if not the grace, of a ballerina, turning head full on towards me. He had me lined up in his horns, which now seemed to serve as a front sight. He was locked on. To reinforce the fact, he snorted and angrily scraped the ground with his rear feet, a clear warning.

I looked around for a tree to climb, but the only suitable tree was shading the rhino – typical. Rhinoceros eyesight is poor, or so we are told. However, research has demonstrated that the rhinoceros can see as well as a rabbit or a dolphin, and certainly well enough to spot me behind my bush, which now seemed even more ridiculous. Feeling exposed and vulnerable, I waited as the breeze oscillated, the rhino trotted a tight circle, repeatedly scraping the ground for effect, and then returned to his original position and locked on again. It was a magnificent sight.

Gently and very, very quietly, I backed away, leaving him to settle. We had recorded his presence, and he was safe, which was our intended purpose. The trackers were highly amused. It turned out that they were so well acquainted with the rhino that they could easily recognise it from its foot tracks alone and therefore knew that it was an animal with a reputation for aggression, something they had neglected to tell me, wanting to see my reaction. They were confident I could handle myself – it was a compliment, really – so it was a funny end to a great day of tracking.

Thanks to the dedication and professionalism of those humble trackers and others like them monitoring and protecting this endangered species, the poachers do not have things all their own way, but despite this it is estimated that currently three rhinoceros are killed every day, mainly as a result of the increase in demand for their horns. This is almost certainly a conservative estimate. With the African continent home to 70 per cent of the world's rhinoceroses, it is inevitable that African conservation organisations are on the frontline of this conservation war.

But while the African rhinoceroses are the most well known, there are three other species of rhino. The smallest and most ancient of the species is the Sumatran rhinoceros (*Dicerorhinus sumatrensis*). This is the closest living relative of the long extinct woolly rhinoceros, which once roamed across Europe and was so vividly portrayed in the rock art at the Grotte Chauvet in southern France. The Sumatran rhino is consequently hairier than its other living relatives. These small, twin-horned rhinoceros are retiring in nature and have suffered from the loss and fragmentation of their habitat, making it increasingly difficult for individuals to meet and to breed. While they were once found in Thailand, Cambodia, southern China, northeastern India and even in the foothills of Bhutan, today they are critically endangered, found in only a few places within the dense tropical forest of Sumatra and Borneo. Their population is difficult to measure, but estimates range from 100 individuals to possibly as low as thirty.

The Javan rhinoceros (*Rhinoceros sondaicus*) is the rarest large mammal currently living in the wild. Once distributed widely across Southeast Asia, today the only location where these rhino are found is the Ujong Kulong peninsular, at the western tip of Java, Indonesia. Here the population has increased from thirty individuals in 1967 to around sixty to seventy today. However, the species depends wholly on conservation efforts. It is hoped that introducing breeding animals into suitable habitat with full legal protection will allow the population to recover to a more genetically viable size (perhaps 2,000 to 2,500), a process predicted to take 150 years, highlighting the fact that it is more difficult to restore a species from the edge of extinction than it is to prevent it reaching that point in the first instance.

The Indian or greater one-horned rhinoceros (*Rhinoceros unicornis*) is found in India and Nepal, particularly in the foothills of the Himalayas. The largest rhinoceros species found outside of Africa, by the early 1900s it had nearly been hunted to extinction, the population falling to less than 200. Today, with legal protection in India and Nepal, the population has risen and is now believed to stand at 3,580. However, this species still falls victim to poaching and will require continued dynamic conservation efforts for the foreseeable future. It does, however, provide some hope, demonstrating that effective conservation management and enforced legal protection have the potential to reinstate a species.

I have heard it said that extinctions are inevitable, that they are a part of the natural process and we should not intervene but simply accept them. This is an argument that in some cases is valid, but not when we are discussing the needless extinction of species caused by human ignorance, callousness and greed.

Just three years ago, I found myself once again standing beside the carcass of a rhinoceros killed for its horn. It was a sad, emotionally charged scene. I felt a deep sense of personal loss, for I had followed the spoor of that rhino more than once. The animal had been shot three weeks earlier. Since then the scavengers had picked the carcass clean; atop the greasy stain on the soil, the skin was already hard and desiccated, and the bones were beginning to whiten. Even the nauseating, sickly sweet stench of death that proclaims each of these crimes was starting to fade.

Not far away in a deep thorn-scrub thicket was the camp where the poachers had operated from. There had been two of them. Here the ground was all boulders, and they had cleared just enough space to lie out, leaving behind some food tins and a loaded AK-47 automatic rifle. This was not the weapon used to kill the rhino; it was simply brought along for self-defence. The stakes are deadly in the trade in rhino horns. It also indicated that they knew that they were committing a crime and that they were willing to take human lives as well.

Through the efforts of expert native trackers following their trail through the night by torchlight, combined with the swift efforts of the local farmers, these poachers were apprehended while they celebrated in the bar of a nearby town. At their feet there was a holdall containing the rhino horn with their blood-sticky fingerprints on it. From their car outside, a heavy-calibre hunting rifle was recovered. The poachers were not impoverished locals; they were specialist contract killers brought in from neighbouring countries, employed by a yet unidentified boss.

I have no pity for them. They clearly knew what they were doing and what the consequences would be if they were caught. I hope that they will feel the full weight of the law, for it is impossible to bring that animal back to life.

Rhino horn is made from keratin, the same as fingernails. That it should be valued more highly than gold by weight is ridiculous. The greed associated with this value is driving the rhinoceros into extinction. Moreover, unlike many other illegally harvested animal products, rhino horn has the potential to be farmed. Horns are now routinely removed from rhino without ill effect in conservation reserves to lessen the risk from poaching.

Sometimes I have nightmares in which I see rhinoceros sliding helplessly on a polished sheet of metal that angles downwards, ever steepening, into the darkness of oblivion. But they are not alone. Sliding helplessly around them in confusion are elephants, tigers, pangolins, who slide even faster on their scales, mountain gorillas, snow leopards, lemurs, sea turtles, and countless other creatures of all shapes and sizes.

. . .

As I write these words, I have in front of me on my desk an anatomically perfect replica of a predator skull. From its size, its muzzle and prominent canine teeth, it resembles the skull of a medium-sized dog. But it is not a dog. This skull was given to me by Nick Mooney, a naturalist and tracker who was responsible for investigating and validating sightings of this creature from 1982 until he retired in 2009.

We had travelled together while filming a documentary in Australia and discovered that we shared a common bond as trackers and conservationists. As he gave it to me, I realised it symbolised more than a friendship born of tracking; it represented what we were both committed to preventing: the needless extinction of a species, for this is the skull of a thylacine (*Thylacinus cynocephalus*), more commonly known as the Tasmanian tiger, whose story is a cautionary tale that we should all be familiar with.

The thylacine was a predator and had vertical stripes around its hindquarters. However, it more closely resembled a cross between a wolf and a wallaby, with a long, dog-like snout but with a stiff, thick-based tail and very powerful rear legs. It was an apex predator and the last member in its genus of large marsupial predators, both male and females possessing a pouch. Typical of marsupials, its tracks showed with four toes in the rear feet and five in the front. It is an example of convergent evolution, where different genera evolve to fill the same ecological role in different localities, the thylacine occupying a wolf-like role in the ecology of Tasmania. From fossil evidence and rock art it has been established that the thylacine once lived in New Guinea and across Australia and Tasmania. On the mainland of Australia, it appears most likely to have become extinct around 3,000 years ago.

When sea levels rose at the end of the Ice Age 10,000 years ago, Tasmania became an island, separated from the Australian mainland, isolating a thriving thylacine population along with the indigenous Aboriginal community. Despite their isolation, the thylacine population survived in coexistence with the Aboriginal hunter-gatherers. Then, in 1803, European settlers began to arrive in Tasmania and set about modifying the land to suit their farming needs. Their arrival coincided with the increasing industrialisation of the world and the onset of a hastening decline in species that has continued unabated to this day.

To the farmers scratching a living from the Tasmanian bush, both the Aboriginal population and the thylacines were an inconvenience, and both would ultimately suffer a similar fate. The Aboriginal story is a shocking and painful tale of ethnic cleansing, which respectfully requires more space to relate properly than is available here.

The thylacine, meanwhile, was considered a direct threat to the farmers' flocks of sheep and therefore their livelihoods. To protect their livestock, they set about its destruction, at first in an arbitrary way, later with bounties paid by the Van Diemen's Land Company from 1830, and from 1888 by the Tasmanian government, which offered £1 for each animal killed. There is no doubt that the settlers were adept at hunting and trapping, showing considerable energy to rid themselves of what they considered to be a pest species.

The bounty records show a stable cull of around 100 animals per year until the early 1900s when the numbers being killed show a rapid decline: forty-two in 1907; seventeen in 1908; two in 1909; and zero

1910. This almost certainly reflects a decline in the thylacine population, but whether this resulted solely from their persecution or from disease is debatable. It is worth considering, however, that for 10,000 years, until the arrival of industrial society, the Tasmanian thylacine survived nature's challenges. If ever a smoking gun was left at a crime scene, it must surely be this. In 1930, Wilf Batty is recorded as having shot the last Tasmanian Thylacine in the wild. Finally, in 1936, 133 years after the arrival of farmer settlers, and just two months after becoming wholly protected in Tasmania, the last-known thylacine died in Hobart Zoo from hypothermia, having been locked outside of its night enclosure.

It is possible that some thylacines survived by retreating into the vast tangle of the Tasmanian bush. Almost as soon as they vanished, their absence was mourned, and considerable effort was then made to locate them. Casts of thylacine footprints were made in 1938, but no animal was found. In a strange change in circumstances, between 1968 and 1972 a very different bounty was offered, this time $100 for hard evidence of their footprints, in the hope of locating a population of thylacines still in existence. The bounty was never claimed.

Today, people regularly claim that they have seen thylacines, yet despite our remote cameras and the ubiquitous phone camera, none of these sightings have been confirmed. Most of these claims can be accounted for as wishful thinking or misidentification, and some are simply fraudulent, hindering proper research, but a few, a very few, seem credible.

One of the most convincing sightings was recorded in 1982 and was exhaustively investigated by Nick Mooney, conducting the most thorough search yet made, covering 250 square kilometres. But to no avail. Today, the thylacine has become a mythical creature, like the Loch Ness Monster or the Sasquatch. Amateur investigators spend time searching and set out cameras; some become obsessed, even leading to their financial ruin. It is a strange phenomenon that we seem unwilling to accept that this species may now be extinct. Two thylacine even adorn the Tasmanian coat of arms, just as the grizzly bear can be seen on the flag of California. The grizzly bear has been extinct within California since 1924.

In amongst all the gloomy news of extinctions, every year researchers do occasionally happen across species thought to be extinct, usually small remnant populations no longer able to contribute to the ecosystem as they once did. Perhaps likewise there are some thylacines still living in a remote corner of Tasmania, Australia, Papua New Guinea or Irian Jaya in Indonesia; if so, they wisely choose to remain elusive to humanity. I am ever hopeful that one day we shall learn that they have survived. Maybe then we will be able to make amends for our foolishness and instead of despising them, come to know them and to understand their role in nature.

But until there is certain proof, the Tasmanian tiger is consigned to the growing list of animals forced into extinction by human activity, along with the dodo, the passenger pigeon, the Saudi gazelle, the Arabian ostrich, the Japanese river otter, the Cuban macaw, the eastern elk, the northern Sumatran rhinoceros, the western black rhinoceros, Haast's eagle, Steller's sea cow, the Formosan clouded leopard, the sea mink and many, many, many more ...

It is notoriously difficult to accurately estimate the rate at which species become extinct, but there is worldwide consensus amongst the scientific community that the rate of species extinction is currently far higher than the normal base rate and that the loss is accelerating – conservative estimates place it at a rate 100 times higher than the norm. It has even been suggested that the actual rate could be ten times greater still. What is certain is that every taxon of life is affected, shrinking and endangering the complex web of interactions between species upon which our ecosystem is built.

It should be obvious that our own welfare as a species is at threat. Our actions are unwittingly endangering our economies, our health, our incomes and our food security, to say nothing of our quality of life.

Nature faces many challenges from humanity: global warming, pollution, destruction of habitat, reduction of biodiversity and a bewildering range of direct acts of cruelty. As I grow older, I feel increasing frustration, both at the continuing stupidity of some of my fellow humans, but most particularly at the sense of personal helplessness I feel. Can we ever reverse the tide?

I believe that we can. There is much to be hopeful about. Increasingly, countries are taking to the cause of conservation. For example, China has delisted rhinoceros horn as a traditional medicine, now legally protects its endangered species and is establishing national parks. Worldwide, environmental issues are at last higher on the political agenda.

But there remains a great deal of work to be done if we are to extinguish the fire of environmental destruction that is currently burning. Conservation is no longer a luxury. It is now essential to the future survival of our own species. Just a few months ago, I stood on a train surrounded by young people carrying homemade banners, striking from school to attend an environmental rally in central London. I asked one of them what they were doing. 'We are saving the planet!' was the defiant reply, full of the implication that my generation had failed. Bravo, I thought.

But I also thought, it is not the planet that is at threat. Whether humanity survives or perishes is of no concern to our planet; nature is dispassionate in the extreme. It is time to be brutally honest. We need to protect our environment for the future survival of our own species. In so doing, we will also protect the welfare of the incredible diversity of life we share it with.

But conserving the environment will require more than simply holding on to what we currently have. Certainly, we must preserve what remains; that is a basic concept of conservation. But try holding on to a handful of sand. The tighter you squeeze, the more grains slip through your grasp, until eventually there is so little left that there seems no point in continuing. That is how conservation is.

There are always gaps – the seemingly rational arguments for development, felling this forest, drilling in that reserve. In the most extraordinary volte-face, the US president Donald Trump recently decided to permit hunting in his nation's national parks, wildlife sanctuaries that are the envy of the world and were the inspiration for similar parks around the globe.

If you want to hang onto the sand, you must constantly be topping it up, adding to the sum. This is how we should think of conservation: the core of what is most precious is deep in our palm, but at the edges the leakage must be constantly replenished and restored.

Most importantly of all is the mind that guides the hand. We must celebrate the joy of nature, share her wonders with children, scrutinise the policies of shallow politicians, invest our savings in schemes that improve our environment, not those that fund environmental destruction, while upholding the laws that protect our wildlife. It is essential to understand that our lives are connected to every other living lifeform and as such crimes against nature are equally crimes against humanity. Those grey suits who commit these crimes should be held accountable, unable to evade justice through wealth or influence.

With so many problems, it is easy to feel morose and despondent, but we should not. Nature continuously demonstrates her ability for self-repair, particularly when we give her the opportunity and lend a helping hand. I have also witnessed nature's astonishing capacity to reach inside of people and to heal them too. When I observe nature, I feel more than simple awe at her diversity and astonishing beauty. I feel a deep intrinsic lifeforce connection. Travelling and guiding groups in wild places has taught me that in wilderness there is hope – hope that wildlife will continue in all its biodiverse glory, and hope that humanity will once again be moved by the rhythm of nature's song.

In many ways, wilderness defines us. It reveals our hidden abilities, the origins of our intelligence and provides us an opportunity to test our philosophies, courage and wisdom. But just as we need the wilderness, so the wilderness needs us.

Every year there are multitudes of crimes committed against wildlife. Globally, police forces deploy incredibly well-motivated and capable officers to tackle these crimes. But the crimes are committed in rural areas, at odd hours, usually when no one is about to witness them. With the crimes being many and the police officers to detect them few, they are difficult to solve. Astonishing as it may seem in the twenty-first century, in Britain there are still people illegally pitting fighting dogs against badgers, deer and hare. These cruel activities have gained new impetus by the gangs involved, who broadcast the crimes online, betting on the outcomes. Peregrine falcon and other raptor eggs continue to be stolen from nests and smuggled to Arabia, where hawk racing has become a multimillion-pound sport. Despite efforts to keep the breeding of racing hawks crime free, the black market is fuelled by the persistent belief that the best birds are those born from hardy, wild birds. The list of wildlife crimes is seemingly endless.

In the earlier chapters, I have hopefully given you the tools to notice more when you are outdoors. I ask you now on behalf of all those animals threatened by these crimes to keep your eyes open when you are out and about. If you notice suspicious activities, keep a record and, if necessary, pass on your observations to the relevant authorities. In the appendix, you will find details of how to record the sort of data that can help make for a successful prosecution. An army of naturalists together can make a difference.

. . .

So, our journey together nears the parting of our ways. While writing, I have imagined you beside me; we have been on many walks together as I searched my memory for inspiration. I trust that you have had the chance to explore and experiment with the skills I have shared. Perhaps you have discovered that when walking discreetly in silence, even a small farmland copse is its own wilderness, and in so doing you are becoming familiar with your own inner wildness. If so, I hope that you have been able to witness some of nature's miracles that you might otherwise have missed. I urge you, pass on your enthusiasm and share your experiences with others.

Nature and wild places have been my life; they have provided me with extraordinary stimulus and excitement, along with the privilege of meeting other like-minded people, many of whom have an astonishing wealth of nature knowledge. If there is one thing we all agree on, it is that one lifetime is not long enough to answer all the questions that we will ask. But then, life is not about its destination; it is about the journey. Which is just as well, for nature is apt to surprise us; just when I think I am beginning to understand something, she often reveals another view that turns my understanding on its head.

The more I learn, the more I realise how much I do not know. But one thing I can say with certainty …

Everything in nature is connected, thus ultimately …

Newport Community
288
Learning & Libraries

WE ARE NATURE.

APPENDIX
Reporting Wildlife Crime

Here is some guidance for recording suspicious activity or evidence of wildlife-related crimes within the United Kingdom. In other countries, please seek advice from your local police department or authority that has responsibility for wildlife-crime investigation.

Sadly, wildlife crimes are not a thing of the past. Far from it. The use of mobile phones and social media has enabled the perpetrators of such crimes to communicate and share details of their activities with each other, encouraging further transgressions. Every day, our wildlife is being persecuted in acts of mindless cruelty and needs our protection. To prevent wildlife crime requires a team effort, with the police, the public and other agencies working together. Given the remote nature of these crimes, it is often members of the general public out enjoying their surroundings who first encounter or notice indications of these offences. Do not hesitate to contact the police if you suspect that a wildlife crime is occurring and ask for the information to be brought to the attention of the local wildlife crime officer. These police officers have specialist training and knowledge relating to such crimes and their investigation. There is never any criticism of individuals reporting suspected wildlife crimes. Indeed, without the general public's watch, many more crimes would pass each year without detection. The police never encourage the general public to approach or confront perpetrators involved in these criminal acts. Experience shows that many are likely to be involved in other high-level criminality, and personal safety must come first. However, much can be achieved with accurately recorded observations, descriptions and photographic or video records.

To bring offenders to justice, the police need solid evidence. To be used in court, this evidence must admissible, having been obtained by methods acceptable within law. Evidence cannot be anonymous, meaning that in most cases the identity of the witness must be made known. Thus, the evidence provider must be prepared to both present their evidence to a court and for their evidence to be scrutinised thoroughly by both the prosecution and the defence. Evidence must never be altered or falsified, which may be considered an offence.

It is the job of the police to collate the evidence and carry out further investigations that may be deemed necessary. On the basis of the evidence, they may charge offenders to court or present it to the Crown Prosecution Service (CPS) for a charging decision. In this case, the CPS will decide whether or not to prosecute.

There must be an unbroken chain of evidence from the witness to the police. If this is not correctly documented, compromising the continuity of the evidence, a case may be jeopardised. It is important to always provide the 'best evidence'. Evidence largely depends on the resources and expertise available. Written witness statements are often the only evidence to be relied upon. As the passage of time can often affect recall, incident details are best recorded immediately, or at the earliest convenient moment, when the observations are still fresh in the memory. Issues regarding evidence arise when individuals differ in what they are able to recall or in what parts of an incident they saw.

Supporting evidence greatly helps securing a successful prosecution. Here photographic or video evidence is ideal but needs to be of good quality. Failing the availability of a suitable camera, a mobile phone may be used. It is worth noting that mobile phones frequently do not have sufficient telephoto range to record rural crimes with imagery of reliable resolution, although they can provide impressive results when combined with a binocular or spotting scope. Either way, some evidence is better than no evidence. Even if it does not directly lead to a prosecution, evidence can provide important intelligence relating to other crimes under investigation. The police have even made successful prosecutions when a witness has written a suspect's car registration number in mud with a stick when no other means was available.

Common Wildlife Offences in the UK and What to Look For

Badger persecution

These offences include badger baiting, where a dog is encouraged to fight a badger, typically resulting in the latter's death, although it is also common for the dog to receive severe injuries and sometimes die. Badger baiters will typically be in a group, will have terrier-type dogs with them, which may have large collars used for tracking them underground, and, crucially, they will have spades with them for digging down to the dog and badger. Badgers may also be coursed with lamps. Offenders will use high-powered lamps to identify a badger before releasing their dogs, typically lurchers and the like, to catch and kill the badger. It is not uncommon for those involved to also purposefully injure the badger before the dog fights it.

Man-made holes, usually square in shape, in the area of badger sets are typical of the sets having been targeted and are worthy of investigation by the police. Terrier-type dogs with facial injuries, particularly to the lower jaw, are also an indication that they may have been used to fight badgers.

Offences relating to badgers often increase and peak following harvest due to the prevalence of open, flat freshly cropped fields. This allows for more 'sport' to take place. Badger offences also increase in late winter and early spring when young are present; it is thought that the badgers have more 'fight' in them at this time of year due to the presence of their cubs.

Bat persecution

This takes the form of disturbing, injuring or killing bats, and damaging or obstructing their roosts. This is most typically seen in property development, new or old. Any such work should be mindful of bats and a survey carried out if in any doubt. Blocking and damaging roosts is an offence and should be brought to the attention of the police if discovered.

CITES

Convention on International Trade in Endangered Species of Wild Fauna and Flora (CITES) offences involve the illegal trade of endangered species, examples of which can be found in a range of places, from antique shops and auction houses to eBay and other selling sites. These offences can be very difficult to identify, and even experts sometimes struggle; however, it is worth contacting the police should you believe an item is from an endangered species. Common articles include fur, ivory, skins, turtle/tortoise shells and the body parts of endangered animals, such as teeth and bone. Individuals can commit offences unknowingly, buying souvenirs on holiday and attempting to bring them back into the country. If you suspect an item may be subject to CITES legislation, call the police. The following website is also useful: https://speciesplus.net

Poaching/coursing

The most commonly poached or coursed animals are hare, deer and fish. Hare and deer coursing usually takes the form of groups running long dogs (lurchers and bull lurchers) after their desired quarry. Coursing increases when there are no crops on the fields. Signs to look out for are groups of vehicles parked in rural areas, by gateways to farmland or on farm or bridal paths. Vehicles will usually be 4x4s, estates or vans, and they may be equipped with high-powered lamps; evidence that dogs are transported in the vehicle may also be seen. The vehicle will usually be older and will be considered an acceptable loss to the poacher should the police seize it.

Coursers often use binoculars to spot their quarry while walking the edges of fields to flush hares into the open. Groups of men with dogs on open land are worthy of a call to the police. Deer coursing usually occurs at night. Offenders will use their vehicle to try and split a herd and then release dogs from the vehicle to run the deer down. Large powerful bull lurchers that are capable of taking down a red stag are often used for this purpose.

Fish poaching occurs on closed and open water. The simplest way to identify a fish poacher is that they usually aren't dressed for the occasion and have very little equipment, often consisting of only a small rod and spinner.

Raptor persecution

The illegal trapping, poisoning or shooting of raptors is very much in the spotlight at present. Raptor persecution can occur anywhere but is most common in isolated areas. Unless the cause of death is immediately obvious – for example, if it is clear that the bird has been killed by a cat, fox or by collision with a car – any bird of prey that is found deceased should be considered suspicious. The police should be contacted before any other agencies so that the continuity of evidence can be preserved and proper procedures can be put in place. Poisoning of raptors does occur, so care should be taken when dealing with any dead birds. When contacting the police, provide an accurate location reference: grid references or ///what 3 words (see page 298) are accepted methods. Unless the deceased raptor can be recovered, the investigation will fail at the first hurdle.

All wild birds, their nests and their eggs are protected by law – it is an offence to destroy or damage any nest. Certain species are afforded even greater protection. These are defined as Schedule 1 birds, a list of which can be found in the legislation of the Wildlife and Countryside Act 1981. The list includes birds such as the barn owl (*Tyto alba*), short-toed treecreeper (*Certhia brachydactyla*) and merlin (*Falco columbarius*). It is an offence to merely disturb the nest of Schedule 1 listed birds.

Raptor eggs, especially peregrine falcons' (*Falco peregrinus*), are commonly taken from the wild. This can be to supply the black market for breeding stock, for the prestige of owning a wild caught bird, or simply to be destroyed in the pursuit of protecting other birds such as pigeons. Egg thieves will typically scope out areas weeks before they commit the crime. They need to gather intelligence to establish where the birds have nested and to formulate a plan to retrieve the eggs. The thefts often happen very quickly and in fading light. The most obvious sign is often the presence of individuals with ropes and climbing harnesses in an area where climbers don't frequent – peregrines especially nest in difficult to reach areas. As offenders approach the birds and their nests, the birds are likely to display signs of stress and agitation, such as leaving the nest and making distress calls. Any suspicious activity around nesting birds should be reported to the police.

Invasive species

Non-native species can have a devastating effect on native British wildlife. Possibly the best example of this is the introduction of the grey squirrel and the resulting decline of the native red. Another example is the introduction of the signal crayfish to UK waters, which has driven the native white-clawed crayfish towards extinction. The impact of releasing non-native species cannot be underestimated, and any suspected release should be reported immediately so the relevant authorities can investigate and deal with the issue. The priority will always be to stop the release, contain the released alien species and stop its spread. DEFRA, the Animal and Plant Health Agency (APHA) or the police should be the first point of contact for any non-native species issues.

Hunting with dogs

This has already been covered in some respect with badger, hares and deer. Since the inception of the Hunting Act in 2004, hunting a wild mammal with dogs is illegal. There are a few exemptions to the act, the primary one being the flushing of a wild mammal from cover to a waiting gun with no more than two dogs. The Hunting Act is a worthwhile read if only to see how difficult it can be to prosecute offenders under the act and its exemptions.

Plants

It is an offence to intentionally pick, uproot or destroy certain plants, a list of which can be found in Schedule 8 of the Wildlife and Countryside Act 1981. In addition, if you are not an authorised person, most commonly the owner, it is an offence to uproot any wild plant not included in the schedule, 'uproot' being the key word.

Sites of Special Scientific Interest and ancient schedules monuments

A common issue is damage to Sites of Special Scientific Interest (SSSI) or ancient scheduled monuments caused by camp fires (these designations can be found via https://magic.defra.gov.uk). For example, rare orchids can be damaged by fires or by individuals collecting firewood or foraging for edibles. Care must therefore be taken when wandering in certain areas, and fires should not be lit on the ground in any circumstances in designated areas and certainly not without landowner permission. Ancient scheduled monuments are often obvious – stone circles, castles, abbeys, etc. – however, many are not visible, and damage to the archaeology below the surface can result in criminal proceedings. An interactive map showing listed historic sites can be found at www.historicengland.org.uk

///what3words

Available as a mobile-phone app, ///what3words has become the preferred method of supplying a location reference to the emergency services. Using this system, ///what3words assigns a unique three-word address for three-metre squares covering the whole planet.

Compared to a six-figure grid reference, which identifies a 100-metre square, the advantage of reporting the location of an incident using this method is obvious, as it is easy to communicate the precise location of a specific farm gate or other site of significance. That is not to say that a map reference cannot be used, or even generated to greater accuracy with eight or ten figure references, particularly where there is no mobile-phone coverage; however, this requires both the sender and recipient to be fully conversant with grid references, which is sadly not always the case. In practice, it is the simple convenience and ease of use that has commended the ///what3words system. If you search for the ///what3words address ///smile.wage.clouds, it will lead you to one of the lions at the base of Nelson's Column. Give it a spin and zoom in with the aerial view to discover which one.

GLOSSARY

bag – game that has been shot

basha – a bivouac, shelter or tarp

Bayaka – the term used to describe the combined populations of the Baka and Aka peoples. Sometimes referred to as Pygmy, these nomadic hunter-gatherers follow an ancient lifeway, maintaining an extraordinarily close physical and spiritual relationship with their rainforest home

Bedouin – a traditional desert-dwelling Arab population of North Africa, the Arabian Peninsula, the Levant and Upper Mesopotamia. While many have abandoned their nomadic way of life, their connection with and understanding of the desert continues

billabong – an Australian word for an oxbow lake

bryologist – an expert in the study of mosses, liverworts and hornworts

cut for sign – to look for physical evidence of any disturbance of the environment left behind by animals, humans or objects

donga – a dry gully, formed by the eroding action of running water, particularly in Australia and South Africa

dew lap – a fold of loose skin hanging from the neck or throat of an animal

envenomation – the process by which venom is injected by the bite or sting of a venomous animal

Ju/'hoansi – San hunter-gatherers found in Botswana, Namibia and Angola. Famed for their tracking prowess and ability to live in an extraordinarily hostile desert environment, they lived a nomadic life until the latter part of the twentieth century. They continue to proudly maintain their traditional skills and knowledge

jury rig – a makeshift repair; nautical in origin

kopje – an isolated hill or small mountain, often made from rock, that rises abruptly from an otherwise flat landscape

Mau Mau – a term of mysterious origin, widely used to describe freedom fighters of the Kenya Land Freedom Army (KLFA) during the Kenyan emergency in the early 1950s, mostly recruited from the Kikuyu ethnic group from the highlands of South Central Kenya

Nez Perce – the Nez Perce are a federally recognised tribe in North Central Idaho, more correctly called the Niimíipuu. Historically a self-governing nation, the Niimíipuu first-nation people were the indigenous inhabitants of a vast area of the Columbia River Plateau, occupying parts of the present-day states of Idaho, Oregon and Washington. Seasonally, they would travel throughout this region, as well as parts of Montana and Wyoming, to hunt, fish and trade. Today they work to protect, preserve and perpetuate *nimíipuu'nee-wit*, their traditional cultural values, which amongst other principles enshrines the protection of the natural environment

outfit – encompassing term for food, clothing and equipment

outfitter – organises logistics, food, equipment, canoe-hire drop-offs and pick-ups, etc.

Pitjantjatjara – Aboriginal people or tribe who inhabit the Central Western Desert in the region of Uluru. They are part of the Anangu, a cultural group that includes the Yankunytjatjara and the Ngaanyatjatjarra peoples. To the Anangu, the principle of

looking after the land, in both a physical and spiritual sense, is a
central feature of their culture

rack – an established or regularly used deer trail

San – *see Ju/'hoansi*

scat – animal faeces

spoor – the track or scent of an animal

swung high – to suspend an item; for example, from a branch

ACKNOWLEDGEMENTS

Jane Goodall, thank you for your wise words and the powerful example that you have lived. All of today's conservationists walk in your shadow and owe you a debt of gratitude – www.janegoodall.org

PC Andrew Shaw from the Derbyshire Police, Rural Crime Team, thank you for providing me with up-to-date insights into the range of crimes currently being perpetrated against wildlife across the UK. Nationwide, the Rural Crime Teams deserve better recognition for their dedication and professionalism in tackling what are often difficult, complex investigations.

Nick Mooney, I often think of our journey together in Tasmania. Thank you for sharing your passion for the Tasmanian tiger; let's hope that the thylacine story can prevent future tragedies.

Phil Coles and Matin Hayward-Smith, thank you for your photographs from past adventures, when we have baked, shivered, sweated and been feasted on by insects together, in forgotten corners of the globe, pursuing a brief glimpse of some rare and brilliantly camouflaged creature. Apart from considering how crazy we must all be, I have often thought how lucky I am to work with such skilled and dedicated fellow naturalists. Phil, you are without doubt the best wildlife spotter alive, and Martin and I can always find you by following the pointy-toed commando-soled shoes you wear – it makes me chuckle every time, 'old bean'.

Alan Steele, a kindred spirit, thank you for providing your wise council on African politics.

Peter Antoniou from Swarovski UK, thank you for your advice, wisdom and tireless support in all matters optical – www.swarovski optik.com

Lee Adams, thank you for your advice and wisdom regarding the latest advances in thermal-imaging optics – www.thomasjacks.co.uk

Jackie Gill, thank you for making the business side of my work light-hearted and enjoyable; your stories are far more shocking than mine.

The Woodlore team, thank you for your tireless support. No one could ask for a better team to work alongside. Every day your diligence and hard work enables so many to make their dreams come true – www.raymears.com

To Lorna Russell, who proposed this book. With your brilliant team at Ebury, you have made the whole experience a joy in what has certainly been the most difficult year imaginable. Thank you for your professionalism and boundless enthusiasm.

To Paul Murphy – my heart sank when I had to review the multitude of typos and punctuation errors that you had corrected. But without your diligence my meaning might have otherwise been misconstrued. Thank you, and guess what? You have to check these words too.

Patsy O'Neill, who masterminded the presention of this work to the world. Thank you! Without your dedication all of this work would be in vain.

Lastly, and most importantly, to my fans and readers. Thank you for believing in me – your strength is my strength.

INDEX

RM indicates Ray Mears.

Index

Jodrell Laboratory, Royal Botanic
　Gardens Kew 44
Ju/'hoansi bushmen 166, 301, 302

Kakadu National Park, Australia 147
Keller, Helen: *The World I Live In* 11
Kepler, Johannes 80, 81, 82
kestrel (*Falco tinnunculus*) 61–2, 101
King, Simon 138
kitten crawl 184

lammergeier (*Gypaetus barbatus*) 100
Laska, Matthias: *Human and Animal
　Olfactory Capabilities Compared* 18
lekking 138–9
leopard 60, 71–2, 78–9, 105–10, 119,
　159–65, 170–4, 176–7, 181, 183–4, 188,
　228, 229, 232, 284
　common leopard (*Panthera pardus*) 106
　crawl 183–4
　footprint 162, 165–6
　hunting of 171
　lions and 171
　snow leopard (*Panthera uncla*) 105–10,
　　165, 281
　speed of 239
　staring at 229
　stealth 159–65, 170–4, 176–7, 181,
　　183–4, 188
　tracking 159–62, 170–4, 176–7
leucophore cells 115
Lichen candelaris 75
ligands 14–15, 24
lion (*Panthera leo*) 119, 120–1, 163–4,
　165, 166, 171, 172, 228, 235–6, 239,
　256, 274, 299
Lipperhay, Hans 79–80
living outdoors 212–15
Longleat Wildlife Safari Park 270–1
loreal pits 192
loupe or hand magnifying lens 75–7,
　82, 99
Luther Standing Bear, Chief: *Land of the
　Spotted Eagle* 1

maps 202, 203, 205, 220, 266, 267, 298,
　299
　map reconnaissance 130–1, 134
marmot (*Marmota marmotai*) 100
mating, danger posed by animals when
　235–6

Mau Mau emergency 21, 301
megafauna 273
Meissner's corpuscles 49
memory
　animal 233
　sight and 67, 68
　smell and 12, 15–16, 67
Merkel discs 49
military-hiking boots 169
Milne, Joy 23
misidentification, danger posed by
　animals and 236
moccasins 169
montagu's harriers (*Circus pygargus*) 100
mongoose, banded (*Mungos mungo*) 78
Mooney, Nick 281, 283
Moore Hall, Chester 80
mosquitoes/malaria 130, 255–6, 258
motionless, ability to remain absolutely
　145, 152–8
motor vehicles, watching wildlife from
　140–1
Muir, John 191
multi-day walking load (temperate –
　summer – lowland) 202–4
mushin (state of consciousness) 199
myelin 48

Namibia 77–8, 118, 159–62, 170, 224–5,
　301
nasopharynx 29
national parks 8, 105, 147, 159, 191, 216,
　285, 286
natural selection 122
navigation 205 *see also* compass *and* map
Nez Perce nation, Native American 8–9
Nickwax Techwash 127
night dives 111–16
nightjar (*Caprimulgus europaeus*) 118
night vision 65, 68, 72, 73–4, 104–5, *104*,
　119, 172, 213
　devices 104–5, *104*
Northeastern Arnhem Land, Australia
　143–9, 151
Northern Ontario 63
northern white rhino (*Ceratotherium
　simum cottoni*) 273–4
Norwegian Jerven Bag 137

observation places, identifying potential
　132

Index

PILLGWENLLY